I0813740

The Story *of* Idaho

Consultants:

William Kirtland, Ed.D.
Reading Education
Boise State University

Betty Waller, M.Ed.
Fourth Grade
Boise Public Schools

Joseph T. Kelly, Ed.D.
Professor of Education
University of Idaho

Contributors

Laverne Sheppard, Editor
Sho-Ban News

Mamie O. Oliver, Ph.D.
formerly Professor of Social Work
Boise State University

Dixie L. Ehrenreich, Ph.D.
Laboratory of Anthropology
University of Idaho

Santos Salinas
Instructor in Bilingual Education
Boise State University

Robert C. Sims, Ph.D.
Dean of the School of Social Science
and Public Affairs
Boise State University

Susan Hendricks Swetnam, Ph.D.
Professor of English
Idaho State University

Virgil M. Young, Ed.D.

Boise State University

University of Idaho Press

Moscow, Idaho

Millennial (Fourth) Edition published 2002 by the
University of Idaho Press
First Edition published 1977

Printed in the United States of America
05 04 5 4 3

Cover: *Images of the Palouse,* alkyd on canvas by Gaylen C. Hansen, federal building, Moscow. Courtesy General Services Administration, Moscow, Idaho.

A CIP catalog record for this book is available from the publisher or the Library of Congress.

ISBN 0-89301-259-9

Visit our website at www.uidaho.edu/uipress

Dedicated to Idaho's two most precious gifts:
Kathy, my wife, and Susie, my daughter

Table of Contents

A Millennial Note to the Teacher

Dear Teacher:

This Millennial Edition has been refined with the young readers in mind. It has been written for young readers—and teachers—to present them with an exciting story of Idaho.

I think Idaho history is exciting! Students and teachers should love to study Idaho. *The Story of Idaho: Millennial Edition* gives a comprehensive history of Idaho—and more. It also gives an up-to-date look at Idaho. Chapter 1 begins with an overview of our state, and highlights many of its interesting features. Chapter 3 acquaints the reader with Idaho's Indians as they lived when the first explorers arrived. The story continues with the progress of the explorers, trappers, missionaries, and first immigrants.

Later the reader follows the gold rush, and then the development of ranches, farms, and towns. Chapter 8 examines pioneer life with many stories and photographs. Chapters 9 and 10 describe our three most important industries: farming, mining, and lumbering. Chapter 11 is devoted to Idaho's governments: state, county, and city. Last but not least, Chapter 12 describes our people—our ethnic groups and a sampling of famous Idaho people.

I love learning about Idaho, and I hope you—the teacher—will share my enthusiasm. I hope you will become a "miniexpert" on our state.

I do not expect every young reader to read every page and learn every fact in this book. It is much more important that students become excited about Idaho and continue to learn about their state as they grow older. As the teacher, you need to be selective in what you expect of your students. I encourage you to pick and choose the areas and units that fit your particular classroom needs.

The following are seven objectives that I think are important to the teacher of Idaho history. I encourage you to borrow them for your own.

The teacher should strive to:

1. Arouse student awareness and interest in Idaho.
2. Motivate students to like Idaho history.
3. Teach the students facts and ideas about Idaho and its history.
4. Help students think about the place they live.
5. Give the students a broad and varied view of Idaho.
6. Help the students understand some of the cause-and-effect relationships of Idaho's development.
7. Help the students understand that Idaho's history is a continuous story that is still unfolding.

Teaching Tips

Most young people should have no difficulty with the material in *The Story of Idaho: Millennial Edition*. However, it is important to consider the independent reading levels of your students.

All textbook material (regardless of subject) should be taught in the same way that you approach a reading lesson. Introduce the story or material to them before they read the material. Then teach the vocabulary contained in the reading assignment. Every reading assignment should be preceded by a vocabulary lesson. If you follow this procedure, your students should have little trouble reading this book.

Study Aids

This textbook contains certain features that should aid you and your student.

1. **Vocabulary.** Certain words are printed in **bold** print. These words will be found in the Glossary, where they are defined and pronounced.

2. **Pronunciation.** The Pronunciation Guide (included in the Glossary) will help your students (and you) learn to pronounce many of Idaho's unique place names. Only a seasoned Idahoan will know how to pronounce some of them. (Yes, there is a "Peek-a-boo," Idaho, except that it is spelled "Picabo." Also, natives say "BOY-see." If you hear someone say "BOY-zee," you will know he probably is not a native Idahoan.)

3. **Captions.** Each photograph and drawing has been chosen to illustrate a certain idea. Many of them include a question in the caption. The question is meant to focus attention on some aspect of the idea being illustrated.

4. **Study Questions.** Two kinds of student questions are distributed through each unit. "Re-

view Questions" are simple fact-type questions. They aid comprehension and memory by focusing attention on facts or ideas. They also give practice in the study skills involved in looking for information.

"Ideas to Talk About" are intended for oral discussion. These are open-ended and should stimulate higher-level thinking. They will assist in developing critical thinking—analysis and evaluation of ideas. They can also serve as excellent springboards for motivational activities.

Please do not grade your students on the open-ended questions. Some students are not able to handle abstract ideas, and it is not fair to penalize them for that. These ideas are meant to be challenging and fun, not a source of fear and failure.

5. **Skill Activities.** At the end of each unit, you will find a variety of student activities. They involve map skills, vocabulary development, research reports, and creative activities. These activities will encourage a variety of thinking skills and study skills.

Other Teaching Resources

You will want to enrich your teaching in every way possible. The following resources should prove very helpful to you.

The *Idaho Compass* Web Site.

http://education.boisestate.edu/compass

This web site is maintained by the author to support the teaching of Idaho history and geography. It provides specific teaching suggestions, resource materials, and additional student activities. You will find many geography activities, interesting tidbits about Idaho and its people, updated information about state officials, and other changes that affect our state. New and interesting resources will be reported as they become available. Last but not least, the site includes an annotated bibliography of books and electronic media that can provide you with a foundation from which to launch your teaching about Idaho. **The *Idaho Compass* Web Site** is a permanent *work in progress* providing a variety of ideas and materials to help keep your teaching fresh and stimulating.

The World Wide Web.

Do not hesitate to search the Internet for ideas and materials for teaching. There are both commercial and non-profit organizations that maintain web sites for teachers. Among these are many kinds of subject matter and data banks, including lesson plans. The National Geographic Society maintains several educational web sites, which can be accessed from the *Story of Idaho* web site.

The Idaho Official Highway Map.

This is one of the best Idaho maps available. It is a full-color map that unfolds to approximately 18 by 36 inches. It shows towns, cities, counties, mountains, lakes, rivers, dams, reservoirs, Indian reservations, and many other items of interest to students of Idaho. You may want to laminate several copies so they can be used again and again.

Free copies are available from the Idaho Department of Commerce. Call toll free 1-800-635-7820 or write to P.O. Box 83720, Boise, Idaho 83720-0093. Orders for the highway map and other free publications can also be placed through the Internet at the State of Idaho web site http://www.visitid.org/Planner/order_form.html.

Films.

Idaho Public Television has dozens of excellent films on Idaho scenery, Idaho history, and other Idaho topics. All are reasonably priced from $16.95 to $19.95 each, and some are discounted in sets. Details can be obtained from Idaho Public Television, 1455 N. Orchard Street, Boise, Idaho 83706. You can also call toll free 1-877-224-7200 or visit the web site at www.idahoptv.org. The local Boise number is 208-373-7220.

Out of Print Books.

It might seem strange to include out-of-print books in the "Further Readings" lists. However, the few that I have included are excellent and may still be in many libraries. Most are still available from sellers of used books. Particularly the Time-Life Series of the Old West will never be outdated, and these books are widely available from used-book sellers. If you don't know where to find out-of-print books, you will find some dealers listed on the *Story of Idaho Web Site.*

Life In Idaho

Jimmy Culp

I like to pick berries. Idaho has many tasty wild berries. Among them are huckleberries, strawberries, blackcaps, and thimbleberries. Huckleberries are my favorite.

Nida Kinnavongsa

I like playing soccer. I learned how to play by watching my brother. It's really fun keeping the ball away from others and scoring points. At home I play soccer with my brother in the back yard.

Dean Buckmaster

I like to ride horses, because you can go places you can't in a car. Boating is the most fun of all. Why do I think it's the most fun? Because when you are on the lake, you can see the town of Sandpoint.

Stacie Woodall

What I like to do in Idaho is to go on nature walks. It is fun to find paths and make bridges across a stream. I like to look at rocks and gather wild flowers. I like to hear birds singing, and squirrels going up and down trees. I like to see fish swimming in streams and bees buzzing around flowers.

When we go camping, I can do all the things I can't do in a city, such as fishing, hunting, exploring, and a lot more. I especially like Idaho because it has lots of wildlife, and because it is beautiful. Idaho is number one!

Tami Veatch

I like snow skiing because I just learned how. There's all kinds of slopes, and it's fun. You don't get too hot or too cold. It seems like you're free to do anything you want to.

Shauna Lee

I love to take long walks on paths that I have found. I walk to a pond and fish awhile, then I feed the ducks and geese. Then I go back and feed the bluebirds and bluejays. Sometimes I go to the back of the cabin or camper and read books about Idaho.

Tami Jo Yaw

I live in the woods. There are birds and deer around our house. I've seen a lot of wild animals outdoors. But one time I was indoors. We were almost ready to go outside, when a moose walked through our back yard!

Joshua Smith

I like to go to our family reunion. It is fun. You get to water ski, and go on the boat, and play lawn darts and eat, and it's good! We play until nighttime, and then we go home. I would like to stay at the reunion forever and ever, but it only comes around once a year.

Shannon Laughlin

I like horseback riding. When I lived in North Shoshone, I would get the horse out on a warm spring day. I would ride down the road to my friend's house. Then we would ride together.

Chapter 1
Welcome to Idaho

Idaho is an exciting state. The mountains, valleys, and rivers are beautiful, and there are many interesting things to see and do. It will be fun to read about the many things that make Idaho a great state.

Our state also has an exciting **history**. We will meet the first explorers and settlers who came to Idaho and learn why they came. We will learn the story of the gold rush, see farms and towns being built, and watch the railroad connect Idaho with far-off places. We will watch Idaho grow, first into a **territory**, then into a state. As you read and learn about Idaho, you will be glad you live here.

Hells Canyon is the deepest canyon in North America. How deep is it? What other state shares Hells Canyon? IDAHO DEPARTMENT OF COMMERCE

Idaho Is An Exciting Place.

Idaho is exciting and fun. It is great to explore because there are so many things to do and see. We find things in Idaho that are not found anywhere else in the world. Did you know Idaho's **Hells Canyon** is the deepest canyon in North America—and perhaps the world? Did you know that **Shoshone Falls** on the Snake River is higher than the famous Niagara Falls in New York? Did you know Idaho has a huge **wilderness area**—the largest one in the United States outside of Alaska?

Idaho has other surprises. Did you know about the **Craters of the Moon**? This part of Idaho looks so much like the moon that **astronauts** have come to see it before flying to the real moon. Did you know that an Idaho city, Arco, was the first city in the world to be lighted by **nuclear power**?

Did you know that Philo Farnsworth, who invented television, went to **Rigby** High School? Did you know that Idaho still has Old West ghost towns like **Silver City** and **Rocky Bar**? Such towns were once full of miners, stage coaches, bandits, sheriffs, and six-guns.

Idaho Is a Proud State.

Doesn't it feel good to be proud? There are many, many things we can be proud of. We can be proud of our family. We can be proud of our school, our team, our friends, our home. We **should** be proud of our state.

We should be proud of Idaho for many reasons! We have the beauty of mountains, lakes, rivers, canyons, and streams. Great forests, deserts, and wide open spaces stretch across our state. Wild animals, birds and fish live only a short way away from our homes. Our many farms and ranches raise first-rate crops and fine animals. Our towns are pleasant towns and our cities are clean. We have good highways and good weather. Most of our air and water is clean, and we are working to make them even cleaner.

Most of all, we should be proud of our people. Each of us, you and I, are part of the great Idaho family. We are honest and hardworking, and we get along well together. We are white and black, yellow and red. We belong to Protestant, Mormon, Catholic, Jewish, Buddhist, and other churches. We have built a great state across the mountains and desert, and someday you will likely help take care of it and keep it great.

Our Symbols Tell About Our State.

Every state has symbols that tell something about it. Idaho has many state symbols and a state song, *Here We Have Idaho*. Each of these shows something beautiful about our state. We also have a state flag with a Great Seal in the center. Let us look closely at each symbol.

The mountain bluebird is Idaho's state bird. IDAHO HISTORICAL SOCIETY

State Bird. The **mountain bluebird** is our state bird. It is very bright blue and smaller than a robin. You may see one along a country road or in the mountains the next time you visit there. Because they eat insects and weed seeds, they are valuable birds. They build their nests mostly in holes in trees or in spaces between rocks. They leave Idaho each winter but return early in the spring.

The Syringa is Idaho's state flower. OFFICE OF IDAHO SECRETARY OF STATE

State Flower. Have you ever seen our state flower? Or smelled it? The **syringa** is a lush bush with white blossoms that have a powerful sweet perfume. It grows on hills and along streams in many parts of Idaho. When you find a syringa, it is all right to pick some of the flowers. They smell oh so good!

The Appaloosa horse is Idaho's state animal. VIRGIL YOUNG

State Animal. The next time you see a horse in a field, look for one with spots on it. If it has a lot of spots, it is likely to be an **Appaloosa**, Idaho's state horse. The Appaloosa is used for racing, for jumping, for show, and for pleasure.

The Appaloosa was named for the **Palouse** country. When trappers and explorers first came to Idaho, the Nez Perce Indians were already grazing large herds of these fine horses on the grassy prairies of the Palouse. Many believe that "a Palouse" became the word "Appaloosa." In 1519, Spanish explorers brought several spotted horses to America from Spain. These horses spread, and by 1730 the Nez Perce were riding them in northern Idaho.

The Western White Pine is Idaho's state tree. A. B. CURTIS #13–5011 U OF I LIBRARY

State Tree. The western white pine is Idaho's best known and most valuable tree. It may grow more than 200 feet tall, and live for hundreds of years. The largest forest of western white pine in America is found in Idaho, mainly north of the Clearwater River. The world's tallest western white pine tree stands near the town of Elk River. It is more than 219 feet tall! Why not plant one on Arbor Day and watch it grow!

State Gem. The star garnet is a breathtaking stone. People wear it in rings, pins, and other kinds of jewelry. If you want to see some, visit a shop that sells gem stones. The star garnet most often has a star with four rays against a very dark red or purple. A few have six rays instead of four. The star garnet is found mainly along stream beds in Benewah and Latah counties.

The Hagerman horse is Idaho's state fossil.
VIRGIL YOUNG

State Fossil. Three million years ago, the **Hagerman Horse** was a fine, healthy horse. It was grazing on grassy land near Hagerman, when it got stuck in a muddy swamp and drowned. Its bones lay buried in the mud until they became **fossilized**. This horse was almost a "modern" horse, but its ancestors were quite small, about the size of a dog. These horses died out. After that, America had no horses until the Spanish explorers brought them from Spain in 1519. The Hagerman Horse stands on display at the Hagerman Museum in Hagerman.

State Flag. The state flag flies over our state capitol along with the American flag. There may be one in your school. It is dark blue with the Great Seal in the center. The flag is five feet, five inches long and four feet, four inches wide. Three sides have gold fringe. Below the Great Seal is a scroll with the words "State of Idaho" in block letters.

State Insect. The beautiful orange and black **Monarch Butterfly** is Idaho's state insect. Females lay their eggs on the underside of milkweed plants. Monarchs live from a few months up to a year and travel many miles during their lifetimes.

State Dance. The **square dance** is the American Folk Dance of Idaho. The modern square dance came from earlier dances brought from France and England by early white settlers.

State Fruit. Several kinds of **huckleberries** are native to Idaho. They are found in forest areas, particularly between 4,000 and 6,000 feet elevation. Bears love huckleberries!

State Fish. The **Cutthroat Trout** is native to Idaho. Its name comes from a reddish slash mark under its lower jaw. Lewis and Clark found cutthroats on their journey west. They are found in both northern and southern Idaho.

State Vegetable. Of course, the **potato** is Idaho's state vegetable. Idaho is known around the world for its fine potatoes, and Idaho grows more potatoes than any other state.

Great Seal of the State of Idaho OFFICE OF IDAHO SECRETARY OF STATE

Great Seal. The Great Seal of Idaho is a picture that has many symbols. It stands for the State of Idaho and is used to mark things that belong to our state. You will find it on state buildings, office doors, and on letters mailed from state offices. Look for the Great Seal the next time you visit a state office.

Idaho's is the only state seal designed by a woman. Emma Edwards Green designed it in 1890. It is a round picture with a shield in the center. Each part of the picture is a symbol of something important to Idaho. In the shield, the pine tree stands for our forests, and the river stands for irrigation. Above the shield is the head of an elk, which stands for Idaho's many wild animals. Above that are the words "Esto Perpetua," the state motto, which means "May it be forever."

The larger picture in the seal shows other symbols. The woman holding the scales is Justitia, goddess of justice. A miner holds a pick and shovel, standing for Idaho's great mineral wealth. Below is a bundle of grain and two "horns of plenty" overflowing with harvested food. These stand for the richness of Idaho's soil.

Review Questions

1. Our state symbols are:
(a) State Bird ____________ [*14*]
(b) State Flower ____________ [*15*]
(c) State Tree ____________ [*16*]
(d) State Animal ____________ [*15*]
(e) State Gem ____________ [*16*]
2. In the Great Seal of Idaho, what does each symbol stand for?
(a) Pine tree ____________ [*17*]
(b) River ____________ [*17*]
(c) Miner ____________ [*17*]
(d) Elk ____________ [*17*]
(e) Grain ____________ [*17*]
(f) Woman ____________ [*17*]

Ideas to Talk About

1. Choose your favorite symbol and tell why you like it.
2. What do our symbols tell about Idaho?
3. Each state has its own state bird, state flower, and state tree.
(a) Why do states choose such things for their symbols?
(b) Would an alligator be a good symbol for Idaho? Why or why not?
4. Nevada's state bird is also the mountain bluebird, but its state flower is the sagebrush. Montana chose the bitterroot for its state flower. Both the sagebrush and the bitterroot grow in Idaho, but Idaho chose the syringa for its state flower. How do you think people decide which bird, flower, or tree to use as a state symbol?

Idaho Has Many Parts.

Idaho is a Big State. How big is Idaho? Idaho is bigger than the states of New York, New Jersey, Massachusetts, and New Hampshire put together! Thirty-seven of the 50 states are smaller than Idaho. We have 83,557 **square miles** of land. Idaho is about the size of England and Scotland together. Some people like to say that if all the mountains and hills in Idaho were spread out flat, Idaho would be bigger than Texas. Now that would be big!

What does Idaho look like? If we could look down from an airplane, we would see many kinds of land: high and low, forest and desert, rocky plains and rich farms. Some of the land looks the same today as it did before settlers came here to live. Idaho has many parts, and sometimes these seem like separate countries. Let's go up in an airplane and look down at the different parts of Idaho.

Desert Country. Before us stretches the giant Snake River Plain. Below us the gray-green desert lies baking in the sun, and the strong smell of sagebrush is everywhere. At first, the desert seems to be just bare, dry land. If we drop down for a close look, we will see that this is not true. The desert is a busy place. There are many animals living here—mice, ground squirrels, snakes, lizards, and dozens of others. We might even see some coyotes, foxes, deer, or antelope. In springtime there will be green grass and tiny young flowers. Some people love to take a picnic and go hiking or biking in the desert. Most of the year, there are beautiful bushes and flowers to delight visitors.

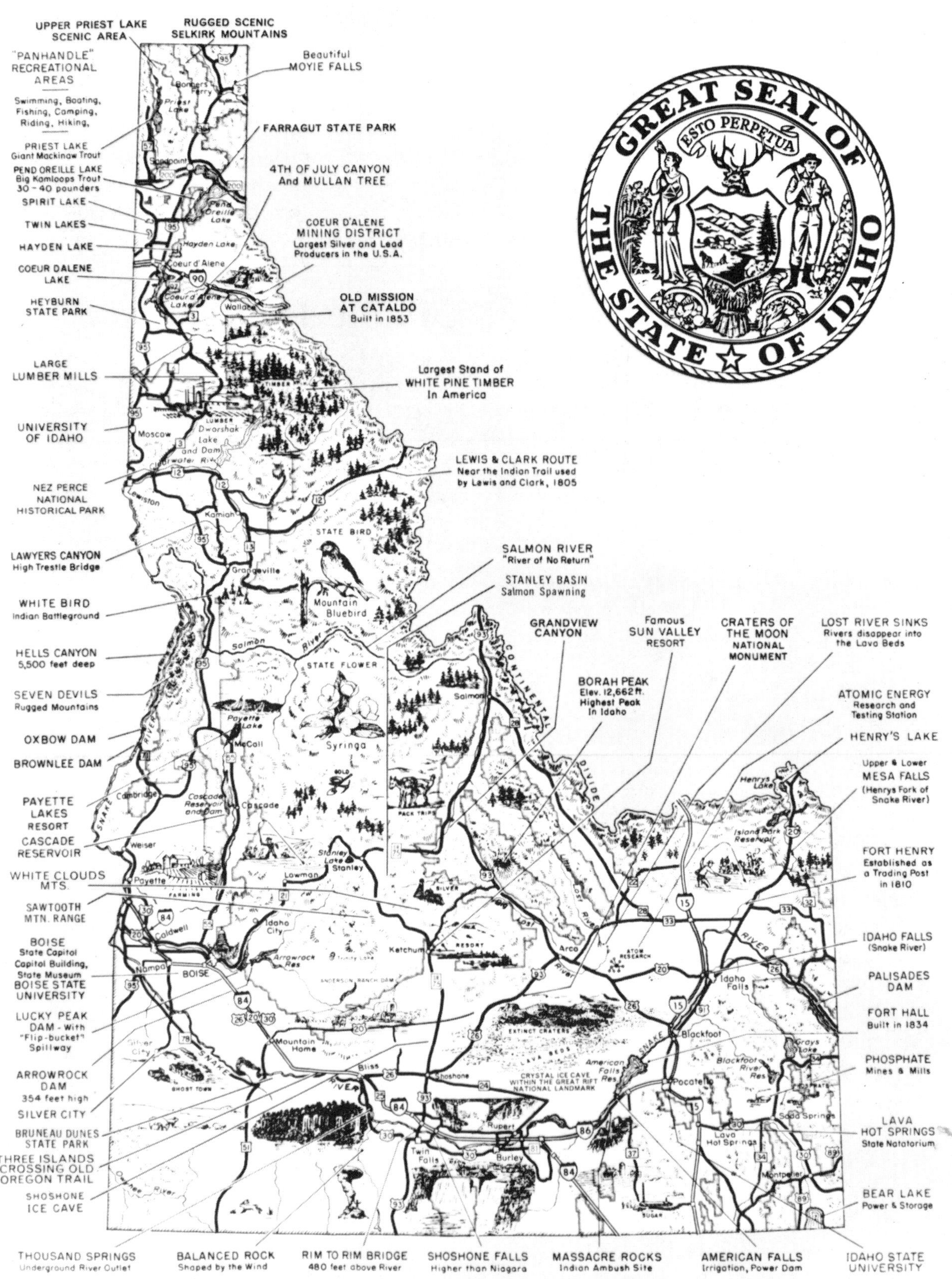

Idaho is an exciting place to live. IDAHO TRANSPORTATION DEPT. & RAND MCNALLY & CO.

Mountain Country. Let's head our airplane north. Do you ever think about the fresh smell of pine trees? Cool, quiet mountain lakes? Sparkling-clear mountain streams? If you like mountains, you are lucky to live in Idaho. Mountains cover about half of our state. We go there to ski, camp, fish, hunt, or just explore. This is where we look for many of our wild animals: fish and birds, deer and moose, squirrels and chipmunks, and bears, to name a few. Mountains have other important uses, too, as we will see later on. Idaho's many mountains have many names, but all of them are part of the great Rocky Mountain Range.

Lake Country. As we fly over the mountains, we will see many lakes. Idaho has more than 2,000 lakes with names, and thousands of others without names. Some can't be found on any map! People say that **Lake Coeur d'Alene** and **Lake Pend Oreille** are two of the most beautiful lakes in the world. Perhaps you have visited Payette Lake, Redfish Lake, Bear Lake, or one of Idaho's other beautiful lakes.

Wouldn't you like to try catching one of these Idaho trout? VIRGIL YOUNG

River Country. We can't fly far without seeing a river. Rivers begin high in the mountains. Small, swift streams carry the water out of the mountains into larger rivers. The Snake River is the biggest and longest river in Idaho. Many smaller rivers flow into the Snake, making it the twelfth largest river in the United States. Idaho's other large rivers are the Salmon, the Clearwater, the Clark Fork, and the **Pend Oreille**.

Schweitzer Basin, near Sandpoint, is a favorite ski area. IDAHO DEPARTMENT OF COMMERCE

Idaho's rivers have many dams. From above, we can see a lake spread out behind each dam. The lake made by the dam is called a **reservoir**. Dams are built to store water for **irrigation**, to make electricity, and to keep flood water from destroying farms and cities. The Snake River has several important dams and reservoirs. Perhaps you have seen the dam at American Falls, Salmon Falls, or Hells Canyon.

Canyon Country. A canyon is made when a river cuts a deep path into the earth's crust. Idaho's rivers run through many canyons, large and small. Have you heard of Hells Canyon or some other Idaho canyon? Our three most important canyons are the Salmon River Canyon, the Clearwater Canyon, and the Snake River Canyon.

Some canyons have interesting waterfalls. Let's go down closer and look at some. Big Fiddler Creek has one of the highest falls in the state—600 feet high. This is above Arrow Rock Dam on the South Fork of the Boise River. Moyie Falls is known for stone shapes that make the water seem to be full of colored glass. We

Lake Pend Oreille is one of the world's most beautiful lakes. IDAHO DEPARTMENT OF COMMERCE

can see this on the Moyie River near Bonners Ferry. On the Snake River near the city of Twin Falls, we can see the giant Shoshone Falls. This great waterfall is higher than Niagara Falls in New York. Some Idaho towns have "Falls" in their names: **American Falls**, **Idaho Falls**, **Post Falls**, and **Twin Falls.**

The Salmon River has been called the "River of No Return." Indians and early explorers learned that once they floated down the canyon, they could not go back up again. The water was too swift, and the canyon was too narrow, rocky, and rough. There are many places where you can't get through on foot. Now we can go up the Salmon River Canyon by jet boat.

The Clearwater Canyon is not as deep, narrow, or rough as the Salmon River Canyon. Its height above sea level is low, and its winters are warm. The Nez Perce Indians made this canyon their home for thousands of years, and many still live there. Towns are now found in the Clearwater Canyon. The largest is Lewiston, where the Clearwater River flows into the Snake River. The canyon is large enough for small farms, and its long growing season is good for growing fruits and vegetables. You will learn more about the Clearwater country later on.

Jason Lewis caught this 26-pound 6½-ounce kamloops trout in Lake Pend Oreille. It took two hours to reel it in. VIRGIL YOUNG

Snake River Canyon. The Snake River Canyon is divided into several interesting parts as it cuts its way across Idaho. Just before reaching the city of Twin Falls, the river drops over two giant waterfalls: Twin Falls and Shoshone Falls. The city was named for Twin Falls, but Shoshone Falls is higher and more exciting to look at. At Shoshone Falls, the river drops 212 feet into a great boiling pool below. Five miles later at the edge of the city, the Snake flows through Blue Lakes Canyon. Blue Lakes Canyon has farm land and a country club almost 500 feet straight down from the desert floor!

Another interesting part of the Snake River Canyon is Hagerman Valley. This small farming valley is a wide part of the canyon. Along the north wall of the canyon is Thousand Springs. Here, water gushes out of the rocky canyon wall and pours into the Snake River. This water has flowed under the ground for many miles. Some of it has come all the way from Big Lost River and Little Lost River near Arco. Both of these rivers disappear into rocky ground about 150 miles north and east of Hagerman Valley.

Bruneau Canyon is about 800 feet deep at this spot. Notice the steep canyon walls. VIRGIL YOUNG

The best-known part of the Snake River Canyon is called Hells Canyon. We can fly through this canyon if we are very careful. Hells Canyon is the deepest canyon in North America. It measures 7,900 feet from the bottom of the canyon to the top of He Devil Peak. This is almost a mile and one-half deep, which makes it 2,250 feet deeper than the Grand Canyon of the Colorado River in Arizona.

Prairie and Plateau Country. As we fly along the Snake River in southern Idaho, we can see broad strips of land rising above the valley. These are called **plateaus**. This land is very dry, so only desert plants grow here unless someone brings water to it. These plateaus are used for grazing cattle and sheep.

At Shoshone Falls, the Snake River drops 212 feet into the canyon below. Shoshone Falls is higher than the famous Niagara Falls of New York.

HELEN LEE

Cattle ranches are found in many parts of Idaho.
#6-55-85 U OF I LIBRARY

In northern Idaho, we can look down on a huge plateau that drains into the Clearwater River. This is the Clearwater Plateau, a great piece of rolling **prairie** land. This land receives enough rain and snow to raise fine crops. It is important farm country. Much of Idaho's wheat and green pea crop grows here.

Ranch Country. Looking down from our airplane, we can see animals grazing over wide stretches of land. This is ranch country. Ranches are often found in mountain valleys and on desert plateaus. In summer, cattle, sheep, and horses may graze in mountain meadows and on forest land. For winter, however, they must be taken to warmer places such as lower valleys or desert land. Though some ranches are small, others have thousands of acres of land.

People have great fun riding kayaks down Idaho's wild rivers. IDAHO DEPARTMENT OF COMMERCE

Farm Country. Idaho is a farming state. We can see farms in almost every direction we look. There are farms north, south, east, and west. Some are large, and some are small. Some must be watered to grow crops, while others get enough water from the rain and snow. We will find farms in nearly every valley in the state. Most of Idaho's farms, however, lie in the giant Snake River Valley.

Idaho farms can grow almost any kind of food. We even have farms that grow rainbow trout for sale to restaurants and food stores. Our farms grow much more food than Idaho people can eat, so a lot of it is sold in other states and other countries. Idaho farms are important to every one of us. They not only grow the food we eat, but they also make jobs for Idaho families.

Review Questions

1. Idaho is bigger than which other states put together?
(a) ____________ (b) ____________
(c) ____________ (d) ____________ [*17*]

2. How many states are smaller than Idaho?
____________ [*17*]

3. What are some animals that we might see in the desert?
(a) ____________ (b) ____________
(c) ____________ [*17*]

4. What Idaho lakes are said to be two of the most beautiful lakes in the world? (a) Lake ____________ (b) Lake ____________ [19]

5. A lake made by a dam is called a ____________. [19]

6. Idaho's biggest and longest river is the ____________ River. [19]

7. A canyon is formed when a river ________________________ [19]

8. Some Idaho towns with "Falls" in their names are:
(a) ____________ Falls
(b) ____________ Falls
(c) ____________ Falls
(d) ____________ Falls [20]

9. The Salmon River was called "The River of No Return" because ________________________ [20]

10. Hells Canyon is ____________miles deep. [21]

Ideas to Talk About

1. How are the parts of Idaho different from each other?

2. Why are reservoirs important to Idaho?

Nature Has Given Idaho Many Great Gifts.

Do you like outdoor fun? Idaho is an "outdoor" state. People love to spend time in our mountains and forests or in the wide-open spaces. They come from far and near to camp, hike, fish, hunt, and ski, or just enjoy the clean air and water. No matter where we live in Idaho, outdoor fun is close to our front door.

Nature's gifts are called **natural resources**. These gifts give us more than fun, however. We need them to live. Our soil, water, trees, and wild animals are all natural resources. We use these things to make food, clothing, houses, heat, and other things we must have to live. In Idaho, we are lucky to have many kinds of natural resources. Let us take a closer look at some of them.

Soil and Water. Idaho's land has some of America's richest soil. Rich soil is found in all parts of our state, north, south, east, and west. Soil needs water to make things grow, and Idaho is lucky to have a lot of water. Our water comes from rain and snow and from our many fine rivers. Water also makes electricity for our homes, farms, factories, and businesses.

Trees and Forests. Forests cover about one-third of Idaho. Our forests grow much of America's lumber and paper. The most important are pine, fir, and cedar. Our most valuable tree is our state tree, the western white pine. White pine makes high-grade lumber that is used for making many things, even toothpicks and matches. Northern Idaho has America's largest forest of western white pine.

Wealth From Under the Ground. Idaho is rich in valuable ores. The most important of these are gold, silver, **lead**, and **zinc**. Idaho has large amounts of **gypsum** (used to make wall board) and **phosphate** (used for making fertilizer). In our canyons and deserts, people find valuable gem stones such as our State Gem, the star garnet. Idaho has 72 kinds of gem stones, such as **agates**, **rubies**, and **jade**. In the whole world, only Africa has more kinds!

The snowy owl is sometimes seen in northern Idaho, but lives mainly in the Arctic. This large owl hunts in the daytime, rather than at night.

IDAHO DEPARTMENT OF FISH AND GAME

Deer can be seen in many places. IDAHO DEPARTMENT OF FISH AND GAME

Wild Animals. Wild animals are perhaps our most exciting gift from nature. Deer or trout might come to mind first, but Idaho has hundreds of different kinds of wild animals. There are fish, birds, and all kinds of fur-bearing animals, large and small.

Our lakes and streams have dozens of kinds of fish. You may know about trout, salmon, and bass, but there really are many kinds. Birds are everywhere, too. You often see robins, ducks, and geese, but you can also find cranes, hawks, eagles, and lots of others. Idaho is rich also in large animals such as elk, deer, moose, bighorn sheep, and cougar. Small animals are easy to find: skunks, squirrels, rabbits, beaver, bobcats, and many, many more.

Review Questions

1. Three of Idaho's natural resources are:
(a) ____________ (b) ____________
(c) ____________*[23]*

2. Idaho's most valuable tree is the ____________. *[23]*

3. What are four kinds of wild animals found in Idaho?
(a) ____________ (b) ____________
(c) ____________ (d) ____________ *[24]*

In Idaho, a mountain lion is called a cougar. This large cat may be more than five feet long, not counting the tail. Cougars like to avoid people.
IDAHO DEPARTMENT OF FISH AND GAME

Strange and Surprising Things From Nature.

Did you know that hot water flows out of the ground in some places? These are called hot **springs**. Hot spring water is used in the swimming pools of some Idaho vacation spots. Near **Bruneau** Canyon is Hot Creek. This mile-long creek of hot water empties into Indian Bathtub. Indians once came here to bathe in the hot water. In Boise, many homes and other buildings are heated by hot water pumped from the ground.

Caves are another surprise. Idaho's largest cave is **Minnetonka Cave** near the town of Paris. It has an unknown number of huge rooms under the center of a mountain. Idaho has many interesting caves. Wind Cave, near Milner, whistles as the wind blows through small openings. Kuna Cave, near Kuna, is a long dry tunnel. The Hot Caves, near Twin Falls, were once filled with hot water. Some of our caves have no names, and a few have been "lost" because people have forgotten where they are.

Perhaps Idaho's strangest caves are the ice caves. Deep under the hot desert floor in southern Idaho are three caves of ice. Shoshone Ice Cave is under a **lava** field near Shoshone. The

These swimmers are having fun in warm water. The water comes from a natural hot spring.

VIRGIL YOUNG

Here is the "throne room" of Minnetonka Cave. Minnetonka Cave is found in Bear Lake County.

IDAHO DEPARTMENT OF COMMERCE

This geyser can be seen near Soda Springs.

IDAHO DEPARTMENT OF COMMERCE

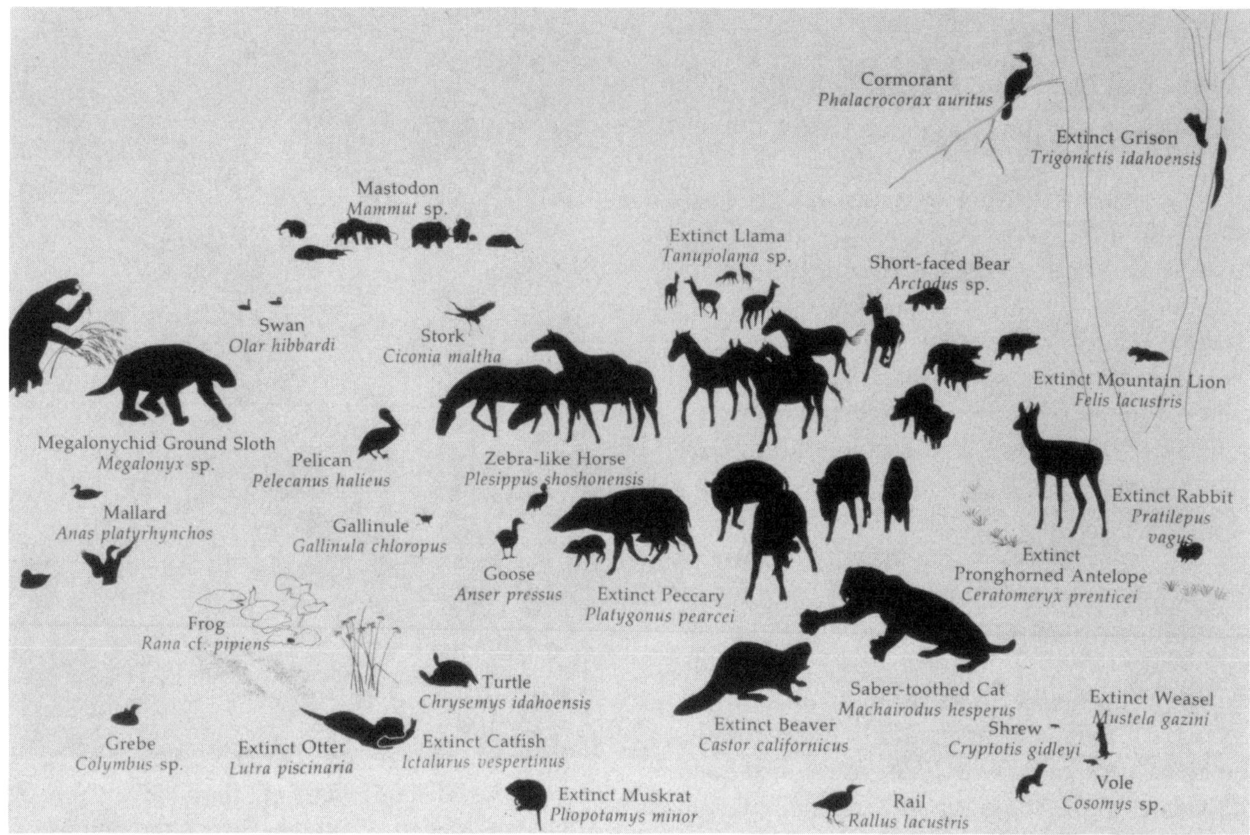

Fossils of all these animals have been found near Hagerman. The animals lived there about 3.4 million years ago. PHOTO NO. 76- 8502 THE SMITHSONIAN INSTITUTION

floor, walls, and ceiling of this large cave are covered with ice. Crystal Falls Cave is near St. Anthony. It has large spaces and a frozen "river" along part of its length. The third is Crystal Ice Cave in the Great Rift National Landmark near Aberdeen.

Idaho has other strange rocky shapes, too. **Fossils** are buried in Hagerman Valley. The bones of ancient horses and many other animals have been found there. Balanced Rock near Castleford has been shown in pictures around the world. Shaped like a giant balloon 40 feet tall, this huge rock is balanced on a small piece of stone. There is a "City of Rocks" near Gooding, and another in Cassia County. The huge rocks seem almost like old broken buildings made from stone. Towers and sky scrapers reach from 100 to 250 feet into the air. Some rocks look like castles with stairs and pointed peaks. Others remind us of animals and people. These shapes were made by wind and water over many thousands of years.

Idaho has a lot of interesting lava. The Craters of the Moon near **Arco** is formed from lava. Other lava fields cover much of the Snake River plateau. Two rivers get "lost" in the lava. Big Lost River and Little Lost River flow into lava fields and disappear north and east of Arco. It is believed that they flow under the lava into the Snake River at Thousand Springs near **Hagerman** and **Bliss**.

The famous Balanced Rock can be seen near Castleford. This huge rock stands high above the valley and rests on a very tiny base. VIRGIL YOUNG

At Thousand Springs, water pours out through many holes in the wall of the Snake River Canyon. The water has traveled hundreds of miles under the desert floor from Idaho's "lost rivers." TWIN FALLS PUBLIC LIBRARY

Let us stop to think about all the things found in Idaho's great outdoors. We have read about swift rivers, deep canyons, interesting waterfalls, and beautiful lakes. There are rich farmlands, rough lava fields, caves, and rocks with strange shapes. Also don't forget the wild animals and the mountains. About half of Idaho is mountain country! The things to see and do in Idaho's great outdoors are almost endless. Truly nature has given us many great outdoor gifts!

Ideas to Talk About

1. If you were writing to a pen pal in another state, what kinds of things would you write about to describe Idaho?

Idaho Is Both Old And New.

As America grows, Idaho grows. In Idaho we find new things growing next to the old. We see new shopping centers and tall office buildings. Boise's airport keeps expanding to meet changing needs. Several large companies have built their head offices in Idaho. Our state is crossed by freeways.

Idaho is connected to the world through nuclear research, computers, and satellites in space. Computers help run Idaho factories, businesses, and schools. Idaho "high-tech" companies make computer chips and other computer parts and provide technology services across Idaho and around the world. Nuclear scientists work at Idaho's nuclear research center near Arco. Satellites in space carry television programs between Idaho and faraway places.

Idaho is always growing and changing, and this keeps Idaho new. However, it is important to understand how our state became what it is. To truly understand Idaho, we must learn about the old as well as the new.

Idaho is as old as the earth itself. Of course, we mean the rocks and hills. People came much later. Indian people have lived on Idaho soil for many thousands of years. In 1805, the **explorers** Lewis and Clark first entered what is now Idaho. They had been sent to discover what lay west of the now United States.

In 1805, the United States was just 29 years old. Columbus had come to America 313 years earlier. By 1805, people who sailed across the ocean from Europe had lived along the **Atlantic coast** for almost 200 years. You can see that settlers took a very long time to go all the way west across America to Idaho.

The Idaho National Engineering and Environmental Laboratory (INEEL) is a center for nuclear research. It is located between Arco and Idaho Falls. This picture shows only a small part of INEEL. IDAHO HISTORICAL SOCIETY

Idaho's first permanent white settlement was not built until 1860. That was really a short time ago. The settlement was called Franklin, and it was started in Cache Valley by Mormons from Utah. Only three years later, in 1863, Idaho was made a United States **territory**. Then in 1890, only 27 years after that, Idaho became the 43rd state. Your grandmother's grandmother may have been living when Idaho became a state.

A worker at Micron Technology in Boise works in a fabrication corridor where computer memory chips are made. Micron Technology is one of the world's largest makers of computer memory chips. The company began in 1978 in the basement of a dentist's office in Boise and now has factories in several states and foreign countries.
MICRON TECHNOLOGY

You can see that settlers from the United States have made their homes in Idaho for only about 130 years. We are lucky that most of our state is still as fresh and clean as it was when Indians lived here alone. Most of our air is still clean, and many of our streams are still sparkling clear.

The place you live is different from other parts of Idaho. It will be interesting for you to get a closer look at the part of the state where you live. It is also important to know something about other parts of Idaho. Each part of Idaho is an adventure by itself. Idaho is a great place to live, to work, and to play. Our state deserves to be studied so we may know more about it.

Review Questions

1. The first explorers in Idaho were ____________ and ____________.[27]
2. The first explorers came to Idaho in the year ____________.[27]
3. Idaho's first permanent white settlement was built in the year ____________.[28]
4. The name of Idaho's first permanent white settlement was ____________. [28]
5. Idaho became a state in the year ____________. [28]

Chapter 1 Skill Activities

Words and Ideas

In Chapter 1, you will find a number of key words printed in **bold** print. Each key word stands for an important idea. Answering these questions will help you understand some of the key words.

You can find the key words in the Glossary at the back of the book. The number after each question is the page where the idea is found in the book. Answer each question with a complete sentence.

1. What was the Appaloosa named for? [*15*]
2. Idaho's state fossil was found near what town? [*16*]
3. What is the name of Idaho's state gem? [*16*]
4. Where can you see the mountain bluebird? [*14*]
5. What are some examples of Idaho's natural resources? [*23*]
6. Where would we look to find a plateau? [*21–22*]
7. What is the star garnet used for? [*16*]
8. Explain what a symbol is. [*14*]
9. Where would you look to find a syringa growing? [*15*]
10. In what part of Idaho does the western white pine grow? [*16*]

Fun With The Idaho Map

How do you go from your town to another place in Idaho? Look at a highway map of Idaho. Find your own town and the place you want to go.

See what **directions** you must travel: east,

west, north, south, northeast, northwest, southeast, southwest. Then find which **highways** you need to follow:

Example: You live in Lewiston and want to drive to Kellogg. Find Lewiston and Kellogg on the map. You will see that you can't simply drive northeast to Kellogg.

Answer: "To get to Kellogg, go north on Highway 95 to Coeur d'Alene, then go east on Interstate 90."

Activity: Write the directions for getting from your town to the following places:

1. Balanced Rock
2. Bruneau Canyon
3. Craters of the Moon
4. Hells Canyon
5. Lake Coeur d'Alene
6. Lake Pend Oreille
7. River of No Return
8. Shoshone Falls
9. Thousand Springs

Using Your Imagination

1. *Choosing a Place to Live.* On our airplane ride, we looked at deserts, mountains, lakes, rivers, canyons, ranches, and farms.

(a) Choose the place that you would like to live.

(b) Make a **diorama**, 3-D model, or drawing of the place.

(c) Write a story about the place you have chosen.

2. *Wildlife.* Do you like fish, birds, and other wild animals? Make a chart, booklet, or bulletin board of Idaho's wild animals. You may cut out pictures or draw your own.

You can write for information from: Idaho Department of Fish and Game, 600 South Walnut, Boise, Idaho 83707.

Research Projects

1. *Endangered Animals.* Some of Idaho's wild animals are **endangered**. Two of these are the bald eagle and the osprey.

(a) What does it mean for an animal to be endangered?

(b) Are any other Idaho animals endangered?

(c) Write a report about endangered animals, using the encyclopedia or other sources. Give your report to the class.

2. *Oral History.* Grandparents and other older people can remember things that happened many years ago. Interview an older person who grew up in Idaho. Ask the person to describe his or her early life and tell about the changes that he or she has lived through. Be sure that you know what years are being described. Perhaps the person would let you tape-record the conversation so you could play it to your class.

Reviewing Chapter 1

Main Ideas In This Chapter

1. Idaho is an exciting place with many things to see and do.
2. Idaho is proud of our fine people.
3. Our symbols show the beauty of our state, as well as some important ideas about the way we live.
4. Idaho has many parts: deserts, mountains, lakes, rivers, canyons, prairies, and plateaus.
5. Nature has given Idaho many gifts: soil and water, trees and forests, wild animals, and wealth from under the ground.
6. Idaho has things that are very old standing next to things that are very new.

Picture Books of Idaho

The following books have excellent color photographs showing many Idaho landscapes and other scenes. Children will enjoy visiting Idaho through these beautiful pictures.

Anderson, Kirk. *Idaho Discovered*. Ketchum, Idaho: Stoecklein Publishing, 2000.

Schwantes, Carlos Arnoldo. *So Incredibly Idaho: Seven Landscapes that Define the Gem State*. Moscow, Idaho: University of Idaho Press, 1996.

Wells, Merle, and Arthur Hart. *Boise: An Illustrated History*. Sun Valley, California: American Historical Press, 2000.

Wuerthner, George. *North Idaho's Lake Country*. Helena, Montana: American & World Geographic Publishing, 1995.

Life In Idaho

Danielle Olsen

Horses are my favorite kind of animal. I like to ride them. I have a horse named Princess. She is brown and white. Princess bucked me off twice because I got on the wrong side.

Geoffrey Fisher

What I like to do is go camping. It's fun because I get to go fishing and ride in the canoe, if we are by a lake. When we are getting ready to leave, I am very excited thinking about all the fun we are going to have there at the camp site.

Corey Chambliss

I like to go up into the mountains and explore. I really enjoy fishing. I like to fish for steelhead and trout. Sometimes I fish in my back yard, which is on the Little Salmon River.

Cathy Schulz

One day we went camping by a stream. It was a nice sunny day, and my father picked up my aunt and threw her in. I told him to throw somebody else in, so he threw me in, too.

Mitchell Green

I like to run outdoors. You can enjoy scenery that you can't in a car. When you run, it's almost silent, so you don't disturb the wildlife. In a car, you just pass things by and don't really see anything.

Seth Larson

On Sunday our family goes for a ride. If it is winter, we go snow tubing and ride snowmobiles. My dad, mom, sister, and I ride snowmobiles. My brother rides on a tube with a rope tied on the back of mine.

Jeremy Reeves

Sometimes it's nice to be alone. When I go camping, I like to explore the area to see if I can find deer, bear, or raccoon tracks. I like exploring caves, rivers, and mountains. Sometimes I collect bones of animals and make notes of where I was and what I saw.

Monique Henry

I like to go sledding in the winter. We have a big hill behind our house where I can sled.

I like to go skiing. It is fun! In January, all of the fourth-graders went skiing free at Schweitzer.

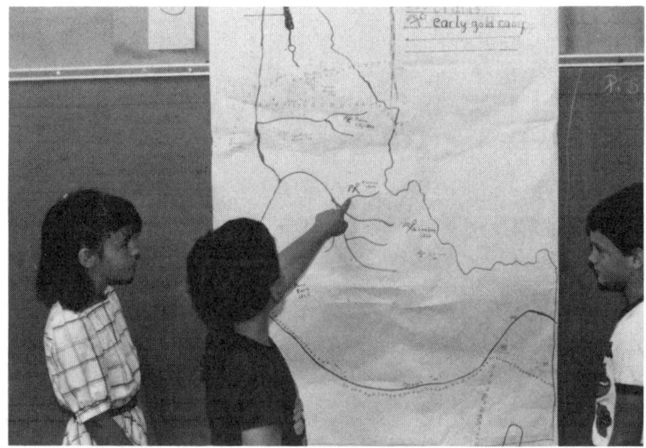

Andrea Beauchene

I like to walk in the woods—
to go mushroom hunting—
to pick wild strawberries—
to swim in Sunnyside—
to fish in Fry Creek—
to watch water bugs, especially a kind that is
green and feathery, like a feathery fish.

Chapter 2
Exploring Idaho's Land

Studying Our Land.

Why should we study Idaho's land? Because there are so many different kinds of it, all in one state. Idaho's land is high or low, flat or hilly, hot or cold, and dry or wet. It is up in the mountains or down in the valleys. Some places get lots of water, while others are too dry to grow crops. Some spots may get ten feet of snow in the winters, and others get almost none. Idaho's many kinds of land are truly interesting.

Geography is Important to Us.

The study of land is called **geography**. Geography helps us understand the shape of the land, its **elevation**, and its **climate**. The shape of the land is like the face of a person. It tells us what the land looks like. **Elevation** is the height of the land above the ocean. **Climate** tells us how hot, cold, wet, dry, windy, cloudy, or sunny

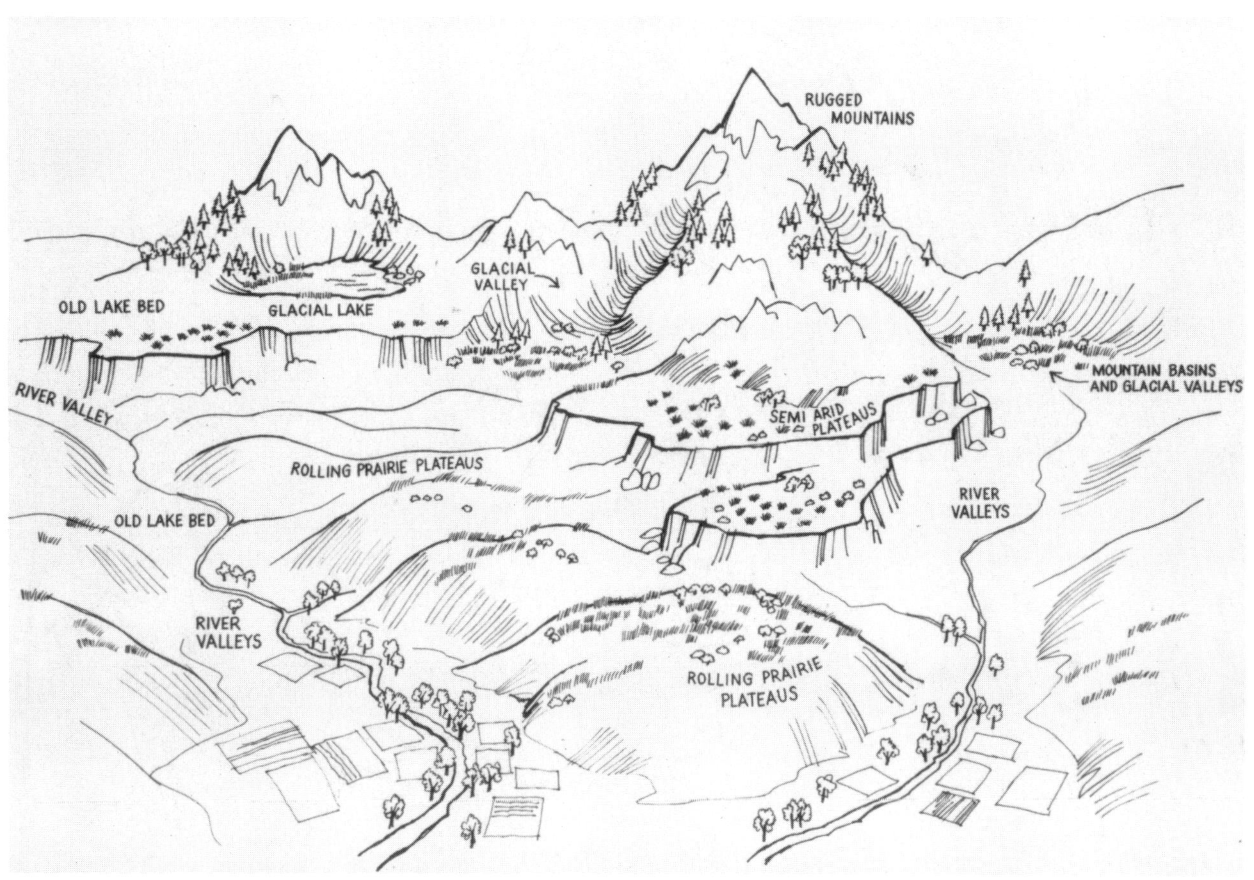

Idaho's land has many faces. What kind of land do you live on? JOHN A. TAYE (DRAWING)

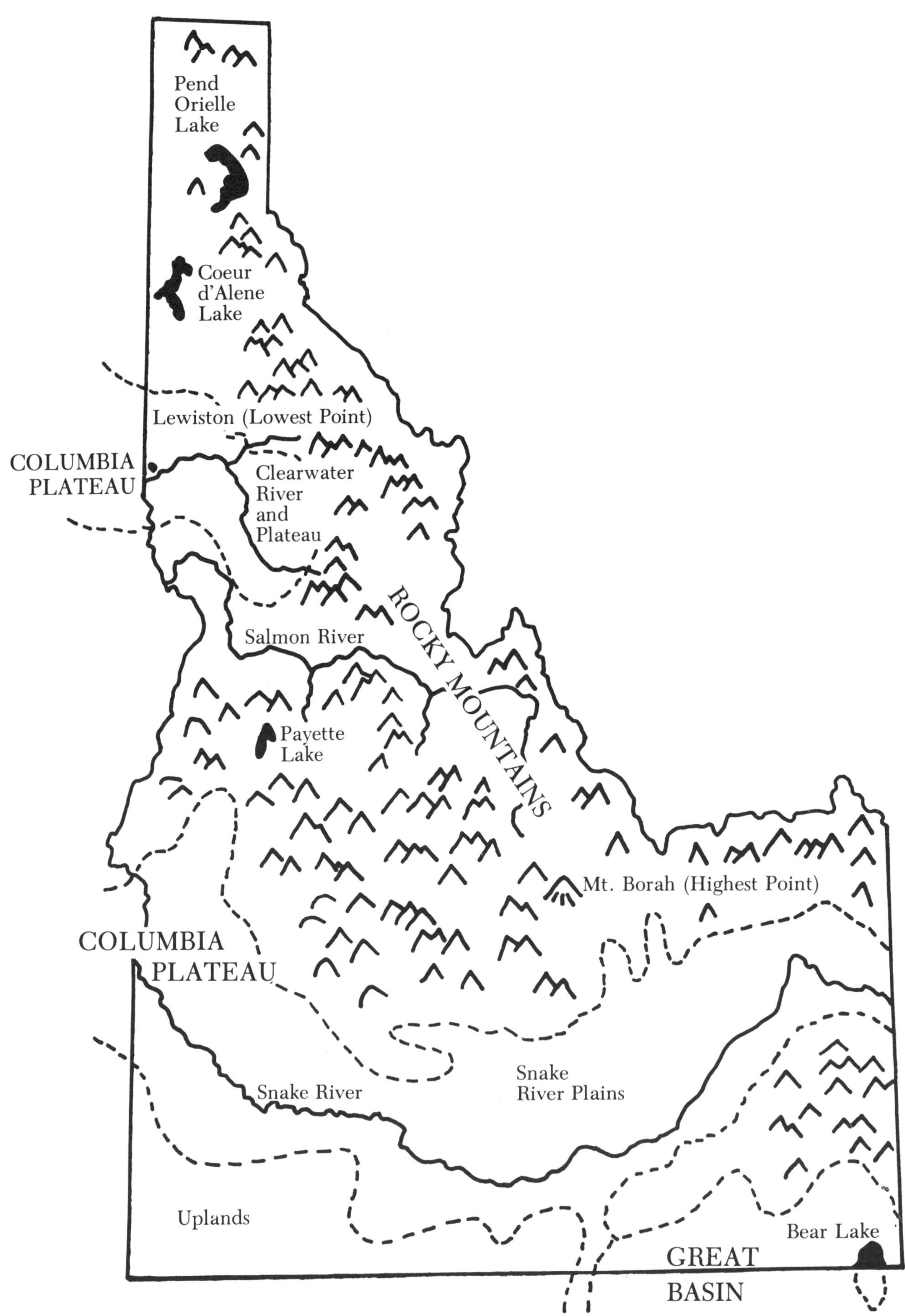
Pend
Orielle
Lake
Coeur
d'Alene
Lake
Lewiston (Lowest Point)
COLUMBIA
PLATEAU
Clearwater
River
and
Plateau
ROCKY MOUNTAINS
Salmon River
Payette
Lake
Mt. Borah (Highest Point)
COLUMBIA
PLATEAU
Snake River
Snake
River Plains
Uplands
Bear Lake
GREAT
BASIN

the weather may be. Why are these things important to us? They are important because they help us understand why people live the way they do.

How much does your daily life depend on the place where you live? A lot! Your home, school, job, and play all depend on the kind of land you live on. It is the land that makes jobs, towns, and homes. If you live near a forest, you may depend on lumber. If you live where there is valuable **ore**, you may depend on mining. If you live in a farming valley, you may depend on farming. If the weather is hot or cold, dry or wet, it helps decide what you will do and how you will do it.

When people go somewhere to live, they make changes in that place. They build homes and settlements. The record of the things people do is called **history**. Because the land helps decide how people live, it also decides many things about their history. For this reason, we cannot study Idaho's history without also studying its geography.

When the Indian or Native American people first came to Idaho from faraway lands, what did they find? They found a land that gave them food—wild animals, fish, and plants to eat. The land also gave them **shelter**—places to live while they hunted and gathered food. Idaho's forests, streams, valleys, canyons, and caves gave them comfort and safety. In these ways, Idaho's first people depended on the land and geography for their families, homes, and settlements.

Why did other people come to Idaho? They came first to **explore** the land—our geography. Fur trappers came to make money by trapping the fur-bearing animals that lived in our mountains and along our streams. That was part of our geography. Later, miners came to dig gold out of the mountains and streams. That also was part of our geography. Still later, farmers came to farm our rich soil. More geography! From this, you can see that geography is quite important for understanding history.

In Chapter 1, we saw maps of Idaho and the country around us. These maps showed where Idaho is and how big it is. In this chapter, we will look at the land itself. In words and pictures we will see the many faces of Idaho's geography. Try to imagine, as we discover different parts of Idaho, how it would be to live in those places.

Review Questions

1. Geography is the study of the ____________. [*31*]

2. When we study the land, we want to know its ____________, its ____________, and its ____________. [*31*]

3. Elevation means ________________________. [*31*]

4. History is ________________________. [*33*]

5. When the Indian people first came to Idaho, the land gave them ____________ and ____________. [*33*]

6. What are three reasons that people came to Idaho after the Indians:

(a) ____________________

(b) ____________________

(c) ____________________ [*33*]

Ideas To Talk About

1. Why is geography important when we study history?

2. How do people's lives depend on geography?

3. How do people decide where they want to live?

The top of Mount Borah is the highest point in Idaho. What is its height above sea level?

IDAHO DEPARTMENT OF COMMERCE

Idaho's Land Has Many Faces.

Few places on earth have so many kinds of land as Idaho. In our state you will find forests, deserts, and rolling farmland. You will find mountain lakes, rivers, deep canyons, and high water falls. You will find low spots and very high spots. The lowest place is 728 feet above **sea level** near the edge of the Snake and Clearwater rivers in **Lewiston**. The highest spot is the peak of **Mount Borah**, 12,662 feet above sea level. The number of feet above sea level is called elevation. Most of the state is much higher than Lewiston and much lower than Mount Borah. The **average** elevation for all of Idaho is around 5,000 feet.

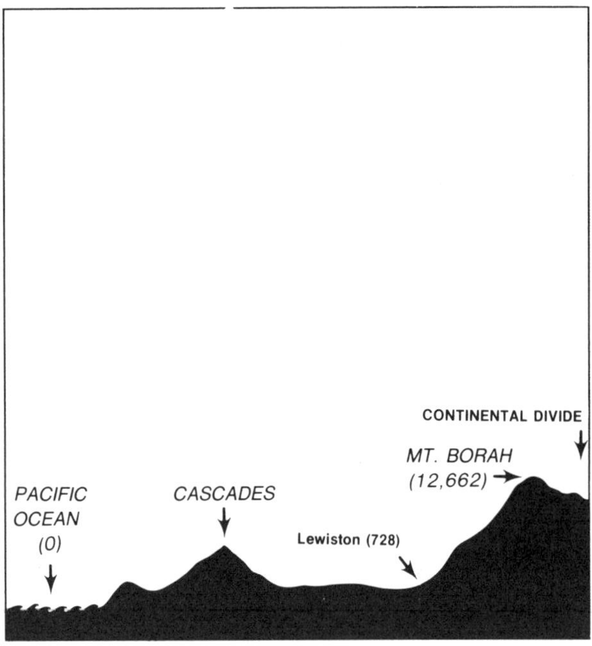

Geographic Regions of Idaho. The United States has many **geographic regions**, and Idaho is divided among three of them. The three are the **Rocky Mountains**, the **Columbia Plateau**, and the **Great Basin**. These Idaho lands will show us many different faces.

A little more than half of Idaho is in the Rocky Mountains. This is a land of mountains, forests, lakes, and streams—and many kinds of wild animals. It lies north of the Snake River Plain and reaches all the way to **Canada**. Idaho shares the Rocky Mountains with several other states: Montana, Wyoming, Utah, Nevada, and Colorado.

The Columbia Plateau lies mostly in Oregon and Washington, but parts of it reach into Idaho. It is huge. In southern Idaho, the great Snake River Plain stretches from **Oregon** almost to **Wyoming**. This is desert land. Other desert land reaches south to **Nevada**. In northern Idaho, the Columbia Plateau is rolling prairie land. Northern Idaho land is green, not desert land like southern Idaho.

The Great Basin is land where the rivers can't drain into an ocean. The water runs into salt-water lakes and dries up. The Great Basin covers most of Nevada and parts of California, Oregon, **Utah**, and Idaho. Idaho's part of the Great Basin is called the Bear River Basin. It lies next to Utah. Water from the Bear River Basin flows into Utah and drains into the Great Salt Lake.

Review Questions

1. The lowest place in Idaho is in ____________. It is ____________ feet above sea level.[*34*]
2. The highest spot in Idaho is ____________. It is ____________ feet above sea level.[*34*]
3. The average elevation in Idaho is ____________ feet above sea level. [*34*]
4. Idaho is divided among three geographic regions: (a) ____________, (b) ____________, and (c) ____________.[*34*]

Ideas To Talk About

1. What geographic region do you live in?
2. What does the land near your town look like?
3. What do you think we mean when we talk about the "face" of the land?

The Rocky Mountains Cover About Half of Idaho.

Do you like the mountains? Maybe you like camping or hiking. Maybe you like fishing or swimming in the clear mountain water. If you do, you are lucky to live in Idaho. Mountains cover about half of our state. Most of them lie north of the Snake River, and they reach all the way to Canada.

Idaho's mountains are part of the huge Rocky Mountain Range. We share the Rockies with several other states. The Rocky Mountains have the interesting job of separating the Pacific Ocean from the Atlantic Ocean. High up in the Rockies is a line of peaks that look both east and west. This line of peaks is called the **continental divide**. The land facing west slopes away toward the Pacific Ocean. Those rivers flow into the Pacific. The land facing east slopes away toward the Atlantic Ocean. Those rivers flow into the Atlantic. Part of this divide runs along the peaks of the Bitterroot Mountains that separate Idaho from Montana.

Wilderness Areas. The most interesting parts of Idaho's mountains are our seven **wilderness areas.** These are mountain areas that are still much the same as they were before the explorers came. The wilderness is kept for people to visit and enjoy. Laws protect it from being changed or damaged. There are no roads, and people are not allowed to live there. Trees cannot be cut for lumber. No cars or trucks of any kind are allowed. Idaho has more wilderness than any other state but Alaska.

When you visit these parts of Idaho, you must

Mountain goats live on the high rocky peaks of Idaho's mountains. IDAHO DEPARTMENT OF FISH AND GAME

Many people like to backpack or ride horses in Idaho's wilderness areas. Why are cars, trucks, motorcycles, and other machines not allowed in the wilderness areas? #6-63-10 U OF I LIBRARY

Elk like to graze in mountain meadows.
IDAHO DEPARTMENT OF FISH AND GAME

Bears are often seen in Idaho's mountain areas.
IDAHO DEPARTMENT OF FISH AND GAME

walk, ride horseback, or fly. There are trails for people and horses, and also a few landing fields for small airplanes. When you camp, you will have only the things you and your horse can carry. You will find steep mountains, tall trees, and clear, cold water. The lakes and streams are alive with fish, and you will see wild animals of many kinds.

A few people lived there many years ago. That was before laws were made to protect these places. You may still find some old cabins and fences left from ranching days. There are also a few old mines. The old things are rotting away, and nothing new can be built. Someday, everything that people built there will be gone, and then people can enjoy the land just as nature made it.

Life In Idaho's Mountains. People do live in the mountains. Often they work in mines, lumber mills, ranches, or vacation spots. Mountain towns are small because jobs are hard to find there.

When you visit the mountains, you may see lumber mills, large trucks, and trains loaded with logs, lumber, and wood chips. You might also see mines, mills, and piles of ore and waste. In summer, cattle and sheep graze on mountain sides and in the mountain valleys. Wild animals live all around, mostly out of sight. However, along the roads, streams, and lakes, you can often see exciting birds and animals—hawks, eagles, bears, deer, moose, porcupines, chipmunks, and lots of others.

Of course, you will see people! Thousands come to visit—to fish, swim, boat, camp, or hunt. Some like to hunt for rocks, wild flowers, and insects, or just take pictures of the beautiful things all around. In winter, they come to ski, ride snowmobiles, play in the snow, or just sit by a cheerful fire.

Trout fishing is a favorite Idaho sport. VIRGIL YOUNG

Snow and Water. Snow is nature's way of storing water to use at a later time. We use that water in our homes, and farmers use it to water their crops.

Snow melts slowly in the mountains. The mountains are high, and the air is colder than in the valleys. As the sunshine melts the snow, the water runs into the streams and rivers. Dams have been built in the rivers to catch and store much of this life-giving water in **reservoirs**. Farmers use it later in the summer to water their fields. Much water sinks into the ground. From there it is pumped out for use on farms and ranches. Towns also get their water from the rivers or by pumping it from the ground. Without this life-giving water, Idaho would have very few farms, crops, animals—or towns.

Idaho's largest river is the Snake River. Most of Idaho's water drains into the Snake before it leaves the state at Lewiston. The Snake River begins in the mountains of Yellowstone Park in Wyoming. As it flows through Idaho, other rivers empty into it. Though the Snake River flows through long stretches of Idaho desert, its water comes from high in the mountains. Many towns and farms in southern Idaho depend on the Snake River for their water.

The Salmon River is the largest mountain river in Idaho. Because of the great amount of water it carries, it is the most important river flowing into the Snake. It drains most of central Idaho. The Salmon River Canyon is more than a

The rugged Sawtooth Mountains look down on these women bike racers. ORE-IDA FOODS, INC.

This photo shows the Salmon River Canyon in Lemhi County. Gold can still be found here.
IDAHO DEPARTMENT OF COMMERCE

The Bitterroots are among Idaho's most rugged mountains. They lie along the Idaho-Montana border. A. B. CURTIS #13-646 U OF I LIBRARY

mile deep in some places, the second deepest canyon in North America. Only Hells Canyon is deeper. The river is very swift with many **rapids**, and it has steep, rocky walls. You already learned that this river is often called "The River of No Return."

The Salmon River cuts nearly all the way across Idaho from Montana to Oregon. It begins and ends in Idaho. The river starts high in the mountains at more than 8,000 feet above **sea level**. Here tiny streams of melting snow come together to make a larger stream. By the time it passes through the Salmon River Canyon, it is a large river. After a journey of about 420 miles, the Salmon River empties into the Snake River.

By the time the Salmon River reaches the Snake, it has fallen about 7,000 feet! Between Riggins and White Bird, the canyon changes from 1,800 to about 1,600 feet above sea level.

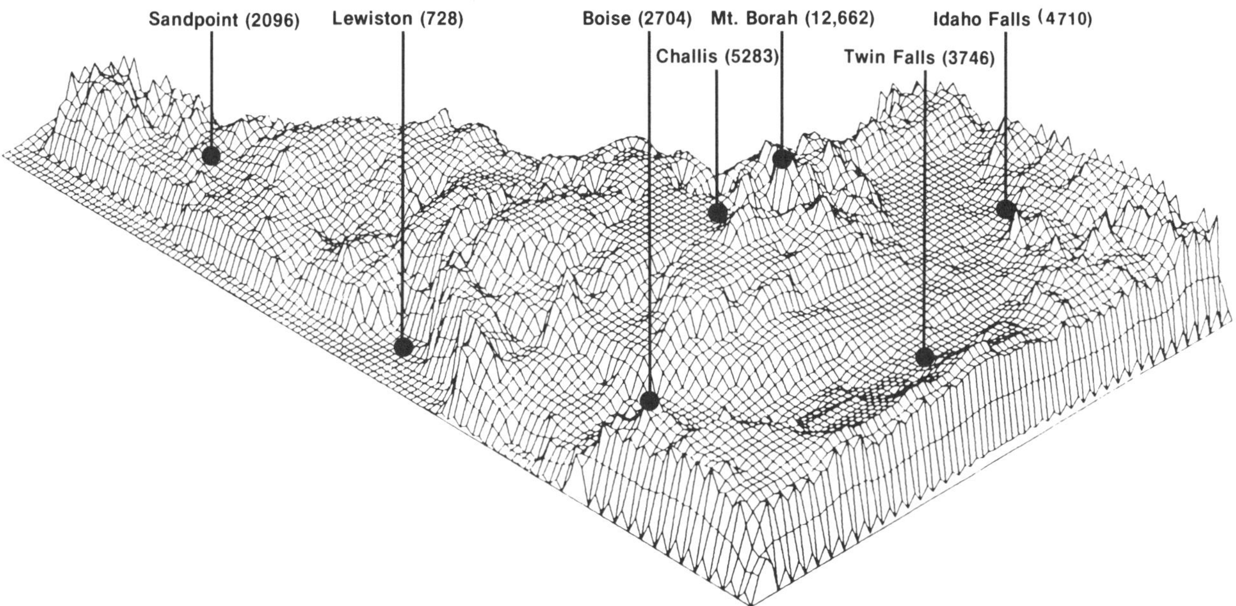

Here the weather is warm, and the growing season is good for crops. People farm small patches of land in the narrow canyon. These are really too small to be called farms, but the people grow fine fruits and vegetables.

Review Questions

1. About how much of Idaho is covered by mountains? ____________. [34]
2. Most of Idaho's mountains lie north of the ____________ and reach all the way to ____________. [34]
3. A wilderness area is ________________________. [35]
4. In the mountains, nature stores water in the form of ____________. [37]
5. Idaho's largest river is the ____________. [37]

Ideas To Talk About

1. Are wilderness areas a good idea? Why or why not?
2. What do you like best about the mountains?
3. Why are our mountains important to all of Idaho?
4. What would happen to most of the farms in Idaho if the mountains didn't get a lot of snow in the winter?

Ice carved Lakes and Valleys. Long ago, thick sheets of ice covered large parts of the earth's surface. In Idaho, ice spread from Canada as far south as Lake Coeur d'Alene. It was more than 4,500 feet thick at Sandpoint! This great piece of ice was a **glacier**. Sometimes smaller glaciers filled our mountain valleys. The glaciers formed when snow piled up year after year without melting. Over time, the snow turned into ice.

An Idaho glacial valley is seen from high above.
PUBLIC AFFAIRS OFFICE, MOUNTAIN HOME AIR FORCE BASE

The glaciers didn't just sit still—they moved! They pushed slowly toward lower land, cutting into mountains, carving out valleys, and moving great amounts of soil. In other places, the great weight of the ice pushed down, making hollows in the earth. These filled with water and became lakes. Of course, Idaho's huge glaciers have long since melted and gone.

A **glacial valley** is made when a glacier cuts a path through the mountains. It leaves a U-shaped path. The valley and the mountains on both sides make the shape of a giant letter "U". This is different from a river valley. A river valley is cut by flowing water, and it makes the shape of a giant letter "V".

Idaho has thousands of lakes left behind by glaciers. Most of them were formed behind dams of rock and earth that the glaciers left behind. Lake Pend Oreille and Lake Coeur d'Alene were made in this way. Glacier-formed lakes are highly praised for their beauty. Lake Pend Oreille and Lake Coeur d'Alene are said to be among the world's most beautiful lakes.

Not every mountain hollow fills with water. If it doesn't, it may become beautiful green meadow land. Stanley Basin is such a place. People come from far and wide to enjoy its beauty. Sharp peaks of the Sawtooth Mountains look down at fat cattle grazing on tall green grass. You can stop for lunch in one of the small towns such as Stanley, where only about a hundred people stay the year round. The exciting Salmon River flows past the edge of town—clear, swift, and full of fish. Only a few miles away, you can camp beside clear, clean lakes such as Redfish Lake and Stanley Lake—glacial lakes, of course.

Review Questions

1. A glacier is a giant piece of ____________. [39]
2. A glacier forms when ____________ piles up year after year without melting. [39]
3. A glacial valley is formed when ________________________. [40]
4. A glacial valley is shaped like a giant letter ____________, while a river valley is shaped like a giant letter ____________. [40]
5. Two of Idaho's glacial lakes are said to be among the most beautiful in the world. They are Lake ____________ and Lake ____________. [40]

A glacier cuts a U-shaped valley. JOHN A. TAYE (DRAWING)

A stream or river cuts a V-shaped valley. JOHN A. TAYE (DRAWING)

Stanley Basin is a popular vacation area. Why do you think people like to vacation here? IDAHO DEPARTMENT OF COMMERCE

Ideas To Talk About

1. How is a glacier like a bulldozer?
2. Have there been glaciers where you live? How can you tell?
3. How could snow pile up deep enough to form a glacier?

The Columbia Plateau Provides Most of Idaho's Farm Land.

Most of Idaho's rich farmland sits on the Columbia Plateau. This giant **plateau** reaches into both north Idaho and south Idaho. It is a giant piece of land with different faces in different places.

In southern Idaho, the Columbia Plateau is called the Snake River Plain. This huge plain stretches 400 miles from **Oregon** almost to **Wyoming**. The Snake River Plain is desert land. This land must be **irrigated** for farming.

In northern Idaho, the Columbia Plateau is **prairie** land. It is separated into a number of smaller prairies, each with its own name. This part of Idaho gets more rain and snow, so it is not desert land like the Snake River Plain. Most northern Idaho farms get enough rain and snow to grow good crops without irrigation.

Idaho's Rich Prairie Lands. What is a **prairie**? A prairie is a large piece of land that grew mostly grass before it was plowed up for farming. It has rich, deep soil well-suited for farming. Many of Idaho's prairies are also **rolling** land. Rolling land has many small hills and knobs. Idaho's rolling prairies have some of the richest farmland in America. They lie close to mountains and get plenty of rain and snow to grow good crops.

Many Idaho towns sit on prairie land. Perhaps you have visited **Moscow**, Grangeville, Fairfield, or Ashton. These towns, spread across the state, sit on prairies. Prairie land grows fine crops of grain, peas, hay, and pasture. Some places grow fruit orchards, but mostly at lower levels. The land around **Mesa** once had the world's second largest apple orchard. Apples were sent from Mesa to many parts of the United States and far-off countries—Norway, Denmark, and even Egypt! The Mesa orchards are gone now, but you can still see a few old apple trees standing on the hillsides around Mesa.

This rolling prairie is part of the Palouse Country. What two important crops are grown here? #6-17-41 U OF I LIBRARY

The prairie land around Moscow is often called the Palouse Country. This is rolling land drained by the Palouse River, which is mostly in Washington state. The soil is dark and very rich. The Palouse Country is known for its heavy crops of wheat and green peas. Moscow calls itself the "Pea Capital of the World." Palouse soil holds the world's record for the most wheat grown on a single **acre** of land.

Idaho's largest prairie is on the Clearwater Plateau in northern Idaho. It begins at Lewiston where the Clearwater River flows into the Snake River. From Lewiston it spreads east and south about fifty miles on both sides of the Clearwater River. It starts at only 728 feet above sea level in Lewiston, but rises to more than 3,390 feet near Grangeville.

The Clearwater Plateau has fewer people than the Snake River Plain. Most of the towns are small, and there are no large cities. Lewiston is the largest with fewer than 30,000 people. Grangeville and Orofino each have fewer than 4,000 people. However, this is an important part of Idaho, with rich soil and many farms.

Review Questions

1. A prairie is land that ________________________. *[41]*

2. Four Idaho towns that sit on prairies are:
(a) ____________ (b) ____________
(c) ____________ (d) ____________. [*41*]

3. Idaho's largest prairie is on the ____________. [*41*]

4. Idaho's prairies are found in the ____________ geographic region. [*41*]

5. Most Idaho prairie land does not need irrigation because it receives enough ____________ and ____________ to grow good crops. [*41*]

Barges are loaded with Idaho grain, lumber, and other freight here at the Port of Lewiston. Where do the barges go when they leave Lewiston? THE PORT OF LEWISTON

Clearwater Valley: Idaho's Great Surprise.

The Clearwater Valley is a surprise because it is different from other parts of Idaho. It has warmer winters and a long growing season. The Clearwater Valley is formed where the Clearwater River cuts deeply across the Clearwater Plateau. The river has cut canyons and carved deep valleys. Lewiston has the lowest point at 728 feet above sea level. Not only is this valley the lowest part of the Clearwater Plateau, it is also the lowest part of Idaho! You already learned that the average elevation for the whole state is 5,000 feet. Lower land has warmer winters than higher land. You can see why the Clearwater Valley has Idaho's warmest winters.

Nez Perce Indians built winter homes in Clearwater Valley long before settlers came from the United States. They had many villages along the Clearwater. Two of them were **Kamiah** and **Lapwai**, which are still towns today. Often the warmer winters bring rain there even if it is snowing at higher elevations. Sometimes the valley gets snow, but it soon melts away.

Clearwater Valley lies at the bottom of Clearwater Canyon. Clearwater Canyon is the deep canyon that carries the Clearwater River through the Clearwater Plateau. It is long and narrow for a valley. It is as wide as three miles in some places, and as narrow as a city block in others. It reaches from **Kooskia** downstream to Lewiston.

If you visit the Clearwater Valley, you will see small farms and small towns. You will drive through such places as **Lapwai**, **Orofino**, and **Kooskia**. In the yards of many homes, you will see fruit trees and vegetable gardens. The long growing season is good for raising fruits, vegetables, berries, and melons. There are fruit orchards around Lewiston. Part of the city is called Lewiston Orchards because orchards grew there before the land filled up with houses. The Clearwater River flows into the Snake River at Lewiston.

The edge of Lewiston is on the Snake River. Here you will see goods being loaded for shipment to far-off places. Lewiston is Idaho's **in-**

You are looking up the Clearwater Valley. Part of Ahsahka is seen on the left side of the river. The Lewis and Clark party spent several days at this spot building dugout canoes in 1805. VIRGIL YOUNG

land seaport. From Lewiston barges carry wheat, logs, lumber, other goods down the Snake and Columbia rivers to Portland. From there those goods will travel to many parts of the world.

About ten miles up the Clearwater from Lewiston, Henry and Eliza Spalding built a Nez Perce Indian mission in 1836. They built a house, school, and church. They also planted fields and gardens and began raising cattle, pigs, and sheep. The mission is no longer there. In its place stands the village of Spalding and a beautiful park on the banks of the Clearwater. The area is now part of the Nez Perce National Historical Park, and it is a favorite spot to visit.

Ideas To Talk About

1. How is the Clearwater Valley different from other parts of Idaho?
2. Why would the Nez Perce choose to settle in the Clearwater Valley?
3. Lewiston is hundreds of miles from the Pacific Ocean. How can it be called a seaport?

The Snake River Valley Is "Magic" In The Desert.

Who would stare openmouthed if they could see the Snake River Valley today? Idaho's early explorers and settlers! When they first saw it, the Snake River Valley was just dry desert land. There was only sagebrush, other desert plants, and patches of rock. It was much too dry for farming. In many places the desert came right to the edge of the river. The river flowed right on by without wetting the nearby land.

Bringing Water To The Desert. Today the Snake Valley is Idaho's largest farming area. It now has more farms than all the rest of Idaho. It also has more towns and more people. Two out of every three Idaho people live in the Snake River Valley. This has been made possible by **irrigation**. Irrigation means watering the land with ditches or pipes. Water has made the desert bloom with crops, farms, and towns. It is

Irrigation has made southern Idaho's desert land bloom. Notice the small ditches (corrugations) that carry water down the rows. Where does this water come from? U.S. BUREAU OF RECLAMATION

no wonder that part of the Snake River Valley is called Magic Valley!

Desert land needs to be irrigated because it receives very little rain and snow. The lack of rain and snow makes the soil too dry to grow crops. There may be enough desert plants to graze cattle and sheep, but the land can't be farmed unless someone brings water to it. The Snake and the other rivers running into it carry huge amounts of water. Our people have found ways to bring the water onto the land.

The amount of water that falls on land is measured as **rainfall**. This means all rain, hail, and snow—melted. Idaho's desert land gets less than twenty inches of rainfall a year. Much of it receives less than ten inches. With less than ten inches, the land is dry indeed, and barely enough plants grow to graze cattle and sheep.

Today huge canals carry water from reservoirs to hundreds of farms in the Snake River Valley. Some farms use huge electric pumps to take water from the Snake River. Other farms get water by pumping it from wells deep in the ground. Far more than half a million people depend on this water.

Review Questions

1. Desert land receives very little ____________ and ____________. [44]
2. Rainfall is ____________________________. [44]
3. Idaho's desert land gets less than ____________ inches of rainfall, and much of it receives less than ____________ inches. [44]
4. Desert land must be ____________ if it is to grow crops. [44]
5. Irrigation is ____________________________. [43]
6. Huge ____________ carry irrigation water to hundreds of farms. [44]
7. Some farms use electric pumps to take water from the ____________ River or pump it from ____________ deep in the ground. [44]

The Snake River Valley Is Divided Into Parts. To some people, the Snake River Valley means only the valley from Ashton south to Pocatello. The Snake River Valley is really more than 400 miles long, reaching all the way to Oregon. In most places it is 50 to 75 miles wide. Other places are as narrow as 25 miles. Some parts have their own names. Hagerman Valley, Swan Valley, and Grand Valley are really parts of the Snake River Valley. The wide plain around Mountain Home and all of the Boise Valley belong to the Snake River Valley.

The Snake River Valley has three natural parts. These parts are separated by plateaus that come almost to the river. (1) The Upper Snake River Valley begins in Teton Valley and around Island Park. It reaches down the river below American Falls. (2) The Magic Valley is the middle part. It reaches down to Twin Falls County and Gooding County. It includes Hagerman Valley. (3) The Lower Snake River Valley begins below Bliss and stretches to Oregon. Another part of the valley lies in Oregon.

If you live in the Snake River Valley, you know what a surprising place it is. Green fields lie next to dry sagebrush land. Irrigation canals run everywhere. You can stand on the hot desert floor and see beautiful mountains towering above the valley. Some of these mountains still have snowcaps in August.

You see towns and cities, broad freeways, and country roads. You see fields of sugar beets and potatoes; tall fields of corn; and hay, grain, seed beans, and dozens of other crops. Thousands of cattle fill feed lots and pastures.

Factories can be seen here and there. These factories make sugar, flour, and animal feeds,

The Grand Tetons look down on Idaho's Teton Valley. The mountain peaks lie just across the border in Wyoming. HELEN LEE

These horses live on an irrigated farm in the Snake River Valley. VIRGIL YOUNG

bricks and fertilizer, mobile homes, and lots of other things. There are businesses and stores everywhere. You can see colleges and universities. In Boise, you can see the beautiful state capitol building. Last but not least, you can see people. Everywhere, people are working, playing, building, and making Idaho a fine place to live.

Review Questions

1. The Snake River Valley is more than ____________ miles long, reaching all the way from Ashton to ____________. [44]
2. The three natural parts of the Snake River Valley are: (a) The ____________, which begins in Teton Valley and reaches ________________________,
(b) The ____________, the middle part, which reaches ________________________,
(c) The ____________, which begins below Bliss and stretches ________________________. [44]

Idaho's Desert Plateaus. Desert plateaus are the higher lands that lie between the valleys and the mountains of southern Idaho. Most of these are part of the Snake River Plain. This land is without trees or other tall plants. Mostly they have a thin cover of sagebrush, spring grass, and desert wild flowers. Much of this land cannot be farmed because it is too far from irrigation water.

Lava rock covers great stretches of desert plateau land. Much lava is found in Butte, Lincoln, Minidoka, and Power counties. Smaller patches are found in many places. Some of the lava-covered land is nothing but hard, rough rock. Other land has just enough soil for desert plants but not enough for farming. Such land can be used for grazing cattle and sheep.

What is **lava rock**? Lava is rock that melts and flows out of the ground. It melts deep in the earth and comes out through **volcanoes** and large cracks in the ground. Often it spreads out and covers wide stretches before it cools. When it cools, it becomes hard and rough.

The **Craters of the Moon** is America's best-known lava plateau land. This rocky stretch of land is between the towns of Arco and Carey. It was named Craters of the Moon because it looks so much like the surface of the moon. The land is rocky and rough, and it is without life as we think of it. The surface is made up of broken rock, cones, cracks, caves, and holes.

How old is the lava in southern Idaho? Scientists believe that it flowed at different times between 2,100 and 15,000 years ago. This may seem to be a very long time ago. However, it was only yesterday when we think of the age of the earth.

Lava rock covers great stretches of desert plateau land. VIRGIL YOUNG

Review Questions

1. Some desert plateau land cannot be farmed because ________________________. [45]
2. Lava is rock that ________________________. [45]
3. The Craters of the Moon got its name because ________________________. [45]

The Craters of the Moon are America's most famous lava beds. What kinds of things can you see at Craters of the Moon? IDAHO DEPARTMENT OF COMMERCE

Ideas To Talk About

1. Look at the picture of the Craters of the Moon. Describe what you see.

The Great Basin Is Small In Idaho.

The Great Basin is a huge desert area that lies mostly in Utah and Nevada. However, a small part of the Great Basin reaches into Idaho. Idaho's part is called the **Bear River Basin**, which is in the southeast corner of our state. All the streams in the Bear River Basin drain into the Bear River. In turn, the Bear River flows into Utah and drains into the Great Salt Lake. The Great Basin was once filled with Lake Bonneville, which you will read about later.

Today no water can flow out of the Great Basin because it is lower than the land around it. All of its rain and melted snow runs into streams that drain into one of its salt-water lakes. (Some of the streams are used to water farm land.) The lakes are salty because the water evaporates, leaving its salt behind.

The Bear River Basin. The Bear River Basin isn't like the land around the Great Salt Lake. Its lower valleys have valuable farm and ranch land. Most of the farmland must be irrigated, but there is plenty of water from the Bear River and other nearby streams. There are also mountain valleys and basins that are used for grazing cattle and sheep.

Besides farming, the Bear River Basin has large amounts of phosphate rock. There are several phosphate mines near Soda Springs and Conda. Phosphate mining is a growing industry in this part of our state.

When you visit this part of Idaho, you will see small, beautiful valleys. Fields of hay and grain grow along the roads, and dairy and beef cattle graze in the valleys. The towns are small and the people are friendly. Idaho's oldest town, Franklin, sits very close to Utah. The larger towns are Montpelier, Preston, and Soda Springs. A favorite vacation spot is Bear Lake, which lies in both Idaho and Utah. Bear Lake is one of the most beautiful lakes in the West.

Review Questions

1. Most of the Great Basin is in the two states of ____________ and ____________. [46]
2. Idaho's part of the Great Basin is called the ____________. [46]
3. All water from the Bear River Basin flows into ____________ and drains into the ____________. [46]
4. Besides farming, the Bear River Basin has several ____________ mines near Soda Springs and Conda. [46]

Ideas To Talk About

1. The Great Basin is unusual because no water drains out of it. Why doesn't it drain into the ocean?
2. Where does the Great Salt Lake get its water?
3. How does a lake become salty?
4. Why aren't all lakes salty?

Half of Bear Lake lies in Idaho and half lies in Utah. What famous mountain man explored the Bear River? IDAHO DEPARTMENT OF COMMERCE

Most Idaho People Live In River Valleys.

We hear the word valley quite a lot. You most likely live in a valley. Perhaps you know some valley names like Cache, Clearwater, Magic, Payette, Treasure, or Wood River. Of course, the Snake River Valley is the greatest of them all because it is so much bigger.

Still, what is a valley? A **river valley** is the land starting at the river and running to the higher land above it. It lies on both sides of the river. The land above it may be a plateau or it may be mountains. The Snake River Valley has high plateau land all along it. Long Valley and Round Valley near McCall touch the edges of the mountains. A valley may be huge, or it may be tiny. Often the valley is named for the river that flows through it.

Idaho has many mountain river valleys. You can tell a mountain river valley by its shape. When you look up the stream, the valley and the mountains make a V-shape. Because their elevation is high, their growing season is too short for most kinds of farming. Grass and hay grow well, however. These valleys are important for raising cattle and sheep.

Idaho's most important farming valleys are found at lower elevations. They have rich soil and longer growing seasons. In southern Idaho they are mostly irrigated from nearby rivers. Idaho's largest cities all sit in river valleys: Lewiston, Nampa, Boise, Twin Falls, Pocatello, and Idaho Falls. We have already looked at two of Idaho's important valleys: the Clearwater Valley and the Snake River Valley.

Review Questions

1. A river valley is the land ______________________. [47]
2. Mountain valleys are important for ______________________. [47]
3. Idaho's largest valley is the ____________. [47]
4. Idaho's largest cities sit in ____________. [47]

Ideas To Talk About

1. How are mountain valleys different from farming valleys?

2. How can you know a mountain valley when you see one?

Idaho Weather and Climate We all like to talk about the weather. Today the **weather** may be sunny and warm, or it may bring rain or snow. Perhaps the weather is dry, but cold and windy. When we talk about the weather, we talk about a small amount of time.

Weather can change very quickly. **Climate** is different. The climate describes the weather over many years.

Climate is the pattern of **rainfall** and **temperature** over a long time. We think of mountains as having snow in the winter. This is part of their climate. Mountains also have warm weather, and that is part of their climate too.

Temperature. High mountains are cooler than low valleys. Climate changes with **elevation.** Remember that our elevation rises from 728 feet at Lewiston to 12,662 feet on Mount Borah. Our warmest climate lies in our lowest valleys. The Clearwater Valley and the Snake River Valley between Bliss and Lewiston have the warmest climate. They get very hot in the summer, and they stay warmer in the winter. The hottest temperature ever recorded in Idaho was at Orofino in July 1934. It was 118 degrees.

As we move up in elevation, the climate gets cooler. In the summer, Twin Falls (about 3,800 feet) is a little cooler than Boise (about 2,700 feet). Idaho Falls (about 4,700 feet) is a little cooler than Twin Falls. In the winter, Idaho Falls is a lot colder than Twin Falls and Boise. McCall, Hailey, and Montpelier (all higher than 5,000 feet) have even colder winters. The coldest temperature ever recorded in Idaho was 60 degrees below zero at Island Park Dam in 1943.

Rainfall. Much of southern Idaho is desert land. Desert land gets less than 20 inches of rainfall a year. A lot of it gets less than ten inches a year. Desert land must be irrigated to grow crops.

Most of Idaho's desert is found on the Snake River Plain. The Snake River Plain reaches 400 miles across southern Idaho. Touching Oregon on the west, it stretches east almost to Wyoming. Lying between the mountains north and south of the Snake River, it is from 50 to 125 miles wide. Some of the higher parts are lava plateau land. The Snake River Valley is the lower irrigated land closer to the Snake River.

Other parts of Idaho have a desert climate too. These are mostly the low river valleys. Lewiston, in the Clearwater Valley, gets very little rainfall.

All of southern Idaho gets less rainfall than northern Idaho. This is true even in the forests.

Bonneville Flood. The Bonneville flood ripped away huge amounts of lava rock, leaving great holes like this one. This is the Snake River Canyon at Blue Lakes near Twin Falls. It is almost 500 feet deep in some places. The Bonneville flood scattered the lava rock downstream in the form of melon gravel. VIRGIL YOUNG

Because of rainfall, trees in northern Idaho can grow twice as fast as those in southern Idaho.

Northern Idaho gets more rainfall because of the Bitterroot Mountains. Clouds from the Pacific Ocean move east across northern Idaho. Because Idaho's land slopes up toward the Bitterroots, the clouds are pushed higher. As the clouds move higher, they become colder and drop rain or snow. For this reason, Sandpoint, Coeur d'Alene, and Moscow receive a lot more rainfall than southern Idaho cities.

Review Questions

1. Climate is the pattern of ____________ and ____________ over a long time. [*48*]
2. Most of Idaho's desert climate is found on the ____________ in southern Idaho. [*48*]
3. Which gets more rainfall, northern Idaho or southern Idaho? ____________. [*48*]
4. Which is warmer, high land or low land? ____________. [*48*]

Huge Lakes Once Covered Many Idaho Valleys. Long ago, your home may have been on the bottom of a huge lake! Can you imagine Fruitland, Parma, and Emmett under hundreds of feet of water? Thousands of years

Melon Gravel. These large boulders are called melon gravel because of their size and shape. The Bonneville flood scattered thousands of acres of these stones over the Snake River Valley. They got their rounded shape from being rolled along by the flood waters. VIRGIL YOUNG

ago, several southern Idaho valleys were filled with water. Lake Payette filled the Payette Valley and much of southwest Idaho. Lake Idaho and Lake Bruneau filled the Snake River Valley at different times. **Lake Bonneville** filled much of the Bear River Basin. (Preston and Franklin were on the bottom of that lake.) Lucky for us that the water is gone now! These old lake beds have rich soil and make good farmland.

The Bonneville Flood. The best known of these old lakes is Lake Bonneville. About 15,000 years ago, at the time of the glaciers, it was huge. It covered about 20,000 square miles, filling much of the Great Basin in Idaho, Utah, and Nevada. When Lake Bonneville reached more than 1,000 feet deep, its water broke over the edge and cut a path out of the lake. Water poured out in a great flood, down the valley of the **Portneuf** River and into the Snake River. Bigger and bigger became the hole, and bigger became the flood. The lake poured west across southern Idaho, swift and churning, with unbelievable size and power. It filled the Snake River Valley miles wide. Its powerful current carried rocks as big as houses. Within days, the swift and powerful flood had cut into the valley floor, carving out the Snake River Canyon as we know it. The waters of Lake Bonneville thundered across southern Idaho for more than a year. Today's Great Salt Lake in Utah is just a tiny part of old Lake Bonneville.

The Lake Missoula Floods. A series of great floods poured across northern Idaho, perhaps 12,000 to 16,000 years ago. These came from Lake Missoula in Montana, formed by the waters of melting glaciers. The water was held by ice that dammed the Clark Fork River near Lake Pend Oreille. Lake Missoula grew to about 2,000 feet deep near the ice dam, and it covered about 3,000 square miles in Montana.

Whenever water began leaking through the ice dam, within a very few days the whole dam would be destroyed. Water would pour out through Cabinet Gorge and the Clark Fork River. It roared across Lake Pend Oreille and Rathdrum Prairie, then rushed through the Spokane Valley in Washington. For a short time, the flow of water was ten times that of all the rivers in the world! In some spots, it raced along at forty-five miles an hour. On its way across eastern Washington it stripped away soil and rock, leaving a broad path of bare lava. Pushing down the Columbia River, the water carried a great load of rock and soil into the Pacific Ocean. Today these bare parts of eastern Washington are known as the scablands.

The floods would force water up the Snake River from the Columbia, flooding the lower Clearwater Valley. At Lewiston the water could have been 600 feet deep! The Lake Missoula floods would be over quickly. The lake could have emptied in about two days, and most of the flood waters be gone in about two weeks.

Review Questions

1. Old lake beds have ____________ and make good ____________. [*49*]
2. Lake Bonneville covered large parts of what three states: (a) ____________, (b) ____________, and (c) ____________. [*49*]
3. When Lake Bonneville broke, its water ____________________. [*49*]
4. Lake Missoula was located in ____________. [*49*]

Ideas To Talk About

1. What happened during the Lake Missoula Flood?
2. How do floods change the surface of the earth?

Chapter 2 Skill Activities

Words And Ideas

In Chapter 2, you will find a number of key words printed in **bold** print. Each key word stands for an important idea. Answering these questions will help you understand some of the key words.

You can find the key words in the Glossary at the back of the book. The number after each question is the page where the idea is found in the book. Answer each question with a complete sentence.

1. What does an **aquifer** do? [*27, 37*]
2. Part of the **continental divide** separates Idaho from Montana. What is the continental divide? [*35*]
3. What do we mean if we say that Burley has an **elevation** of 4,165 feet? [*31*]
4. How does a **glacier** make a glacial valley? [*40*]
5. If your valley had a **growing season** of 5 months, what would that mean? [*39*]
6. Why must some land be **irrigated**? [*43–44*]
7. Why is Idaho's **prairie** land well suited for farming? [*41*]
8. What do we measure when we measure **rainfall**? [*44*]
9. What is a **river valley**? [*47*]
10. What is unusual about a **wilderness area**? [*35*]

Fun With Maps

1. **Pencil and Paper Map.** Begin with a plain outline map of Idaho. Use a pencil to mark the following:

(a) Mark the highest and lowest points in Idaho. Write in the elevation of each. For the highest point, look between Arco and Challis.

(b) If you can find the information, mark the elevation of your own town.

(c) Along the edges of the map, mark the directions: north, south, east, and west.

(d) Label these parts of Idaho: north Idaho, central Idaho, southern Idaho, eastern Idaho, and western Idaho.

(e) Write in all of our neighbors along the borders of Idaho: Canada, Montana, Nevada, Oregon, Utah, Washington, and Wyoming.

2. **Crayon Map.** (This is a good group or class project). Use an opaque projector to make a large outline map of Idaho (about six feet high). With a pencil, lightly draw in the features described below. When you are sure that you have everything in the right places, color the map with crayons as directed.

(a) Draw in the following major rivers: Clark Fork, Kootenai, Coeur d'Alene, Clearwater, Salmon, Snake, Portneuf, Bear, Boise, and Payette. The Idaho Official Highway Map shows these. Color them blue.

(b) Draw the following lakes: Priest, Pend Oreille, Coeur d'Alene, Payette, and Bear. The Idaho Official Highway Map shows these. Color them blue.

(c) Outline the desert land. See the Snake River Plains on the map [*32*]. This is mostly where Idaho's desert land is found. Color it light brown or tan.

(d) Outline the mountains and forest land. See the mountains on the map [*32*]. Color them medium green.

(e) Draw in Idaho's wilderness areas, and color them dark green. All five are shown on the Idaho Official Highway Map:

(1) Frank Church River of No Return Wilderness Area.
(2) Gospel Hump Wilderness Area.
(3) Hells Canyon Wilderness Area.
(4) Sawtooth Wilderness Area.
(5) Selway-Bitterroot Wilderness Area.

3. **Postcard Map.** Make a collection of picture postcards of Idaho. If you know people who travel around Idaho, ask them to collect some from other parts of Idaho. A gift shop or motel should have postcards from your own part of Idaho.

Once you have a collection of postcards, pin an Idaho Official Highway Map to the bulletin board. Arrange the postcards on the bulletin board around the map. Place colored pins on the map at the spots shown on the picture postcards. Then run a string or a ribbon from each postcard to the pin that locates it on the map.

Using Your Imagination

The Bonneville Flood. A Shoshoni family is living on the Snake River Plain when the Bonneville Flood happened. They hear a great roaring sound off to the east. The ground is trembling. They are on a slope above the valley, and they see a great dust cloud coming toward them. A great wall of water is moving under the dust cloud. Soon the muddy water will roar past carrying whole trees and huge rocks. They will have to climb higher if they are to escape.

You are part of that Indian family. Your brothers and sisters are scared, and so are your father and mother. What do you think? What will you do? Will you make it to high ground? What will happen then?

Rewrite this story and make it your own.

Reviewing Chapter 2

Main Ideas In This Chapter

1. The study of geography helps us understand why people live the way they do.
2. Idaho has many different kinds of land.
3. Idaho is divided among three natural geographic regions: the Rocky Mountains, the Columbia Plateau, and the Great Basin.
4. The Rocky Mountains cover about half of Idaho.
5. Idaho's wilderness areas are protected so people can enjoy the land just as nature made it.
6. Idaho's farms and towns depend on water that is collected and stored in the mountains.
7. The mountains collect snow, which is nature's way of storing water that can be used at a later time.
8. Some of Idaho's mountain lakes and valleys were carved by huge glaciers.
9. Most of Idaho's farmland is located on the Columbia Plateau.
10. Idaho's prairie land is rich farmland, and most of it does not need irrigation.
11. The Snake River Valley is desert land that has been made to bloom by irrigation.
12. Rainfall is the amount of water that falls on the land. It includes rain and melted snow and hail.
13. The Snake River Valley is separated by plateaus into three natural parts: the Upper Snake River Valley, the Magic Valley, and the Lower Snake River Valley.
14. The Craters of the Moon is an interesting and well-known lava area.
15. Idaho's part of the Great Basin is the Bear River Basin in southeast Idaho.
16. The Great Basin does not drain into an ocean.
17. Most Idaho people live in river valleys.
18. Many Idaho valleys were once covered by huge lakes.
19. The Bonneville Flood and the Spokane Flood made important changes on the surface of the land.

More Picture Books of Idaho

Bly, Steve, and Leland Howard. *Idaho Wild and Beautiful*. Helena, Montana: Farcountry Press, 2000.

Gnass, Jeff. *Idaho Magnificent Wilderness*. Englewood, Colorado: Westcliffe Publishers, Inc., 1989.

Lisk, Mark W., and Stephen Stuebner. *Idaho Impressions*. Portland, Oregon: Graphic Arts Center Publishing, 1997.

Technology Resources

Internet Web Sites:

Idaho Compass

http://education.boise state.edu/compass

This colorful geography web site contains interesting, updated information and learning activities for students and classroom ideas for teacher. Great graphics and pictures!

Computer Program:

Oregon Trail 5th Edition, The Learning Company.

Media: CD-ROM. Platform: Mac OS, Windows 95 / 98 / Me / XP / 2000. This is a game for children ages nine and older that pits players against all the hazards a wagon-train voyage can dish out. The program teaches history, map reading, geography, and a variety of other skills.

Time Line

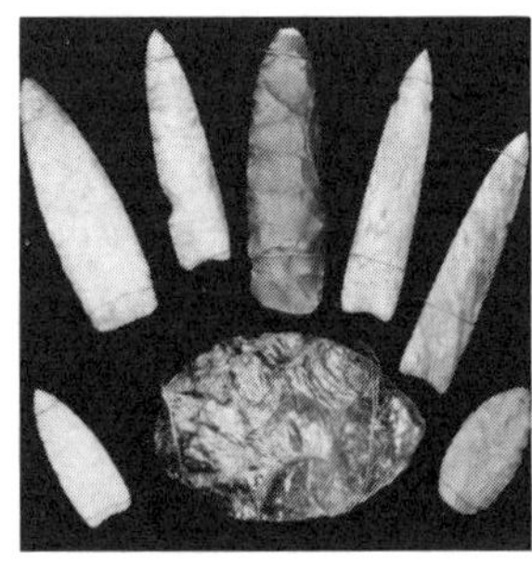

35,000 B.C.		
30,000 B.C.		
25,000 B.C.		Indians come to America from Asia.
20,000 B.C.		
15,000 B.C.		
10,000 B.C.		
5,000 B.C.		
		Birth of Christ
500 A.D.		
1000 A.D.		
1100		
1200		
1300		
1400		
	1492	Columbus lands in America.
1500		
1600		
	1620	Pilgrims come to America in the Mayflower.
1700		
	1730	Idaho Indians get horses.
	1776	Declaration of Independence; USA begins.
1800		
	1805	Lewis and Clark explore Idaho; 1808—Fur trappers come to Idaho.
	1836	Missionaries come to Idaho; 1840—Chief Joseph is born.
	1860	First permanent white settlement in Idaho; 1863—Idaho Territory is formed.
	1890	Idaho becomes a state.
1900		
	1990	Idaho Centennial
2000 A.D.		

Chapter 3
Indians: Idaho's First People

Were There Really Cowboys And Indians?

We have all seen movies about cowboys and Indians. Did you ever wonder if there have been Indians where you live? You can stop wondering. The answer is YES! Wherever you live in Idaho, Indians have lived there, hunted there, or at least been there. Lots of Indians have lived in Idaho, and they still do!

Of course, the Indians we see in movies are not like the real ones. Neither are the cowboys. If you would like to know more about **real** cowboys and **real** Indians, read on. You know that the Indians lived here long before cowboys came. It is only right, then, to meet the real Indians first. Later we will meet the real cowboys.

Wilson Butte Cave. This is one of the oldest known "houses" in North America. People lived in this cave and dined on horse and camel meat 14,500 years ago. We know this because of bones and other artifacts they left. The horses and camels are now extinct. VIRGIL YOUNG

Indians Were The First Americans.

Indians were the first people to live in America. They were living in nearly every part of North and South America when the first people arrived from Europe. Scientists believe the Indians came from Asia between 12,000 and 40,000 years ago. At that time, there may have been a bridge of dry land between Asia and Alaska. Now these two lands are separated by about 75 miles of ocean.

Indians were given the name "Indian" by mistake. When Columbus landed in America, he thought he had found India. He had been trying to reach India by sailing across the Atlantic

You are looking into Wilson Butte Cave. The people who lived here may not be related to Idaho's present Indian tribes. The cave is on a high lava plateau northeast of Twin Falls. The Bonneville Flood could not reach this high. VIRGIL YOUNG

These large spear points and scraper were found buried near Fairfield. They are believed to be between 11,000 and 12,000 years old. The people who left them are called Clovis people. Clovis people may not be related to Idaho's present Indian tribes. VIRGIL YOUNG

Ocean. When he saw people, he called them "Indians." America's Indians had nothing to do with India, but they have been called Indians ever since. Today, they are often called **Native Americans**, because they were the first people to live in America.

Indians Belonged To Tribes And Bands.

An Indian **tribe** was a group of people who shared the same **ancestors**, language, and **customs**. We often hear the names of Idaho's tribes: **Nez Perce**, **Kutenai**, **Coeur d'Alene**, **Shoshoni**, **Bannock**, and **Northern Paiute**. Most of these Indian names are also used as the names of places in Idaho.

Some tribes were small, and others were quite large. The Coeur d'Alene tribe in northern Idaho had only a few hundred people. On the other hand, the Shoshoni were a huge tribe spread across parts of Idaho, Utah, Wyoming, Nevada, and Oregon.

Tribes were made up of smaller groups called **bands**. A **band** was a group of closely related families. In northern Idaho, a band might have 100 people. Bands in southern Idaho were much smaller, with perhaps 30 people.

Villages. Did you know that there were some Indian towns? In northern Idaho, certain Indian villages were **permanent** like small towns. The Nez Perce once had as many as 70 villages, some permanent, along the Salmon, Clearwater, and Snake rivers. Two of these are towns today. Nez Perce lived in **Lapwai** and **Kamiah** for hundreds of years before anyone else came to Idaho.

A Shoshoni mother and child are seen here in the late 1800s. SMITHSONIAN NEG. #45247-C

In northern Idaho, bands would leave their villages in the summer to gather food in far-off places. For winter, they would return to their villages.

In southern Idaho, Indian bands moved from place to place. They had to search over wide areas to find enough food. These bands had no permanent villages. They would settle in a winter camp until spring, then move on to search for more food.

Fort Hall was the home of this Shoshoni girl until about 1910. IDAHO HISTORICAL SOCIETY

Indian Languages. The Indians of North America spoke hundreds of different languages. Idaho's Indians had six languages. Often people from one tribe could not understand people from another tribe. They could "talk" in sign language, however.

Indians did not have a written language. Messages had to be repeated from person to person. This is the reason there was no written history of the Indians before people came to America from Europe. Since then, many Indian languages have been written using the English alphabet.

The Nez Perce village of Kamiah looked this way in 1870. Where is Kamiah located? U OF I LIBRARY

Some people think that Indian rock drawing is "Indian writing". These pictures are not writing. They are really rock art, and often they can't be understood by Indians either.

Review Questions

1. Scientists think Indians came to America from ____________. [53]
2. It is believed that Indians came to America between ____________ and ____________ years ago. [53]
3. A tribe is a ________________________. [54]
4. A band is a ________________________. [54]
5. What two Nez Perce villages are towns today: (a) ____________ (b) ____________. [54]
6. The Indians of North America spoke ____________ of different languages. [55]
7. Idaho's Indian tribes spoke ____________ different languages. [55]
8. Before people came from Europe, the Indians had no written history because ________________________. [55]

Ideas To Talk About

What kinds of problems would people have if they didn't have a written language?

Idaho Indian Houses.

Southern Idaho Indians. Before Idaho's Indians had horses, they had no way to carry heavy loads. Their houses had to be made from things found nearby. A Shoshoni band would build a **wickiup** when they camped. This was a cone-shaped frame made of poles and covered with grass, brush, or strips of bark. A fire pit was built in the middle, and the smoke went up through a hole in the roof. You can see that such a house would have more fresh air than heat. Because the band didn't stay long in one place, they didn't bother to make a better house. When the band moved on, they simply left the wickiup to the wind and weather.

Some Bannock Indians built this wickiup out of rushes and willows. IDAHO HISTORICAL SOCIETY

Northern Idaho Indians. The Indians of northern Idaho lived a more settled life, and their houses showed it. In warm weather, they lived in **lodges** and **longhouses**. The lodge was made with poles and shaped like a cone. It looked much like a **tipi**, but the sides were covered with mats of bark or grass instead of animal skin. The longhouse was just that—a long house. It also was built with poles covered with mats, but it was long enough for ten or more families. It could be made any length, and some Nez Perce longhouses were more than 100 feet long!

When cold weather came, the people gathered in their villages, which were in the warmer valleys. Their winter houses were built partly under the ground. Some were longhouses with earth banked up on the sides. Others were circle-shaped, dug partly into the ground. These were roofed with poles and mats and then covered with earth.

These Sheepeater Indians had their picture taken in about 1871. SMITHSONIAN NEG. #1713

Horses had to be "broken" to make them tame enough to ride. Which Idaho tribe was known for their fine horses? FREDERICK REMINGTON IN *HARPER'S MONTHLY*, JULY 1891.

Tipis and Horses. When Idaho's Indians got horses, they began using the tipi. The tipi was a cone-shaped frame made of poles, but was covered with animal skins. It was well suited for traveling. The poles and skins could be easily carried on pack horses, and they were easy to set up. This was much like present-day Americans who like to take tents and pickup campers along on camping trips.

Horses Changed Indian Life.

The Indians had no horses until the Spaniards brought them from Europe. Before that, Indians could travel only on foot or by canoe. To carry things, they used dogs or else carried the load on their own backs. Even before horses, they sometimes went long distances, but such trips were slow and hard. You must remember that this was long before there were cars, trains, and airplanes.

The first horses were brought to America in the year 1519. **Cortes**, the Spanish explorer, brought them from Spain to Mexico. Other people followed, and they brought more and more horses. These horses multiplied, and many came into Indian hands. Slowly these horses spread to all the tribes in North America. The Shoshoni and Nez Perce had horses by about 1730. When the first explorers arrived in Idaho, they saw many Indian horses.

With horses, it was easy for bands to go great distances. Nez Perce, Kalispel, and Shoshoni bands went on long hunting trips. They rode east over the high mountains, hunting buffalo in Montana valleys and on the prairies of Wyoming. The Nez Perce traded horses with Indians of the Great Plains.

Indians in southern Idaho used jack rabbits for food and for clothing. VIRGIL YOUNG

What Clothing Did Indians Wear?

Early Indians did not have cloth to make clothing like we have today. Each tribe dressed in its own way, making clothing from things they could find where they lived.

Before they had horses, Indians in southern Idaho used rabbit skins for much of their clothing. In cold weather, everyone wore robes made of rabbit skins, and the same robes were used for blankets at night. Both men and women wore **leggings** and **sandals**. In warm weather, a man sometimes wore a **breech cloth** made of animal skin. A women might wear a dress made of sagebrush bark or an apron made of milkweed fiber.

Clothing changed when the Indians got horses. With horses, they could hunt and kill more kinds of animals. Shoshoni and Bannock people began wearing **buckskin** clothing. Buckskin was a soft leather made from the skins of antelope, deer, or bighorn sheep. A man often wore a long buckskin shirt, leggings, moccasins, and a fur cap. A woman might wear a long buckskin dress, leather belt, leggings, moccasins, and a cap woven like a basket.

Indians liked to wear necklaces and other ornaments of bear claws, feathers, brightly colored stones, or copper. They also wore ornaments in their hair. Kalispels sometimes wore earrings made of shells. A few Nez Perce were seen with ornaments in their noses.

Indians used stone scrapers such as this one to scrape the flesh from animal skins. Why didn't they use metal tools instead? #12-2 U OF I LIBRARY

Review Questions

1. A Shoshoni band sometimes camped in a ____________. [55]
2. A wickiup was a ________________________. [55]
3. A lodge was much like a tipi except that ________________________. [56]
4. In northern Idaho, winter houses were built partly under the ____________. [56]
5. The Indians didn't have horses until the ____________ brought them from ____________ in the year 1519. [57]
6. Before the Indians had horses, they had to carry loads ________________________. [57]
7. When Indians got horses, they began to live in ____________. [57]
8. After they had horses, Indians began wearing clothing made from a soft leather called ____________. [58]

Ideas To Talk About

How do people decide what kind of clothing to wear?

What Did The Indian People Use For Food?

Idaho Indians were not farmers. They ate food that grew wild around them. They knew of many roots, bulbs, and berries that were good to eat. Indians spent a lot of time fishing and hunting in order to have fish and meat. Much of the food had to be prepared and stored for winter.

Catching Salmon. The Indians spent a lot of time fishing. Each village had its own places to go fishing. They caught fish with nets, lines and hooks, spears, bows and arrows, and traps built in the water.

Idaho's Indians ate many kinds of fish, but **salmon** was the most important. These big fish are about three feet long and can weigh more than 20 pounds. The salmon were split, cleaned, and hung on poles to dry. Some were smoked on wooden racks over a fire. Cooked salmon was pounded into meal using a mortar and pestle.

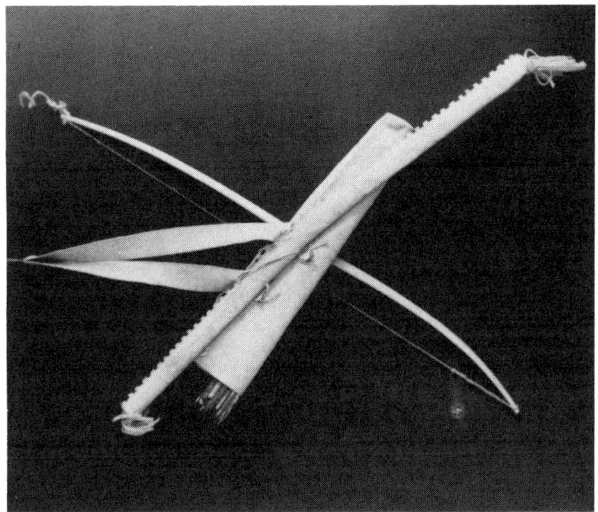

This is an Indian bow and quiver. The quiver was used for carrying arrows. IDAHO HISTORICAL SOCIETY

This was mixed with salmon oil to make salmon **pemmican**. The salmon pemmican was stored in bags made from salmon skin.

Hunting Wild Animals Without Guns. Before explorers and traders came, Indians did not have guns. Can you imagine killing a wild animal without a gun? It takes careful planning and great care. Sometimes an Indian hunter would wear a real deer head when hunting deer. He would try to act like a deer until he was close enough to shoot the deer with a bow and arrow.

Coeur d'Alene Indians liked to chase deer to a river crossing. Hunters would be hiding in the bushes or in canoes to shoot the deer with bows and arrows. Shoshoni Indians would sometimes chase deer toward rows of sticks that had pieces of scorched skin on them. The smell would frighten the deer, and they would bunch together. Then hunters could come close and shoot them with arrows.

Hunters often went on long trips to hunt antelope, elk, mountain sheep, mountain goats, and buffalo.

Idaho's Indians traveled great distances to hunt buffalo. These buffalo were raised on a farm.

IDAHO DEPARTMENT OF FISH AND GAME

Idaho Indians ate small animals, too. They liked rabbits, beaver, porcupines, and sage hens. If they could not find these animals, they might eat prairie dogs, snakes, and even insects like grasshoppers and ants. When there was no other meat, Indians sometimes ate some of their dogs and horses.

The Shoshoni had rabbit drives. Men, women, and children would beat the bushes to chase the rabbits out. The rabbits would be chased into long nets held on poles. The trapped rabbits were then killed with clubs. Indians killed antelope in much the same way. These animals run too fast for anyone to catch. The Indians would chase them into pens. There the antelopes were killed with clubs.

Camas Lily. The Indians' most important vegetable was **camas**. Camas is a wild lily with a beautiful blue flower. The bulb, which grows under the ground, was the part used for food. It was eaten by all of Idaho's tribes, as well as by other Indians of the West. Before farmers plowed up the land, camas grew across prairies and mountain meadows from California to Canada. In springtime, its star-shaped flowers covered the land with a rich blue blanket.

Preparing Camas. From June to September, bands of Indians would camp on meadows or prairies to dig and cook camas bulbs. Women dug the bulbs with the help of the children. Digging was done with a digging stick. The stick was sharp on one end, and the point was made hard in the fire. A bone or antler handle was tied cross-ways on the other end. The bulbs were carried to camp in baskets, where they were cleaned and cooked. Digging and preparing the bulbs for winter would take an Indian band several weeks during the summer.

The bulbs were cooked in earth ovens. These were pits in the ground, where a fire was built to heat rocks. When the rocks were hot, the camas bulbs were put over them between layers of grass. The grass and bulbs were covered with earth and left for several days. The heat from the rocks baked the bulbs.

Baking made the bulbs sweet, and they could be eaten that way. For winter, the baked bulbs were pounded into a mash with a **mortar** and **pestle**. The mash was made into loaves that were then boiled. The boiled camas was formed into thin cakes and dried in the sun. The dried cakes could be stored for winter.

The camas lily was an important food for most Idaho Indians. Where did they go to dig most of their camas? ROBERT BOREN

Other Food Plants. The first vegetable in springtime was the **biscuitroot**. It had corn-like roots that were dried and pounded into meal, then baked into cakes. Another favorite was **bitterroot**. When the root was peeled and boiled, it was ready to eat. For winter, it needed only to be dried. The Coeur d'Alene and Nez Perce would make long trips to dig bitterroot. Bitterroot is now the state flower of Montana.

Indians also gathered and ate many hard-shelled seeds. They used beaters to knock the seeds off the plants into baskets. The seeds were roasted using hot coals, then ground into meal on stone slabs or with a mortar and pestle. The meal was baked into loaves or cakes. Sunflower seeds were a favorite.

Wild berries grew in many places. Blackberries, huckleberries, serviceberries, and chokecherries were eaten fresh or dried for winter.

Review Questions

1. The ____________ was a large fish that was a very important food for all of Idaho's tribes. [*58*]

2. Name three kinds of animals that Indians used for food: (a) ____________ (b) ____________ (c) ____________. [59]

3. Name three kinds of plants that Indians used for food: (a) ____________ (b) ____________ (c) ____________. [*60*]

Ideas To Talk About

1. Why did the Indians spend so much time preparing food for winter?

The mortar and pestle were stone tools used to crush or grind food. D. E. WARREN #6-24-3D U OF I LIBRARY

Idaho Indians Enjoyed Many Freedoms.

The Indians who lived in Idaho were people with many freedoms. Each village chose its own chief, and it might have several chiefs. A chief was a chief only so long as his people wanted him. They could choose a new chief any time they wanted.

Some tribes, like the Nez Perce, had no head chief. Only a spirit chief or a war chief was more important than other chiefs. Important matters were decided by a meeting of the chiefs. A meeting of chiefs from one or more villages was called a council. The Nez Perce didn't believe in majority rule. People were free not to follow the things decided by the council. This made it hard for the United States to make a treaty with the Nez Perce. Chief Lawyer, who signed the treaty, could not sign for the whole tribe.

Review Questions

1. An Indian chief was a chief only as long

____

____

[complete the sentence]. . [*61*]

2. A meeting of chiefs was called a ____________. [*61*]

Ideas To Talk About

1. What is meant by "freedom"?

Indians Passed Legends On To Their Children.

Do you know any legends? A **legend** is a story from the past that is repeated from person to person. It may be a tall tale or a story about people who lived long ago. We have legends about George Washington, Davy Crockett, John Henry, and many others.

Indians had legends to explain how the world came to be the way it is. These stories were told to every child. Indians did not have written languages, so these stories had to be repeated from memory. Indian legends are so old that no one knows how long ago they were first told.

KUTENAIS
Blackfeet Res.
Kutenai Res.
KALISPELS
Kalispel Res.
BLACKFEET
Sacred Heart Mission
Flathead Res.
COEUR D'ALENES
Tensed
Coeur d'Alene Res.
Ahsahka
Spalding Mission
Nez Perce Res.
Kamiah
NEZ PERCES
Camas Prairie
Whitman Mission
SHEEPEATERS
Tendoy
Council
LEMHIS
Indian Valley
Camas Meadow
NORTHERN PAIUTES
Big Camas Prairie
BANNOCKS
Fort Hall Res.
SHOSHONIS
Duck Valley Res.

This rock mound at Kamiah is the Monster's Heart. In Nez Perce legend, how did the Monster's Heart get there? VIRGIL YOUNG

Indian Legend: Birth Of The Nez Perce

The following Nez Perce legend explains why there are different tribes of Indians. **Coyote** and **Fox** are found in many Indian legends.

Iltswetsix was a huge monster from the sea who came to live in the **Kamiah** Valley of Idaho. He had a great hunger and sucked everything he could find into his stomach. Soon he was eating everything in sight.

Coyote heard about this and decided to defeat the monster. When he reached Kamiah Valley, he hid himself under a grass bonnet and tied himself down with a wild grape vine. Then he dared Iltswetsix to suck him into his huge mouth.

The huge Iltswetsix sucked and pulled until Coyote was finally pulled into the monster's stomach. Coyote had hidden a knife in his belt, however. After he got into the stomach, he began cutting out the monster's heart. That killed Iltswetsix, and Coyote cut his way out of the monster's body.

Fox had been hiding and watching the battle. Coyote did not know what to do with the body of the monster, so Fox suggested they cut it up to make people. They cut off the head, and it became the Flathead Indians. The feet became the Blackfeet Indians. Each part of the body became a different tribe.

When only the heart was left, Coyote held it high in the air and drops of blood fell from it to the ground. From these drops sprang other people. They were taller, stronger, nobler, and wiser than the other tribes. These were the Nez Perce.

The Great Spirit Chief who rules the earth was very pleased with Coyote. He turned the monster's heart into a huge stone so that people would not forget this wonderful deed. This stone can still be seen in Kamiah Valley.

Seven Indian Tribes Lived In Idaho.

Seven Indian tribes lived in Idaho when the explorers first arrived. These were the **Kutenai**, **Kalispel**, **Coeur d'Alene**, **Nez Perce**, **Shoshoni**, **Bannock**, and **Northern Paiute**.

Idaho Indians were friendly and helpful to the explorers. The Shoshoni saved Lewis and Clark by letting them have horses. Later, the Nez Perce saved the party by letting them have food when they were sick and starving. Only when settlers began pushing the Indians off their land did trouble break out between the Indians and the settlers.

Review Questions

1. What seven Indian tribes were living in Idaho when the first explorers came:
(a) ____________ (b) ____________
(c) ____________ (d) ____________
(e) ____________ (f) ____________
(g) ____________. [63]

2. Lewis and Clark led the first party of explorers into Idaho. What two Idaho tribes helped them: (a) ____________
(b) ____________ [63]

The Kutenai Tribe

Kutenai Indians were living in only a small part of Idaho when Lewis and Clark arrived. The rest of the Kutenai tribe lived in Montana and Canada. Idaho's Kutenai lived along the Kootenai River near Bonners Ferry. They were known as "river people" who fished for much of

A Kalispel father and son try their luck at fishing.
OREGON HISTORICAL SOCIETY

their food. After they got horses, the Kutenai depended less on fishing and spent more time hunting for large game animals.

The Kalispel Tribe

The **Kalispel** wcrc also known as the Pend d'Oreille Indians. These people were part of the Flathead, a larger tribe that lived in Montana. The Kalispel lived mostly along the shores of Lake Pend Oreille. For food they gathered berries, plant roots and camas. They hunted fish, deer, and buffalo. Each year, their hunters would travel to Montana for a buffalo hunt with their Flathead cousins.

"Pend d'Oreille" is French for "earring." French-Canadian trappers called these Indians Pend d'Oreille because some wore seashells on their ears. (Notice that the Pend d'Oreille Indians and Lake Pend Oreille are not spelled the same way.)

The Coeur d'Alene Tribe

The **Coeur d'Alene** Indians lived mostly around Lake Coeur d'Alene. They were called Camas People, because the beautiful camas was an important food for them. They also gathered wild berries, dug other plant roots, caught fish, and hunted deer.

French Canadian fur trappers called these Indians the Coeur d'Alenes. There is a story that some trappers tried to buy animal skins from the Indians at a very cheap price. The Indians made fun of the price. The trappers were impressed by the trading abilities of the Indians and called them "needle hearted" or "hearts like an awl." Thus the tribe became known by the French word Coeur d'Alene, which means "heart of an awl."

The Nez Perce Tribe

The Nez Perce Indians lived in central Idaho along the Clearwater River and the lower Salmon River. (Other Nez Perce lived in Oregon and Washington.) Their winter villages were in the Clearwater Valley. Winter is warmer there than in the mountains, and there is little snow. In summer they took trips over the high mountains. Some would go to Montana and Wyoming to hunt buffalo. Others would go to summer camp at Lake Wallowa in eastern Oregon. During their trips, they would gather wild foods such as berries, camas lilies, fish, and wild animals.

"Nez Perce" is French, meaning "pierced nose." Early French Canadians named the tribe

Nez Perce because some of the Indians were wearing ornaments in their noses.

The Nez Perce were known for their fine horses. Large herds could be seen grazing on the rich grassy hills of the Palouse Country. The Palouse was the tribe's richest pasture land. Some of their horses were spotted. Later, when the fur trappers arrived, they gave the name "Palouse" to horses with spots. "A Palouse" grew into the word "Appaloosa". Today Appaloosa horses are prized by many horse lovers.

The Nez Perce were friendly from the very first. When Lewis and Clark arrived weak from hunger, the Nez Perce gave them food. Later, when more people, including trappers and traders, arrived, they were still friendly and helpful. War with the Nez Perce came only because settlers were pushing the Nez Perce off their land.

Review Questions

1. Idaho's Kutenai Indians lived near the present town of ____________. [*63*]

2. The ____________ tribe lived along the shores of Lake Pend Oreille. [*64*]

3. The Kalispel Indians were part of a larger tribe, the ____________, who lived in Montana. [*64*]

4. The Indians who lived around Lake Coeur d'Alene were the ____________ tribe. [*64*]

5. The Nez Perce Indians lived in ________________________. [*64*]

6. The name "Nez Perce" was given by early French Canadians. In French, the name means ________________________. [*64–65*]

7. The Nez Perce were known for having beautiful spotted horses. Today these horses are called ____________ horses. [*65*]

Some Nez Perce are camped by the Snake River near Lewiston. #6-24-7B U OF I LIBRARY

Chief Joseph: Thunder Rolling In The Mountains

Young Joseph wandered about the village with his fine black eyes watching everything. The young boy watched the women of the tribe grinding camas into meal with pestle and mortar, and drying wild berries on mats in the sun. Other women were busy scraping skins of deer and elk with sharp pieces of stone.

Joseph also watched young men shaping spear heads and arrow heads from black, shiny rock. He listened to the talk of warriors and of the old men about their adventures in hunting and battle. Like all Nez Perce children, Young Joseph liked to hear again and again the stories of Lewis and Clark's visit to the Nez Perce. Joseph's father had told the story so many times that the boy knew it by heart. To all these things the young boy watched and listened with great interest. These things he must know if he was to grow into a leader of his people.

Young Joseph grew up to be Chief Joseph, a great Nez Perce chief. He was admired as a fair, wise, and brave man by both friends and enemies. **Hin-mut-too-yah-la-kekht** was his Nez Perce name. It meant **Thunder Rolling in the Mountains**. His father also was called Chief Joseph by the settlers. When young Joseph became chief, they called his father Old Joseph.

Chief Joseph is history's most famous Nez Perce chief. Why is he famous? IDAHO DEPARTMENT OF COMMERCE

Young Joseph was born in about 1840 in the **Wallowa** Valley of eastern Oregon. At that time, the Nez Perce lived as free people on their own land. Later, miners and settlers began taking Nez Perce land. Chief Joseph tried to keep peace between his people and the miners and settlers, but he could not. Today he is remembered as a brave leader who almost defeated the U. S. Army while trying to lead his people to freedom. This part of his story is told later in this book.

The Shoshoni Tribe

Shoshoni Indians lived along the Snake River Valley of Idaho. These Shoshoni were part of a huge tribe that spread over a large part of the West. Others lived in Colorado, Utah, Wyoming, Nevada, and California. Those living along the Snake River were called Northern Shoshoni. Northern Shoshoni also lived along the **Boise**, **Weiser**, **Bruneau**, and **Owyhee** rivers.

The Shoshoni are sometimes called Snake Indians. Shoshoni-speaking Indians were called Snakes by Indians of the Midwest. Because of this, explorers and early settlers called them Snakes, too. The name Snake has stayed with the Shoshoni. The river they lived along is now called the Snake River.

Shoshoni leaders liked to meet in **councils** to talk over the tribe's business. Indian Valley and Council Valley are two places where the Shoshoni held their councils. A council began with everyone giving gifts. Then the chiefs held their talks. Later, people traded goods and played games. The Indian games were different from those we play today.

Two groups of Shoshoni are often called separate tribes by mistake. The **Lemhi** Indians and the **Sheepeater** Indians were small bands of Shoshoni. The Lemhi lived mostly in the Lemhi and upper Salmon River valleys. Other Shoshoni called them Salmon Eaters. Like other Shoshoni, they also journeyed over the mountains to Montana to hunt buffalo. Chief Tendoy was a well-known Lemhi chief. The small town of Tendoy is named for this chief, who also is buried there.

The Sheepeaters lived in and around Yellowstone Park and the Salmon River Mountains. Many people thought they were a separate tribe because they lived apart from other Shoshoni. They were called Sheepeaters because wild sheep and mountain goats were an important part of their food. Shoshoni were often called by the food they ate. Others were called Fish Eaters, Ground Hog Eaters, Rabbit Eaters, Seed Eaters, and Buffalo Eaters. Of course, these names changed as the Indians moved from place to place. They ate what could be found there.

Sacajawea: Mystery Woman

The end of **Sacajawea's** life is quite a mystery. As a young girl, she lived in the **Lemhi** Valley of Idaho. While on a family hunting trip to Montana, Sacajawea was captured by another tribe. She was then sold as a slave to a Mandan Indian. Later a French Canadian named **Charbonneau** bought her from the Mandan. She became Charbonneau's wife.

Lewis and Clark hired Charbonneau as a guide, and Sacajawea and her newborn son went along. Sacajawea was more valuable than Charbonneau. A woman with a party of men showed other Indians that the men came in peace. She also knew a lot about the Rocky Mountain tribes. When they reached the Lemhi Valley, Shoshoni chief **Cameahwait** saw that Sacajawea was his lost sister. The Shoshoni gave Lewis and Clark a warm welcome.

It has been written that Sacajawea was only 17 years old when she and Charbonneau joined Lewis and Clark's party. Captain Clark liked Sacajawea very much and called her "Janey". He called her son "Pompey" or "Little Pomp." The child's real name was Baptiste.

The people in this Shoshoni camp are posing to have their picture taken. The photo was taken in 1870. W. H. JACKSON SMITHSONIAN NEG. #1668

This Indian rock art seems to be a map. What would you need to know before you could read this kind of a map? IDAHO HISTORICAL SOCIETY

The mystery of Sacajawea's life began after Lewis and Clark returned to St. Louis. It is known that she and Charbonneau lived at St. Louis between 1806 and 1811. After that, there are two different stories about her life—and death! Some historians believe that she died in 1812. Others believe that she lived to be a very old woman.

A diary written at the time reports that Charbonneau's "Snake" wife died in 1812. Some historians believe that this was Sacajawea. However, Charbonneau had two Shoshoni wives. It isn't clear which one died. There were other reports that Charbonneau was cruel to Sacajawea and that she left him.

A number of people reported seeing Sacajawea in the years that followed. Comanche Indians living in Oklahoma believed that Sacajawea lived among them for about 25 years. This woman married a Comanche man and had five children. After her husband was killed in battle, she became unhappy and left the Comanches in about 1855.

During the 1860s, a number of different people reported seeing or knowing Sacajawea in Montana and Wyoming. One man reported that "everybody" around Fort Bridger knew who she was. Late in life, this woman went to live with a son and his family at the Wind River Reservation in Wyoming. She died there in 1884 as a very old woman.

Why is it hard to know the truth about Sacajawea? Records were not kept well in those days. Often Sacajawea is called by a different name, or no name at all! Lewis often called her "the Indian woman." Clark called her Janey. She was also called "Bird Woman." An Indian was often called by several different names by family and friends, and these names could change over the years.

The woman at the Wind River Reservation was called Chief Woman, Porivo, and Bazil's Mother. She had a friendship medal that she said Lewis and Clark gave her, and some papers that were buried with her. She could speak French, and she told stories of a French husband and a long trip "toward the setting sun."

Another problem is that of time. The study of Sacajawea began after Chief Woman died in

The Lemhi Valley is where Sacajawea lived as a girl. The Bitterroot Mountains are seen in the background. IDAHO DEPARTMENT OF COMMERCE

1884. After that, all information had to come from old diaries and other records, and the memories of people who had known Chief Woman many years before.

Now you know the mystery. Did Sacajawea really die in 1812, or was she Chief Woman, who lived to be a very old? What do you think?

The Bannock Tribe

The **Bannock** Indians lived in the same part of Idaho as the Shoshoni. They came from small bands of **Northern Paiute** who moved in from Oregon. These Northern Paiute got horses and began riding with the Shoshoni. With horses, they could hunt buffalo and have a better life. The Bannock were strong, tall people, who were good hunters and warriors.

Mixing freely with the Shoshoni, the Bannock shared many of their ways. They rode as partners with the Shoshoni when hunting buffalo. If they could not find buffalo in southern Idaho, they would hunt buffalo in Wyoming and Montana.

The Bannock called themselves **Panakwate**. This was their word for being partners with the Shoshoni. Settlers changed the word to Bannock because they couldn't say the Indian word.

Camas was the Bannock's most important food for winter. They dug camas bulbs on Big Camas near Fairfield. Farmers helped start the Bannock Indian War when they destroyed the camas. The farmers pastured cows and horses in the camas fields. They also plowed up much of the land and let their pigs eat the bulbs. The Bannock went hungry for much of the winter because they didn't have enough camas to eat.

The city of **Pocatello** is named for the Bannock chief Pocatello. Pocatello (the city) is in Bannock County.

The Northern Paiute Tribe

Other than the Bannock, few Northern Paiute came into Idaho. Two bands are known to have lived along the Snake and Owyhee rivers on the western edge of Owyhee County. These were family groups with perhaps only about fifty people each. Most Northern Paiute lived in Oregon, Nevada, and California.

The Northern Paiute's land was not as good as that of the Shoshoni and Bannock. Except for a few river valleys, it was too dry to grow much food. Not many deer or other large animals could be found. Their streams had only a few salmon. Because of this, they ate mostly small animals. Rabbits, gophers, squirrels, bobcats, and blackbirds were all used for food. They also ate insects, seeds, roots, and berries. Gathering enough food was hard work for the Northern Paiute. Everybody had to help—men, women, and children alike.

The Northern Paiute didn't keep horses like other Idaho Indians. The land was too poor to feed both people and horses. They killed and ate any horse that came on their land.

Review Questions

1. Shoshoni Indians lived along the ____________ Valley of Idaho. [66]
2. The Shoshoni were also called ____________ Indians. [66]

These two Bannock men are dressed in ceremonial clothing. MAJOR LEE MOORHOUSE #7-14-1 U OF I LIBRARY

3. Shoshoni chiefs gathered in ____________ to talk over the tribe's business. [66]

4. A well-known Shoshoni, ____________, helped Lewis and Clark on their journey to the Pacific Ocean. [67]

5. What two groups of Shoshoni are sometimes called separate tribes by mistake: (a) ____________ (b) ____________ [66]

6. The ____________ Indians mixed with the Shoshoni and rode with them to hunt buffalo. [69]

7. Bannock Indians dug camas near the present town of ____________. [69]

8. The Bannock Indians formed from bands of ____________ who came into Idaho from Oregon. [69]

Chapter 3 Skill Activities

Words and Ideas In Chapter 3, you will find a number of key words printed in **bold** print. Each key word stands for an important idea. Answering these questions will help you understand some of the key words.

You can find the key words in the Glossary at the back of the book. The number after each question is the page where the idea is found in the book. Answer each question with a complete sentence.

1. What is meant by somebody's **ancestor**? [54]
2. **Bitterroot** was a favorite Indian food. Why else is it remembered today? [60]
3. Why was **camas** important to the Indians of the West? [60]
4. What was an Indian **council**? [66]
5. What did Indian **legends** explain? [61]
6. How was a **lodge** different from a **longhouse**? [56]
7. What were a **mortar and pestle** used for? [60–61]
8. Why were **salmon** important to Idaho's Indians? [58–59]
9. How was a **tipi** different from a **lodge**? [56]
10. How was a **wickiup** different from a **tipi**? [55–56]

Mapping The Indian Tribes

Where did Idaho's Indians live? Each tribe had its own home area. Let's make a map that shows these areas.

Begin with a plain outline map of Idaho. You can use this book, Idaho's Official Highway Map, or other sources.

(a) Label the parts of Idaho where each of the following tribes lived: Kutenai, Kalispel, Coeur d'Alene, Nez Perce, Shoshoni, Bannock, and Northern Paiute.
(b) All the tribes lived near water. Draw in the major rivers and lakes where each tribe lived.
(c) Mark the present-day towns and cities that are now found where each tribe lived.

Using Your Imagination

1. *Indian Life*. Write a story about the life of an Idaho Indian boy or girl who lived 100 years **before** Indians had horses.

You can use this book, an encyclopedia, or other sources. Be careful when using an encyclopedia. Most of the Indians described are **not** Idaho Indians. Many of their customs are different from Idaho's tribes.

2. *Appaloosa Horse Show*. Have an Appaloosa horse show. Each student should draw and color an Appaloosa. You can find pictures and names in the *Appaloosa News*.

Think of a good name for your horse. The following are some names that other people have given to their Appaloosas: Time Flies, Nina Syringa, High Flying, Angel Feathers, Mr. Top Bracket, and Comanche Warbonnet.

After everyone has drawn and named a horse, you can have a horse show by putting all the pictures on the bulletin board.

Research Projects

1. *Indian Sign Language*. Learn some Indian sign language. You will find pictures in the Time-Life book *The Indians*, listed at the end of the unit. Others may be found in the "Indians" section of an encyclopedia.

2. *Pemmican*. Pemmican was made from all kinds of meat: buffalo, deer, salmon, or whatever else the Indians had. Today a type of pemmican is used by some snowmobilers, backpackers, and others who need a high-energy food.

Write a report on pemmican. Information can be found in the encyclopedia and in the Time-Life book *The Indians*, listed at the end of the unit. (See what the Sagers thought of pemmican in *Seven Alone.*)

3. *Famous Indians*. Write a report on a famous American Indian. Below are some suggested names:

1. Chief Joseph
2. Sacajawea
3. Chief Crazy Horse
4. Chief Sitting Bull
5. Will Rogers (comedian)
6. Chief Dan George (actor)
7. Buffy St. Marie (singer)
8. Hattie Kauffman (TV/radio newsperson)
9. Jim Thorpe (athlete)

Reviewing Chapter 3

Main Ideas In This Chapter

1. Indians lived in America for many thousands of years before people came to America from Europe.
2. Seven tribes of Indians were living in Idaho when the first explorers came to Idaho.
3. Many Indian villages were like small towns.
4. The Indians of America spoke many different languages.
5. Indian houses were made of simple materials that the people could find nearby.
6. The Indians did not have horses before Cortes brought horses from Europe in 1519.
7. Horses changed Indian life, including their food, housing, clothing, and travel.
8. Idaho Indians harvested and ate a wide variety of wild plants and animals. They were not farmers.
9. Camas was an important food for many western tribes.
10. Salmon was an important food for all Idaho tribes.
11. Idaho Indians enjoyed many freedoms before settlers came.
12. Indians passed legends on to their children.
13. Chief Joseph was a great Nez Perce chief.
14. Idaho's Indians were friendly and helpful to the first explorers to visit here.
15. The Kutenai Indians of Idaho lived near Bonners Ferry.
16. The Kalispel Indians, also called the Pend d'Oreille, lived mostly around Lake Pend Oreille.
17. The Coeur d'Alene Indians lived mostly around Lake Coeur d'Alene.
18. The Nez Perce Indians lived in central Idaho along the Clearwater River and the lower Salmon River.
19. The Shoshoni Indians, also called the Snake, lived along the Snake River Valley and several smaller rivers in southern Idaho.
20. The Bannock Indians lived among the Shoshoni and hunted with them.
21. The Bannock came from small bands of Northern Paiute that moved into Idaho from Oregon.
22. A few Northern Paiute lived in Idaho on the western edge of Owyhee County.

Further Reading For Children

Capps, Benjamin, and editors of Time-Life Books. *The Indians*. New York: Time-Life Books, 1973.

Dramer, Kim. *The Shoshone*. Philadelphia: Chelsea House Publishers, 1997.

Goldin, Barbara Diamond. *Coyote and the Fire Stick*. (A Pacific Northwest Indian Tale) San Diego: Gulliver Books, Harcourt, Brace & Company, 1996.

Moss, Nathaniel. *The Shoshone Indians*. Philadelphia: Chelsea House Publishers, 1997.

O'Dell, Scott. *Thunder Rolling in the Mountains*. Boston: Houghton Mifflin Company, 1992. [A story about Chief Joseph.]

Patent, Dorothy Hinshaw. *Appaloosa Horses*. New York: Holiday House, 1998.

Taylor, Marian. *Chief Joseph: Nez Perce Leader*. Philadelphia: Chelsea House Publishers, 1993.

Sneve, Virginia Driving Hawk. *The Nez Perce*. (A First Americans Book) New York: Holiday House, 1994.

Stone, Lynn M. *Appaloosas*. Vero Beach, Florida: The Rourke Corporation, Inc., 1998.

Time Line

1400 A.D.

1492 — Columbus lands in America.

1500

1600

1620 — Pilgrims come to America in the Mayflower.

1700

1750 — Russians trap furs in Alaska.

1776 — Declaration of Independence; USA begins.

1778 — English Captain Cook trades for furs on the Pacific coast.

1792 — American Captain Robert Gray discovers and names the Columbia River and Captain George Vancouver discovers Puget Sound.

1800

1803 — President Thomas Jefferson buys Louisiana Territory from France.

1804 — Jefferson sends Lewis and Clark to explore to the Pacific Ocean.

1805 — Lewis and Clark explore Idaho and continue west; they return in 1806.

1860 — Franklin becomes Idaho's first permanent white settlement.

1890 — Idaho becomes a state.

1900

1976 — USA celebrates its Bicentennial

1990 — Idaho Centennial

2000 A.D.

Chapter 4
Explorers And Fur Trappers Come To Idaho

The First Explorers Arrive.

Until August 12, 1805, Native Americans were the only people who had ever walked on Idaho soil. On that bright sunny morning, Captain Meriwether Lewis and George Drewyer, having crossed the mountains on foot, stepped into Idaho. They were members of the now famous Lewis and Clark party sent by President Jefferson. Lewis and Clark were to explore the land that lay west of the United States.

Until that day, Idaho had belonged to the Indian people and to them alone. Suddenly, on this day, all of that ended. The rest of the world had found Idaho, and things would never be the same.

William Clark (left) and Meriwether Lewis (right) were the first explorers to visit Idaho. Why did they come to Idaho? G. W. FULLER/IDAHO HISTORICAL SOCIETY

Idaho Was Part Of The Oregon Country.

When Lewis and Clark came west, Idaho was part of the **Oregon Country**. The Oregon Country included Idaho, Washington, and Oregon, and stetched north into Canada. The first explorers in Oregon Country began along the coast. The rivers, mountains, valleys—and Idaho—would have to wait until later.

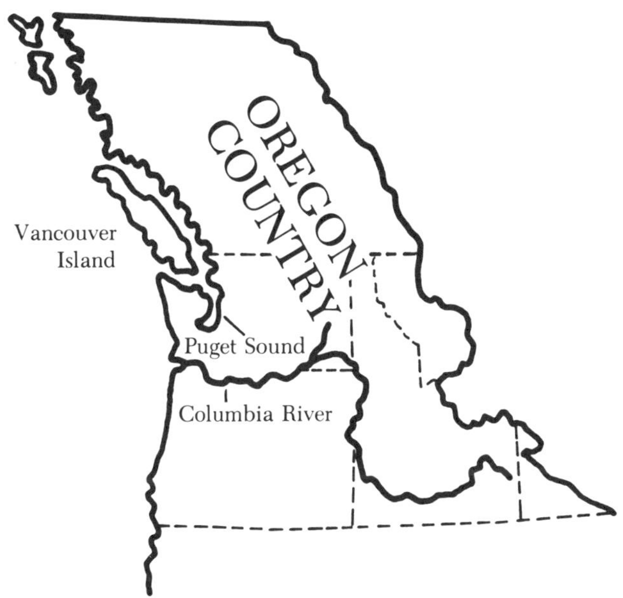

The Oregon country included Oregon, Washington, Idaho, and parts of Canada, Montana, and Wyoming.

Early Fur Business On The Coast.

Because of the fur business, four countries wanted to own land in the Oregon Country. These were Spain, Russia, England, and the United States. Ships came from Spain to **Vancouver Island** to buy furs from the Indians during the 1700s. By 1750, Russians were trapping furs among the islands of Alaska. Captain Cook, of England, was buying furs along the coast by 1778. Other English fur traders soon followed.

The first American to claim land for the United States was Robert Gray of Boston. He started a fur business called the Yankee Triangle Trade. He would buy a load of furs form Indians on the Oregon coast, then sell it in China for a good price. In China, he would buy a load of tea, then take it back to Boston.

On such a trip in 1792, Gray discovered the **Columbia River**. He named it for his ship, the **Columbia**, and made a claim for the United States. After sailing 30 miles up the river, he claimed all the land drained by the Columbia River and its **tributaries**. Gray had no idea how much land this was. The Columbia drains much of Washington, Oregon, Idaho, British Columbia, and smaller parts of Montana and Wyoming.

You can see that all four countries wanted land in the Oregon Country. Still they knew nothing about the land. They had experienced only the coast. The first country to explore the land would have the best chance to own it. Who would make the first move?

This is a model of the *Columbia*, Captain Gray's ship. G. W. FULLER

President Jefferson Changes History. President Thomas Jefferson made the first move in 1803, and changed the history of the United States. He bought the **Louisiana Territory** from France. This included nearly all of the land between the Rocky Mountains and the Mississippi River. It more than doubled the size of the United States. The United States now stretched far to the west, right up to the tallest peaks of the Rocky Mountains. The Oregon Country was just next door, on the other side.

Jefferson was eager to know more about the land he had bought. He knew it must be explored and mapped before Americans could settle there. Jefferson was also eager to know more about the Oregon Country, west of the Rockies. He wanted the United States to own the Oregon Country also.

Jefferson's next move brought about one of the most interesting pages of American history. He picked **Meriwether Lewis** to lead a party to explore America all the way to the Pacific Ocean. Captain Lewis asked **William Clark** to help him lead the party. The story of Lewis and Clark was about to begin.

Review Questions

1. What three states were once part of the Oregon Country: (a)__________
(b)__________ (c)__________[73]

2. What four countries made claims in the Oregon Country: (a)__________
(b)__________ (c)__________
(d)__________[73]

3. The Columbia River was claimed by what country:__________[74]

4. Which U.S. President sent Lewis and Clark to explore the Oregon Country?
__________[74]

Ideas To Talk About

1. What kinds of things would people need to know about the land before they could settle in the Oregon Country?

Lewis And Clark Come West.

Lewis and Clark left St. Louis, Missouri, in the spring of 1804. The land they were to explore was Indian country. Most of it had never been seen by anyone but Indians.

The Lewis and Clark party had about 45 people. Records of the journey do not agree on the number. As a result, we don't know exactly how many people were in the party. We do know there were guides to help find the way through Indian country. There were soldiers to protect them, and other men cooked and made camp. One of the men was a big, strong black man named York. His color and great strength were greatly admired by Indians all along the way.

An important person in the party was the young Shoshoni woman named **Sacajawea**. She was the wife of the party's French-Canadian guide, **Charbonneau**. With her she carried her newborn son, **Baptiste**. Sacajawea had been raised in the Lemhi Valley of Idaho. She was a great help in dealing with the Rocky Mountain tribes. Besides this, a woman with a party of men showed other Indians that the men came in peace. (See Sacajawea in Chapter 3.)

Lewis and Clark wanted peace with the Indians. They were careful to make friends with those they met. When they met a group of Indians, they gave gifts and talked about friendship. Their gifts were things such as brightly colored beads, flags, handkerchiefs, soap, **vermillion** (red powder), **awls**, knives, and clothing. The finest gifts were medals showing President Jefferson on one side, and clasped hands of friendship on the other.

You may think these gifts were of little value, but we must remember that Indians traded for many things. Their money was shells, beads, skins, dogs, horses, guns, and anything else useful. They did not use coins or paper money. When other people traded with the Indians, they used things Indians seemed to like. Lewis and Clark took as many gifts with them as they could carry.

Jefferson medal of the Lewis and Clark expedition. Lewis and Clark gave medals like this one to important Indian chiefs along the way. This medal was found in 1899 at the mouth of the Potlatch River. The photo shows both sides of the medal. AMERICAN MUSEUM OF NATURAL HISTORY

The Journey West. In the spring of 1804, the party left St. Louis and made their way slowly up the Missouri River by boat. There were no motorboats at that time. Boats had to be pushed, pulled, and sometimes carried by hand. It was very hard work pushing the heavy boats against the powerful flow of the river. Winter came before the party could cross North Dakota, so they built a fort there. When spring came, they pushed on up the Missouri River. High in the Montana Rockies, they entered smaller streams. When the streams became too small, they had to buy some Indian horses to ride.

As the Rocky Mountains towered above them, they pushed their way toward the top. At the **summit** of the Rockies is the **continental divide**. This ridge of rocky peaks (running somewhat north and south) divides North America. On the east side, all the land slopes away toward the Atlantic Ocean. All the water on the east side runs into the Atlantic. On the west side, all the land slopes away toward the Pacific Ocean. All water on the west side runs into the Pacific. On the west side lay Idaho and the Oregon Country.

August 12, 1805, is one of Idaho's most important dates. On that morning, Captain Lewis and George Drewyer crossed the summit of the mountains and walked on Idaho soil. Their crossing place is now known as **Lemhi Pass**. As they stood on this high point, it must have seemed like the very top of the world.

They camped at a spring just inside Idaho that night. The next day they met two Shoshoni women and a girl. The women took the explorers to meet Chief Cameahwait, leader of the band that was camped nearby. When the chief saw

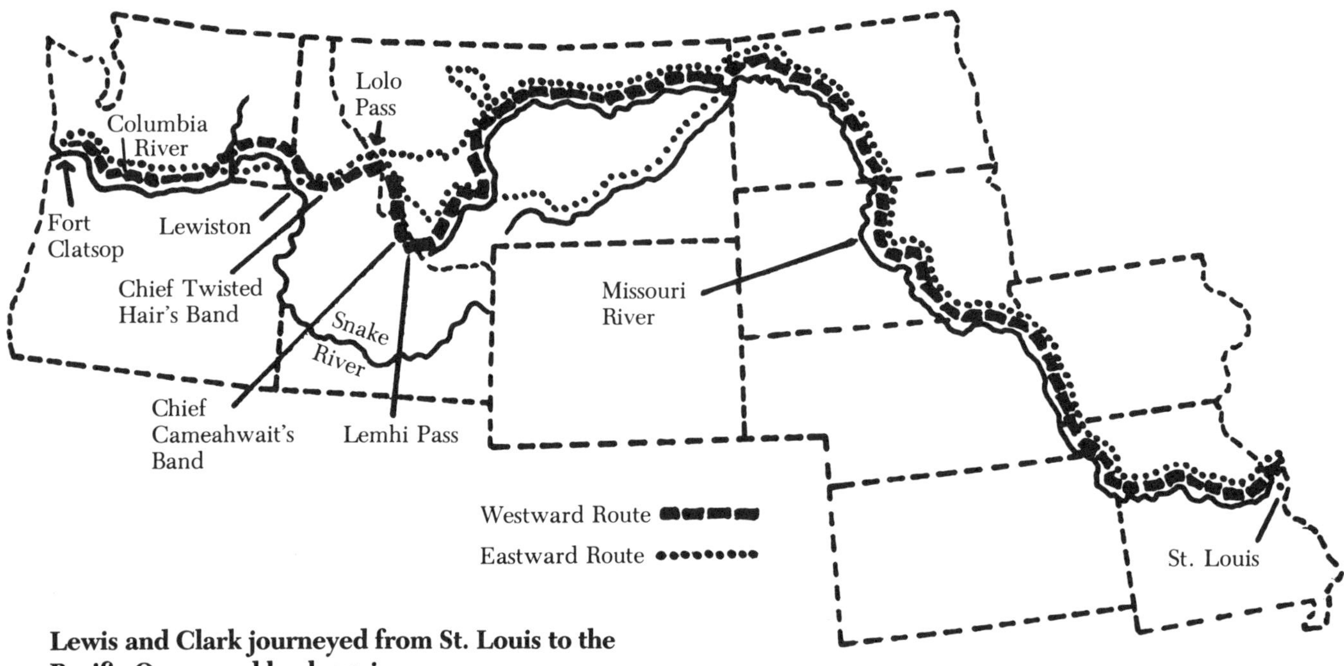

Lewis and Clark journeyed from St. Louis to the Pacific Ocean and back again.

that they had come in peace, he greeted them with a hug and the words **ah hi e**. This meant "I am much pleased." Later, when Sacajawea met Chief Cameahwait, she saw that he was her long lost brother. This happy meeting brought much joy to the Shoshoni.

Lewis and Clark traded gifts to Cameahwait's people for more horses. They had more mountains to cross, but did not know where to cross. Cameahwait told them about the Snake River Valley, but Lewis and Clark were afraid it was too far south. They wanted to follow the Salmon River canyon, but it was too rough and rocky. The Indians told of an Indian trail further to the north. Lewis and Clark decided to follow that trail.

They hired a Shoshoni to guide them to the trail and over the mountains to Nez Perce country. He led them back over the mountains into Montana. Near the present city of Missoula, they turned west up Lolo Creek. Indians had used the Lolo Trail for hundreds of years. High in the Bitterroots, at Lolo Pass, the party entered Idaho for the second time.

Snow comes early in the high mountains. Even though it was early fall, the party had to struggle through deep snow. They didn't have much food, and they found very few animals to kill. Many of the men became sick and weak. Once they killed and ate a horse because they had nothing else. Slowly they made their way down a tributary of the Clearwater River.

Near the present town of **Weippe**, Lewis and Clark found the Nez Perce camp of Chief Twisted Hair. Twisted Hair welcomed the party and gave them food and shelter. The Indian food—dried salmon and camas—was strange to the white men. They were hungry and weak, and the strange food made them ill. They spent several days getting well before they could go any further.

Twisted Hair drew a map on a piece of elk skin. It showed Lewis and Clark how to go down the Snake and Columbia rivers to the Pacific. When they became stronger, the party made **dugout canoes** from large pine trees. With these canoes, they finished their journey to the Pacific. The Nez Perce had agreed to keep their horses until they returned.

The Journey East—And Home.

Lewis and Clark spent the winter on the Pacific coast. When spring came, the party made their way back up the Columbia and Snake rivers. They reached the spot that is now Lewiston on May 5, 1806. To their surprise, the snow was still deep on the Lolo Trail. It was not possible to cross the mountains until more snow melted. For more than a month, Lewis and Clark waited in a camp along the Clearwater River.

While they were there, Captain Clark treated some of the Indians who were sick. He cleaned and drained their sores, and gave them simple medicines. Many healed quickly, so Clark was thought to have strong powers. The Nez Perce were amazed by the spyglass, compass, watches, magnets, and other things the explorers carried. This second visit made Lewis and Clark good friends with the Nez Perce.

During this visit, an interesting council was held with the Indians. Lewis and Clark did not understand the Nez Perce language, and so, everything had to be said through others. First, Lewis and Clark would speak in English to another person in the party, who would repeat it in French to Charbonneau. Charbonneau would say it in Mandan (Indian) to Sacajawea. She repeated it in Shoshoni to a young Shoshoni boy. The boy repeated it in Nez Perce to the Nez Perce chiefs. The Nez Perce chiefs had to speak to Lewis and Clark through the same chain of people.

Lewis and Clark followed the Lolo Trail, which can be seen faintly in this picture. Why do you think there was a trail over these mountains? How do you think the trail got started?

IDAHO DEPARTMENT OF COMMERCE

The Nez Perce had taken good care of the party's horses during the winter. When the snow had melted enough, the party packed their horses and left. Three Nez Perce guides helped them find their way back over the Lolo Trail.

Lewis and Clark arrived back in St. Louis on September 23, 1806. They had been away for more than two years. Traveling by foot, horseback, small boat, and canoe, they had journeyed about 8,000 miles. They had seen unknown lands. They had made friends with—and lived with—unknown Indian tribes. Lewis and Clark were heroes to the American people. They had carved a path for other Americans to follow.

Lewis and Clark had each kept a diary of things they saw and did during their journey. Their diaries were made into a book called *The Journals of Lewis and Clark*. Americans eagerly read the book and became excited about what they read.

Lewis and Clark started Americans moving west into the Oregon Country. A few people came at first, then more and more. Lewis and Clark had written about streams full of beavers. Soon an army of fur trappers was on its way to the Rocky Mountains. They had written about friendly Indian tribes. In only a few years, **missionaries** would journey west to work among the Nez Perce and Coeur d'Alene. After that, a flood of Americans would burst into the Oregon Country. Thanks to Lewis and Clark, the Oregon Country—and Idaho—would someday became part of the United States.

Review Questions

1. The Lewis and Clark party had about ____________ people. [75]
2. Sacajawea was a member of the ____________ Indian tribe. [75]
3. Lewis and Clark gave gifts to the Indians they met. Some of these gifts were:
(a) ____________ (b) ____________
(c) ____________ (d) ____________
(e) ____________ [75]
4. The Lewis and Clark party made their way slowly up a powerful river all the way from St. Louis to the Rocky Mountains. This was the ____________ River. [76]
5. The first Indians Lewis and Clark met in Idaho were members of the ____________ tribe. They were led by Chief ____________. [76]
6. Sacajawea was welcomed by the Shoshoni because ________________________. [76]
7. The second group of Indians Lewis and Clark met in Idaho were members of the ____________ tribe. They were led by Chief ____________. [77]

Ideas To Talk About

1. Since Lewis and Clark came west, there have been many inventions to make travel easier. What are some present-day inventions that Lewis and Clark did not have?

Meriwether Lewis: Was He Murdered?

Meriwether Lewis was a close friend of President Thomas Jefferson. He also had been President Jefferson's private secretary for two years. He was not quite 30 years old when he began the journey west.

When Lewis learned that he had been chosen to lead the party, he prepared himself for the job. Part of the job was to keep a careful record of everything he saw. He decided that he needed to know more about science. Thus he went to Philadelphia to study animals, plants, geography, and astronomy. He also studied with a doctor so he could treat anyone who became sick or hurt.

His studies served him well. He kept a careful diary describing the land, rivers, plants, animals, weather, and Indians. He even drew maps and pictures of animals and plants. His diary, together with the one kept by Captain Clark, were made into a book called *The Journals of Lewis and Clark*. Later the book was read eagerly by people thinking about going west. Today the journals are studied by people interested in learning about America before settlers filled the land.

After the journey, Lewis became Governor of the Louisiana Territory. In 1809, while Governor, he set out for Washington, D. C. He believed that the government still owed him money for the trip, so he was going to try to get it. On the way, he stopped overnight at a place called Grinder's Stand, in Tennessee. That evening he was shot to death.

Lewis's death was very mysterious. Grinder's Stand was an inn deep in the forest, far from towns and policemen. No one ever found out whether it was murder or suicide. President Jefferson believed that it was suicide. However, his friend Captain Clark was sure that it was murder.

William Clark: The Red-Headed Chief.

William Clark was an easy choice when Meriwether Lewis needed someone to help him lead the trip west. Clark could do things that Lewis could not. He knew how to draw maps, handle river boats, and live off the land in wild country. The two had worked together in the Army and had high respect for one another.

Clark was outgoing and even tempered. This was a good balance for Lewis, who was quiet and sometimes moody. The two men became good friends while on the journey. However, they couldn't agree about salt and dog meat. Lewis liked lots of salt, and Clark thought it wasn't needed. Also Lewis liked the taste of dog meat, while Clark thought it was disgusting.

After returning home, Clark married his sweetheart, Julia Hancock. Later he became Superintendent of Indian Affairs at St. Louis. Indians liked him very much, calling him the Red-Headed Chief. They felt he was the one person they could trust, and he was known to all the tribes of the Midwest and the West. In St. Louis, he did what he could to look after Sacajawea and her son, Baptiste.

No other person in the history of the West did as much for the Indians as William Clark. He worked hard to see the Indians treated fairly. When he died at the age of 68, he was well liked and highly thought of by many people.

Beaver Hats Brought Others To Explore Idaho.

Well-dressed men in Europe and America wore tall hats made from beaver fur. The fur came mostly from beavers trapped in North America. Beaver fur was in great demand. Trapping and trading fur was a good way to make money. Lewis and Clark had seen many beavers

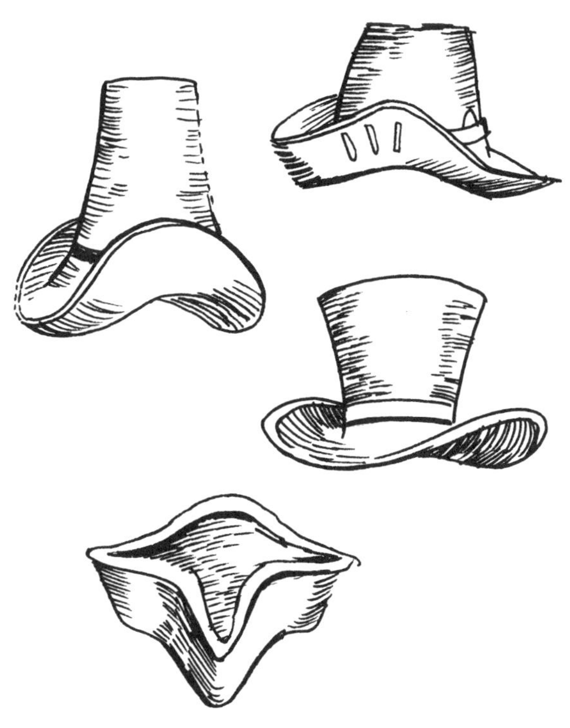

In the early 1800s, well-dressed men in Europe and America wore beaver hats like these. Beaver hats were made from beaver fur. After Lewis and Clark's visit, beaver trapping became important in the Oregon country. JOHN A. TAYE (DRAWING)

on their journey west, and this was good news to people who made money by selling furs. Idaho's next explorers would be fur trappers and traders.

Fur Trading In Northern Idaho. David Thompson was Idaho's first fur trader. His fur trading began with Kutenai and Flathead Indians near Bonners Ferry in 1808. In 1809, he built a **trading post** on the east side of Lake Pend Oreille, near the present town of Hope. This was the first building built by traders on Idaho soil. Thompson called it **Kullyspell House** because of the Kalispel Indians who lived nearby.

Thompson soon built two other fur trading posts. Spokane House was in northeast Washington, and Saleesh House was in northwest Montana. These three trading posts traded with all of the nearby tribes: Spokane in Washington; Kutenai, Kalispel, and Coeur d'Alene in Idaho; and Flathead in Montana.

David Thompson was important to Idaho because of his study of geography. While he lived in Idaho, he studied the land and made careful maps. He was trained as a surveyor, and was one of the few great geographers of all time. In the fur trade he covered over 50,000 miles of North America in 23 years. Everywhere he went, he mapped streams, lakes, mountains, and **passes**. When he didn't visit a place himself, he would carefully question trappers and Indians.

Thompson journeyed around northern Idaho for four years. He made friends with the Indians by his fair and honest trading with them. He mapped the routes used today for railroads and highways. Because of David Thompson, the world would learn about Idaho.

Fur Trading In Southern Idaho. **Fort Henry** became Idaho's second trading post in 1810. Andrew Henry and a party of trappers built several log cabins near the present town of St. Anthony. They called it Fort Henry. They planned to stay through the winter and trade with friendly Shoshoni. It is likely that they had to trap all their own furs, however. The Indians knew that the place was very cold, so they went elsewhere during the winter. Henry's party trapped during the fall and spring, then moved on.

Henry did not return to his "fort". The last we hear of Fort Henry was when the Hunt party stopped there in 1811. The cabins were empty then, and the Hunt party stayed only a short time. We shall see more of the Hunt party soon.

Andrew Henry discovered a lake on this trip into Idaho. Today we call it **Henry's Lake**. The river where his party did much of their trapping is called **Henry's Fork** of the Snake. Years later Henry started a new fur company and returned to travel Idaho's streams again. His lasting gift to Idaho, however, was his name.

Henry and his party were the first people after the Indians to see southern Idaho. However, they explored only Henry's Fork of the Snake. Other fur trappers would explore the rest of the Snake River country.

Review Questions

1. Idaho's first fur trader was ______________ .[79]

2. Thompson built his first trading post near the present town of ______________. He named it ______________ ______________ because of the Kalispel Indians. [79]

3. David Thompson was important to Idaho because of his study of ______________. He drew careful ______________ of streams, lakes, mountains, and passes. [79]

4. Andrew Henry built a fur trading post called Fort ______________. It was built near the present town of ______________. [79]

The Astorians Explore Southern Idaho.

Another party of fur trappers entered Idaho in 1811. These were the **Astorians**, led by William Price Hunt. The party had about 65 people, including one woman and two children. They entered Idaho through **Pierre's Hole**, which is now called **Teton Valley**. The town of Victor now stands where they camped the first night.

The Astorians had started west from St. Louis in 1810. They aimed to make their way across North America to a fur trading post on the Pacific coast. The post was called **Astoria**, after John Jacob Astor, owner of the American Fur Company.

When the Hunt party reached Fort Henry, the Snake River looked smooth and pleasant. Some of the men insisted on going the rest of the way by canoe. They didn't know about the sharp rocks, rough water, and waterfalls further down the river. Other men would call the main Snake the "Mad River" because of its rough,

The Astorians explored southern Idaho.

swift water. You will remember the rocky Snake River Canyon from reading Chapter 2.

At Fort Henry, the party built 15 **dugout canoes**. Hunt left their valuable horses with friendly Indians and sent five men to trap along Henry's Fork. The rest of the party started down the river in the canoes.

Their first two days were pleasant, and they went 60 miles. Then the water became rough and dangerous. At American Falls, they had to get out of the river and carry everything around the falls. In the ninth day, near the present Milner Dam, a canoe was smashed against the rocks. One man was killed. After a walk down the canyon, Hunt knew they couldn't go any further by canoe.

William Price Hunt was the leader of the Astorians. G. W. FULLER

Now the Hunt party had no horses. These had been left at Fort Henry. Using poor judgment, Hunt decided against going back for the horses. He divided the people into three smaller parties, each to search for a different route. They hid the supplies they could not carry, and loaded the rest on their backs.

One party, led by Donald Mackenzie, went northwest across the mountains of central Idaho. They arrived where the Clearwater meets the Snake, then followed the route of Lewis and Clark down the Snake and Columbia rivers. Mackenzie's party arrived in Astoria in the middle of winter.

A second party, led by Ramsay Crooks, stayed on the south and west side of the Snake. They were stopped by Hells Canyon below the present town of Weiser. The Crooks party turned around and went back up the river. By then they were starving and weak.

Caldron Linn. Antoine Clappine died here in 1811 when his canoe was smashed against the rocks. The Astorians called this spot Caldron Linn or the Devil's Scuttle Hole. HELEN LEE

Hunt led the rest of the people along the north side of the Snake. There they were stopped by the great canyons and wild mountains of the Seven Devils country. Going back up the river, they saw the Crooks group on the

Ramsay Crooks and his men were starving when Hunt and his party found them. G. W. FULLER

other side. Hunt sent a canoe and food across the river. Using the canoe, Crooks and his party crossed the river to join Hunt's party. One of Crooks's starving men couldn't wait for Hunt's canoe. He dived into the icy river and drowned.

Now Hunt and his party left their canoes and tried to get help from some Indians. They had poor luck finding help. Most Indians ran away when they saw them coming. Those who didn't run refused to trade for horses. Finally, Hunt found an Indian village along the Weiser River. These Indians traded with him for horses and a guide. With the guide and horses, the party made their way across the Blue Mountains of Oregon. Once on the Columbia, they rode the river to Astoria. They arrived a month later than Mackenzie's party.

The Astorians had taken 11 months to cover 3,000 miles. They crossed plains, mountains, and deserts. They suffered hunger, thirst, and pain. Two died in the Snake River. It is sad to say, but they caused most of their own troubles. They did not plan well, and they didn't have the good sense of Lewis and Clark or of David Thompson.

The Astorians were important to Idaho. (1) They found that the Snake River could not be used as a water route. (2) Small groups of trappers stayed along the streams to trap furs. This gave the United States a better chance to own the land. (3) Much of their route became the Oregon Trail. You will learn about the Oregon Trail in the next unit.

Review Questions

1. The Astorians entered Idaho through ____________, which is now called ____________.[*80*]

2. The Astorians were on their way to a trading post called ____________, which was on the Pacific coast. [*80*]

3. Hunt led the Astorians across southern Idaho along the ____________ River. [*80–81*]

4. Hunt and his party learned that the Snake River was dangerous for canoes because ____________________. [*81*]

5. The Astorians gave the United States a stronger claim in the Oregon Country because ____________________. [82]

Ideas To Talk About

1. Why do you think David Thompson was more successful than William Price Hunt in the fur business?

Other Fur Companies Come To Idaho.

For many years, fur traders were the only people except for the Indians who were interested in Idaho. During these years, many things happened. In January 1814, John Reed and a party of trappers were killed on the Boise River by some unfriendly Sheepeater Indians. This was the first killing of whites by Indians in Idaho. John Day became sick and died in eastern Idaho in 1820, and he left a will to his friend, Donald Mackenzie. This was the first written will in Idaho. Today a river and a town in Oregon, a dam on the Columbia, and a street in Pocatello are named after John Day.

Nathaniel Wyeth was the man who built Fort Hall as a fur trading post. Why was Wyeth forced to sell his business at a great loss? G. W. FULLER

Fort Hall And Fort Boise. In 1834, Fort Hall was built by **Nathaniel Wyeth**. Wyeth was a young man from Boston, who had come to Idaho two years before. He had trapped beavers and learned all he could about the fur business. This year, he brought wagons loaded with supplies. He built his fort on the Snake River nine

Fort Hall was an important fur trading post on the Snake River. This picture shows covered wagons making their way to Fort Hall. Where was Fort Hall located? #5-18-1 U OF I LIBRARY

Old Fort Boise was another important fur trading post on the Snake River. Where was Fort Boise located? What caused it to close? #6-121-1 U OF I LIBRARY

miles above the mouth of the **Portneuf River**. The spot was just a few miles from the present town of Fort Hall. He planned to buy furs from the trappers, and sell them supplies. It was his plan to take over the fur trade along the Snake.

The Hudson's Bay Company (an English company) had most of the fur trade on the Snake at this time. They did not want to let someone else take it over. That same year, the Hudson's Bay Company built **Fort Boise** to compete with Wyeth. Fort Boise was built on the Snake near the mouth of the Boise River. The company then sold supplies so cheaply that Wyeth could not stay in business. Two years later, Wyeth had to sell his fort to the Hudson's Bay Company at a great loss of money. In 1838, Fort Boise was moved to a spot near the present town of Parma.

Fort Hall and Fort Boise never made much money. As years went by, there were fewer and fewer beavers. The trappers had done their work well. They had taken most of the beaver out of Idaho and the Rocky Mountain country. In the 1840s, fur prices dropped, and fur trapping became a poor business. Silk hats had begun to replace those made of beaver fur.

With fewer beaver, Fort Hall and Fort Boise became stopping places for people moving west on the Oregon Trail. In 1846, the Oregon Country became part of the United States. Fort Hall and Fort Boise both closed in 1855. No trace of either fort is left today. Visitors can only read the signs where these well-known posts once stood.

Review Questions

1. Fort Hall was built by ____________ in 1834. It was built on the Snake River nine miles above the mouth of the ____________ River. [82]

2. Fort Boise was built by the ____________ in 1834. It was built on the Snake River near the mouth of the ____________ River. [*84*]

3. Wyeth lost money and had to sell Fort Hall because ________________________. [*84*]

Ideas To Talk About

1. How were fur trading posts like today's department stores?

The Mountain Men: An Exciting Story.

On March 20, 1822, the following notice appeared in the St. Louis Missouri Gazette:

"Wanted . . . 100 young men to ascend the Missouri River to its source, there to be employed for one, two, or three years."

Would you have answered this notice? It left out some important things. The work? Trapping beavers. Living conditions? Dangerous! Rugged country! You will have to kill your own food. You may have to fight for your life—both grizzly bears and Indians! You may be scalped by Indians. The pay? Money, whisky, tobacco, adventure, maybe fame, maybe death.

Jim Beckwourth was a mountain man who wrote about his "Life and Adventures." He was one of the few mountain men who were black. *HARPER'S MONTHLY*, SEPTEMBER 1856.

Peter Skene Ogden was a mountain man. Ogden, Utah, was named after him. G. W. FULLER

The notice was written by two people who were starting a new fur company, the Rocky Mountain Fur Company. You met one of them before. He was Andrew Henry, who built Fort Henry.

Would you want to go? Many were eager to try it. You may read stories about some of those who went: Jim Bridger, Jedediah Smith, "Broken-Hand" Fitzpatrick, Jim Beckwourth, Mike Fink, and others. These became the "Mountain Men" of history and legend.

The Rocky Mountain Fur Company wanted part of the beaver fur trade in the Rocky Mountains and Snake country. Their story isn't just an Idaho story, as you already know. The Rocky Mountains are shared by several states. Trappers of the Rocky Mountain Fur Company worked in Idaho, Wyoming, and Utah. There were no states then, only streams, valleys, and mountains. They followed beaver streams in and out of the states we know today.

Fighting and fur stealing added new dangers to the life of the fur trappers. The men of the Rocky Mountain Fur Company discovered that they had to fight other trappers. The trappers who were already there didn't intend to give up beavers to somebody else. However, the Rocky Mountain trappers were brave. They fought and stayed and added to Idaho's history.

Many of the fur trappers left their names on the pages of our history. Their adventures fill whole books, so only a few names can be told here. John Colter was the first "mountain man". He had journeyed with Lewis and Clark to the Pacific and back to the Rockies. At the Yellowstone River, he left Lewis and Clark and went off to trap beavers. Hugh Glass was known for his fight with a grizzly bear. After the bear left him for dead, he crawled and stumbled 100 miles to safety. Mike Fink, "King of the Keelboaters", drowned in a Montana river. John Johnston was made famous by the movie *Jeremiah Johnson*. The movie was made from the book *Mountain Man*, written by Idaho's own author, Vardis Fisher.

Several places have been named for mountain men. The Payette River and the town of Payette are named for Francois Payette. Ogden, Utah, is named for Peter Skene Ogden. Provo, Utah, is named for Etienne Provost. Jackson Hole, Wyoming, is named for David Jackson. Pierre's Hole,

Jim Bridger explored the Bear River from Idaho to the Great Salt Lake. What did he have to do with naming Cache Valley? UNKNOWN

now called Teton Valley, was named for Old Pierre Tivanitagon. **Cache Valley**, in Idaho and Utah, was named because Jim Bridger cached (stored) his furs in that valley. Later he built Fort Bridger in Wyoming, and was a guide for wagon trains coming west. William Craig became Idaho's first homesteader. He married a Nez Perce and settled near Lapwai.

Another interesting person was Captain Bonneville. On leave from the Army, he journeyed about Idaho, getting to know the Indians and trappers. Some people think he may have been sent by the United States to keep watch on the Hudson's Bay Company. Today Bonneville's name is used for Bonneville County (Idaho), Bonneville Dam (Columbia River), and old Lake Bonneville (seen in Chapter 2).

Review Questions

1. What are the names of some of the famous "Mountain Men"? (a) __________
(b) __________ (c) __________
(d) __________ (e) __________ [85–86]

2. The trappers of the Rocky Mountain Fur Company trapped beaver in which states:
(a) __________ (b) __________
(c) __________ [85]

3. What are some of the places that were named for "Mountain Men"? (a) __________
(b) __________ (c) __________
(d) __________ [85–86]

4. Cache Valley got its name because
____________________. [86]

Ideas To Talk About

1. Would you have answered the notice that appeared in the *Missouri Gazette*? Why or why not?

Captain Benjamin L. E. Bonneville explored much of Idaho while the fur trappers were busy in Idaho's streams. Several things have been named for Captain Bonneville. What are some of them? OREGON HISTORICAL SOCIETY

The Life Of A Trapper.

The fur trappers were special persons. Those who came to trap beavers and stayed, and lived to tell about it, came to be called **mountain men**. Their way of life has fired the imagination of many young people. Exciting stories and books have been written about them, some true, and others just exciting tales or legends.

Mountain men spent years away from towns and civilization. The longer they were away, the more they became like Indians. They learned to eat what Indians ate, and wear the kind of clothing Indians wore. They killed their own food. They learned to fight using knives and tomahawks. Living mostly outdoors, their skin became darkened by sun and weather, and they looked much like Indians. Many of them married Indians.

The mountain man's clothing was a five-piece suit of buckskin, including moccasins. He often made his own buckskin clothing. He carried a bowie knife, a hatchet, a rifle, a revolver, and ammunition. Beaver skins were his money.

Mountain men lived with danger at all times. It has been said they became as brave as a grizzly bear and as sly as a fox. They were happy in what they were doing and felt great joy in life. They sang and yelled in the empty forests. They had a strong code of honor—they helped everyone but their enemies.

Trapping The Beaver. The trappers worked in parties. It was important to find a safe place to camp and to protect each other. When camp was made, the leader would spread the trappers out in different directions. After working their traps, they would come back to camp.

The trapper pushed along the streams lined with willows, cottonwood, alder, and aspen. Much of the time was spent wading in the cold water looking for signs of beavers. The water also kept the trapper's scent from scaring the beavers away. Sometimes the trappers hunted beavers the way the Indians did. The beavers were chased out of their lodges and killed as they tried to get away. Most beavers were caught with steel traps. These were carefully hidden under the water. Six to ten traps would be set in the evening just before dark. Then just before sunrise, the trapper would come back to empty them.

The animals were skinned right there. Only the skins, the castoreum glands, and the tails were kept. Beaver tails boiled or baked in coals were very tasty eating. The trapper then moved upstream. Sticks floating down the stream or muddy water might mean Indians or other dangers were ahead.

The trapper cleaned and dried the skins. The flesh was scraped off, and the skins were stretched to dry on hoops made of willows. Each skin had to be marked, because the trapper was paid for the number brought in. When the skins were dry, they were pressed into packs of about 60 each. This was done by piling logs or heavy stones on the pack. Each pack weighed from 90 to 100 pounds.

The trappers' worst problems were Indians, trappers from other companies, and rheumatism. Rheumatism brought stiff and painful joints and muscles. It was brought on by wading in ice-cold water. Often furs were stolen by Indians or other trappers. This was another reason to mark every skin. Many trappers were also killed by Indians, mostly the **Blackfeet**.

Not all Indians fought the trappers. Most were friendly, and some even married trappers. Often, Indians traded furs to them in return for knives, tobacco, and other things. However, not all Indians were happy to see the trappers come into their country. Some would kill them or try to run them out. There was always danger, so the trappers had to be careful about Indians at all times.

Trapping was done only in the fall and spring months. From June to September, the beaver sheds some of its fur. Then its skin is not valuable. During the heavy winter freezes, the beaver holes up for the winter.

The trapper would hole up for the winter when the beaver did. The trapping party might build an Indian-type tipi, or a rough log cabin. Set for the winter, they would repair their clothing and equipment. They also made new clothing and other things they would need in the spring. These winter lodges were known for their fun and good humor. There would be talk and arguments, and spinning of yarns and tall tales. Great friendships were formed this way. These winters together were thought of as a kind of schooling. However, as soon as the snow began to melt, everyone was back out on the trap lines.

The Mountain Men And The Rendezvous. The **rendezvous** was the high point of the mountain man's year. This was a summer meeting at a place decided ahead of time. Company trappers—and other trappers and Indians in that part of the country—would come and trade their furs. General Ashley invented the rendezvous to supply his trappers

Mountain men dressed much like Indians. Artist Frederic Remington drew this picture of two mountain men and titled it, "I took ye for an Injin." *CENTURY*, NOVEMBER 1890

and pick up the furs. He had found it cost too much to build and keep trading posts.

In June, the trappers would take their furs to the nearest rendezvous. Packs of furs were loaded on horses, two to the horse. If there were no horses, the packs might be carried by dugout canoe. Without horses or boats, the furs had to be carried out.

The furs were traded for money or goods. Then the trapper bought things needed for the coming year. These might be traps, guns, ammunition, clothing, food, tobacco, whiskey, and **foofaraw**. Foofaraw was the name for the things traded to Indians for their good will, and maybe for furs or horses. This might be brightly colored glass beads (blue was the favorite color), colored cloth, earrings, mirrors, or anything else that might please the Indians.

Idaho's rendezvous were held in such places as Bear River Valley, Cache Valley, and Pierre's Hole. These meetings would last two or three weeks or more, and were for fun as well as business. The mountain man had no town to go to, so the rendezvous was the only way of "going to town."

The trappers and Indians had fun in many different ways at the rendezvous. There was racing, wrestling, shooting, and riding. There was also gambling, drinking, and fighting. (The rendezvous wagons brought lots of whiskey.) Trappers liked to sit around the campfire and boast and tell tall tales. Some even got married at the rendezvous. There were always Indians on hand, and many Indian women were eager to marry trappers.

The trappers often spent a whole year's earnings at the rendezvous. This was really very little money. After buying supplies and equipment needed for the coming year, there was little left to spend. When the money was gone, there were only coffee and chocolate left to drink. These were stored in big barrels in the wagons. When the rendezvous was over, the trapper would head back into beaver country.

The End Of The Mountain Men.

As the number of beavers grew less, most of the mountain men gave up their traps. They had to find other jobs and other ways of life. Because they knew the land so well, and because they loved to be outdoors, many became guides. The wagon trains coming west on the Oregon Trail were often guided and protected by mountain men.

Western artist W. H. Jackson drew this picture of a rendezvous on the Green River of Wyoming. Why are there so many tipis in the picture? STATE HISTORICAL SOCIETY OF COLORADO

Pierre's Hole was a famous spot for Indian councils, fur trapping rendezvous, and outlaw hideouts. Today it is called Teton Valley. In this picture you can see the present-day town of Driggs. The Teton Mountains tower in the background. IDAHO DEPARTMENT OF COMMERCE

Some mountain men settled on land and became farmers. Others settled in the new towns of the West. Here they went into business and the professions. Several served in the governments of the new territories and states. As mountain men, they had blazed the trails that brought other people west. In their new lives, they went on to help build America—and Idaho.

Review Questions

1. Mountain men learned to live like ____________. [86]
2. The clothing of mountain men was made of ____________. [86]
3. The trapper spent much of his time wading in ____________ looking for signs of ____________. [87]
4. The trapper needed to mark each skin he caught because ________________________. [87]
5. The trapper's three worst problems were: (a) ____________ (b) ____________ (c) ____________ [87]
6. The ____________ was the high point of the mountain man's year. [87]
7. The mountain man traded his furs for ____________ or ____________. [88]
8. The things traded to the Indians were called ____________. [88]
9. Idaho's rendezvous were held in places such as: (a) ____________ (b) ____________ (c) ____________. [88]
10. Most of the mountain men had to give up trapping because ________________________. [88]

Ideas To Talk About

1. Why was the rendezvous important to the mountain man?

Chapter 4 Skill Activities

Words And Ideas

In Chapter 4, you will find a number of key words printed in **bold** print. Each key word stands for an important idea. Answering these questions will help you understand some of the key words.

You can find the key words in the Glossary at the back of the book. The number after each question is the page where the idea is found in the book. Answer each question with a complete sentence.

1. Who were the **Astorians**? [80]
2. Where does the **Columbia River** go after the Snake River empties into it? [74]
3. What does the **continental divide** do? [75]
4. What was a **dugout canoe** made from? [77]
5. What kinds of things were used for **foofaraw**? [88]
6. How did **mountain men** change after they had lived in the wilderness for a while? [86]

7. What present-day states made up the **Oregon Country**? [73]
8. What did mountain men do at their **rendezvous**? [87–88]
9. What is the **summit** of a mountain? [75]
10. What is a **tributary** of a river? [74]

Exploring Idaho

Where did Idaho's explorers visit? Begin with a plain outline map of Idaho, and draw in the places listed below.

You will need to study a good map of Idaho. The Idaho Official Highway Map has the information you need.

1. Cache Valley—1860
2. continental divide—1805
3. Fort Boise—1834
4. Fort Hall—1834
5. Fort Henry—1810
6. Kullyspell House—1809
7. Lemhi Pass—1805
8. Lewiston—1861
9. Lolo Trail—1805
10. Pierre's Hole—1811
11. Weippe—1805

Research Projects

1. *Beavers*. Beavers are very interesting animals. Write a report about beavers and the way they live. An encyclopedia should be helpful.

2. *Rendezvous*. The rendezvous was the most exciting part of a mountain man's life. Make a report about the mountain man's rendezvous. This could be a written report, a comic strip, or a filmstrip. You may use this book or another source.

Using Your Imagination

Put on a Skit. Plan and act out a skit. (If you prefer, you can put on a puppet play instead. Finger puppets are easy to make.)

1. *Meriwether Lewis and George Drewyer*. On August 12, 1805, these two became the first explorers to set foot on Idaho soil. Write a skit about this famous event, then act it out for the class.

2. *Sacajawea*. Imagine the excitement when Sacajawea met her brother, Cameahwait! Write a skit of this meeting, then act it out for the class.

3. *Lewis and Clark*. Do you remember when Lewis and Clark arrived at Chief Twisted Hair's camp? The explorers were weak and ill from their journey over the mountains. Write a skit about this, then act it out for the class.

4. *The Astorians*. Who had more trouble than the Astorians? Remember the problems they had trying to cross the Snake River above Hells Canyon? Write a skit about the Astorians, then act it out for the class.

Reviewing Chapter 4

Main Ideas In This Chapter

1. Idaho was once part of the Oregon Country.
2. The Oregon Country was made up of Idaho, Oregon, Washington, and part of Canada.
3. President Thomas Jefferson sent Lewis and Clark to explore the Louisiana Territory and the Oregon Country.
4. Lewis and Clark made friends with many Indian tribes, including the Shoshoni and the Nez Perce.
5. The Lewis and Clark party brought the first white people to Idaho.
6. Captain Meriwether Lewis and George Drewyer were the first explorers to enter Idaho. This took place on August 12, 1805.
7. The Shoshoni and the Nez Perce helped Lewis and Clark on their journey.
8. The fur business brought trappers and explorers to Idaho.
9. David Thompson was Idaho's first fur trader. He began trading with the Kutenai and Flathead Indians near Bonners Ferry in 1808.
10. Kullyspell House was Idaho's first fur trading post and the first building built by traders in Idaho.
11. David Thompson made careful maps of northern Idaho.
12. Fort Henry was Idaho's second fur trading post.
13. The Astorians explored southern Idaho along the Snake River. They gave the United States a strong claim to the Oregon Country.
14. Fort Hall and Fort Boise were important fur posts along the Snake River.
15. In 1846, the Oregon Country became part of the United States.
16. Certain fur trappers were known as mountain men.
17. The life of the mountain man was exciting and dangerous.

18. Mountain men learned to live much like Indians.

19. Trappers were not paid much for their work.

20. Trappers took their furs to a rendezvous to sell them or trade them for supplies and equipment.

21. The rendezvous gave the mountain men a chance to have fun and enjoy a good time.

22. The fur business became poor because well-dressed men began wearing silk hats instead of fur hats, and because most of the beaver had been trapped and killed.

23. Most of the mountain men gave up trapping when the fur business became poor.

Further Reading For Children

Anderson, Madelyn Klein. *The Nez Perce.* (An American Indian First Book) New York: Franklin Watts, 1994.

Blumberg, Rhoda. *The Incredible Journey of Lewis and Clark.* New York: Lothrop, Lee & Shepard Books, 1987. [This excellent book shows rarely seen sketches from Lewis and Clark's journals: Indians, animals, birds, fish, and Lewis's dog, "Seaman."]

George, Charles, and Linda George. *Idaho.* (America the Beautiful Second Series) New York: Children's Press, 2000. [Good sampling of Idaho geography and culture.]

Gilbert, Bil. *The Trailblazers.* (Time-Life Series of the Old West) New York: Time-Life Books, 1973. [Interesting photographs and art work.]

Gregory, Kristiana. *Jenny of the Tetons.* (An Odyssey Book) Orlando: Harcourt School Publishers, 1989. [Award-winning book. A girl's parents are killed by Indians and she is wounded, but she is nursed back to health by a Shoshoni woman.]

Kummer, Patricia K. *Idaho.* Mankato, Minnesota: Capstone High/Low Books, 1999.

Marcovitz, Hal. *Sacagawea: Guide for the Lewis and Clark Expedition.* (Explorers of New Worlds Series) Philadelphia: Chelsea House Publishers, 2001.

O'Dell, Scott. *Streams to River, River to Sea.* New York: Fawcett Juniper, 1986. [Story of Sacajawea's journey with Lewis and Clark, told in first person by Sacajawea.]

Rifkin, Mark. *The Nez Perce Indians.* (Junior Library of American Indians) New York: Chelsea House Publishers, 1994.

Rowland, Della. *Story of Sacajawea, Guide to Lewis and Clark.* (A Yearling Book) Bantam Dell Publishing Group, 1989.

Smith, Roland. *The Captain's Dog: My Journey with the Lewis and Clark Tribe.* Orlando: Harcourt School Publishers, 1999. [America's greatest journey of discovery, as seen through the eyes of a remarkable dog. An award-winning book.]

Stefoff, Rebecca. *Idaho.* (Celebrate the States Series) Tarrytown, New York: Benchmark Books, Marshall Cavendish Corporation, 2000. [Good sampling of Idaho geography and culture.]

Thomasma, Kenneth. *Truth About Sacajawea.* Jackson, Wyoming: Grandview Publishing Company, 1997.

Movie

The Trail—Lewis & Clark Expedition. VHS 88 minutes. Filmed and narrated by Robin D. Williams, 1996. Approved by the National Lewis & Clark Bicentennial Council. Available from www.amazon.com. [This film authentically retraces the epic journey of 1803–1806 by carefully following their letters, field notes, and journals. Filmed on many actual sites and features art work of Charles M. Russell, John Clymer, and Bob Scriver. Highly recommended.]

Time Line

1776 A.D. — Declaration of Independence; USA begins.

1800

1805 — Lewis and Clark explore Idaho.

1809 — David Thompson builds Kullyspell House near Lake Pend Oreille.

1810 — Andrew Henry builds Fort Henry near present town St. Anthony.

1811 — The William Price Hunt party of Astorians explore southern Idaho.

1812 — Robert Stuart's party of Astorians return east over the route later to become the Oregon Trail.

1814 — John Reed party of trappers killed by Indians on Boise River.

1832 — Famous mountain man rendezvous at Pierre's Hole; Captain Bonneville explores Idaho.

1834 — Nathaniel Wyeth builds Fort Hall; Hudson's Bay Company builds old Fort Boise; Spaldings and Whitmans visit Idaho.

1836 — Spaldings build mission at Lapwai; Whitmans build mission near Walla Walla, Washington.

1838 — Old Fort Boise is moved to a spot near present town of Parma.

1840 — Colonel William Craig settles on homestead near Lapwai.

1846 — Oregon Country becomes part of the United States.

1855 — Fort Hall and old Fort Boise are closed.

1860 — Franklin becomes Idaho's first permanent white settlement.

1863 — Idaho Territory is formed.

1890 — Idaho becomes a state.

1900

1976 A.D. — USA celebrates its Bicentennial

1990 — Idaho Statehood Centennial

Chapter 5
Settlers Come To Idaho

Most of the Oregon Country is now part of the United States. Three states were carved from this great land because great numbers of Americans came west to live there. This is the story of those people.

Coming West On The Oregon Trail.

The Americans who came west to the Oregon Country followed the **Oregon Trail**. Much of the Oregon Trail began as Indian trails. These trails had been used by Indians for hundreds of years. When the mountain men came, they closely followed the trails already there. After all, the Indians knew their own land best.

For many years, mountain men followed the same general route west. Later, missionaries followed the trail of the mountain men. Settlers followed soon afterward. As more people used the trail, it wore deeper into the ground. Over the years, the Oregon Trail became a very deep track worn in the earth. This track was worn by thousands of wheels, boots, cattle, horses—and tears. It was the Oregon Trail that brought America to Oregon, and Oregon to America.

Immigrants and Settlers. The people who came west to make new homes were called **immigrants**. An immigrant is a person who comes to a new country to make a home. Once these people settled on the new land, they were called **settlers**. There were several kinds, and a great many of them. Trappers, missionaries, and farm families all became settlers. The Indians, too, sometimes settled as farmers on their own land.

Traces of the Oregon Trail can still be seen in certain parts of Idaho. This photo was taken east of Boise. People had to cross many miles of desert such as this to reach the Oregon Country. IDAHO HISTORICAL SOCIETY

Review Questions

1. A person who comes to a new country to make a home is called an ____________. [93]
2. People who settle on new land are called ____________. [93]
3. People who came west to the Oregon Country followed the ____________. [93]

Ideas To Talk About

1. Northern Idaho had at least two other well-used Indian trails. Lewis and Clark used the

Lolo Trail to cross the Bitterroots into Idaho. The Nez Perce also used another trail, called the Nez Perce Trail, to cross the mountains into Montana to hunt buffalo. Why didn't settlers use these two trails instead of the Oregon Trail?

Missionaries Helped Settle Idaho.

Christian **missionaries** began coming to the Oregon Country in 1834. They wanted to bring their religion to the Indians, and to teach them American ways. These people were important in settling the Oregon Country. They taught the Indians simple farming and home crafts. Also they brought many settlers who began to farm the land.

The first missionaries came because Indians had asked for them. The Nez Perce and Flathead Indians had noticed the Christian religion during Lewis and Clark's visit. They thought it was interesting. Later they saw fur traders, such as David Thompson, reading the *Bible* and praying. A number of French-speaking trappers had married Flathead Indian women. Most were Catholic, and this interested the Flathead. Some Indians thought that the Christian religion had more power than their own. They wanted teachers to teach them about this power, and about the *Bible*.

In 1831, four Nez Perce and Flathead Indians journeyed to St. Louis. They found their old friend, William Clark, and asked him to send them religious teachers. Clark was not able to help them at that time. He passed their message on to other people. In later years, other Indians journeyed east to ask for teachers of the new religion.

The first missionaries came to Idaho with Nathaniel Wyeth in 1834. Jason Lee, with a party of three, stayed at Fort Hall for a short time. While he was at Fort Hall, he gave Idaho's first church service. He also held a funeral service for a trapper who had died in an accident. Lee and his party soon moved on to western Oregon.

Lee wanted more Americans to come to Oregon. In 1839, he returned to the East and led a party of more than 50 new settlers back to western Oregon. This started the rush that would fill the Oregon Country with Americans. Soon the Oregon Trail would be alive with people. Thousands more would follow those first settlers to Oregon.

Rabbit skin leggings (left) and no-horns-on-his-head (right). These men journeyed to St. Louis to ask for Black Robes, their name for Catholic priests.

G. W. FULLER

The Spaldings Build A Mission At Lapwai.

In 1836, Reverend **Henry and Mrs. Eliza Spalding** stopped at Fort Hall and Fort Boise. With them were Doctor **Marcus and Mrs. Narcissa Whitman**. These four would become important in settling Idaho and Washington. They had come west to built **missions** among the Indians.

The Whitmans decided to build their mission near the mouth of the Snake River where it flows into the Columbia. Today this spot is near the city of Walla Walla, Washington. The Spaldings decided to build their mission among the Nez Perce. They chose a spot in Idaho near Lapwai.

The Spaldings arrived in Clearwater Valley in the fall of 1836. They found the Nez Perce eager to help them. The Indians brought them food and helped build buildings. The mission began as a rough log building, and was built near the mouth of Lapwai Creek.

Reverend Henry and Mrs. Eliza Spalding built the Lapwai Mission. Why was Lapwai a good place to build a mission? G. W. FULLER

There was much work to be done. The Spaldings discovered that they had to do many things besides teach and preach to the Indians. Reverend Spalding treated the sick. He was not a doctor, but he had been with Doctor Whitman enough to know how to treat simple kinds of sickness.

Spalding showed the Indians how to farm. He had brought seeds with him for gardens and fields. He also brought cattle, hogs, and chickens. The first crops were wheat, oats, buckwheat, potatoes, corn, peas, and other vegetables. This was the beginning of farming in Idaho. Since that time, many of the Indians living around Lapwai have been farmers.

Review Questions

1. Missionaries came west because they wanted to ______________________. [94]
2. Four Nez Perce and Flathead Indians went to St. Louis to ask for ___________. [94]
3. The Whitmans built their mission near the present city of ___________, Washington. [95]
4. The Spaldings built their mission in Idaho near the Indian village of ___________. [95]

Life At The Lapwai Mission.

The Spaldings started Idaho's first school. Mrs. Eliza Spalding was the teacher. The pupils were Nez Perce, young and old. There were children, mothers with babies in their arms, and grandmothers and grandfathers. She taught reading, writing, and religion. She also taught home crafts such as spinning, weaving, knitting, and sewing. There were no books, so she printed her own "books" by hand. This took much of her time, so her time in school each day was short. While she was away, the pupils worked in small groups and taught each other.

Many "first" things happened at the Lapwai Mission. Idaho's first white child was born there on November 15, 1837. She was named Eliza Spalding, after her mother. The Indians liked her very much. In later life, she married an Oregon rancher, and lived to be 82 years old. She wrote a book about her life and the Lapwai Mission.

The Lapwai Mission had the first printing press in the Oregon Country. It came in 1839. The first book printed in the Oregon Country was done with this machine. It was a small eight-page children's book, printed mostly in the Nez Perce language. The press was used also to print a song book and parts of the *Bible* in Nez Perce.

These books were "first" for another reason. Until the Spaldings came, the Nez Perce language had never been written. The Indians only spoke their language. Henry Spalding found a way to write it, using the English alphabet. Then he began teaching the Nez Perce how to read and write in their language. He wanted them to read the *Bible* and to learn his own religion. They could learn to read in Nez Perce easier than they could learn to read in English.

This printing press at the Lapwai Mission was the first one in the Oregon Country. Why did the Spaldings need a printing press? OREGON HISTORICAL SOCIETY

This mill stone once helped grind grain into flour at the Lapwai Mission. #5-13-36 U OF I LIBRARY

The year 1839 was a dry year at Lapwai. Henry Spalding showed the Indians how to irrigate their gardens. This was the first irrigation in Idaho.

A mill was built at Lapwai. It could grind wheat and corn, and it could cut trees into lumber. Now the Indians and the Spaldings could make their own grain into flour. This saved a lot of money. Flour had cost $26.00 a barrel, and corn meal had cost $35.00 a barrel.

In the space of only ten years, many things were done at Lapwai. Many of the Nez Perce settled at Lapwai and farmed instead of spending their summers hunting for food. The few cows had grown into many herds, and the sheep had grown into several flocks. About 500 pupils had gone to Eliza Spalding's school. The Nez Perce language had been written into books. The church had about 100 members. A government had been started, and laws had been written.

Ideas To Talk About

1. What were some of the things that Henry Spalding taught the Nez Perce?
2. What were some of the things that Eliza Spalding taught the Nez Perce?

3. What were some of the "first" things that happened at the Lapwai mission?
4. The Spaldings tried to change the Nez Perce by teaching them new ways. Do you think this was good or bad? Explain your reasons.

William Craig, Mountain Man, Settles At Lapwai.

William Craig, mountain man, left fur trapping and came to Lapwai in 1840. He became Idaho's first homesteader. He and his Nez Perce wife, Isabel, settled on 640 acres of land. Because of Isabel, Craig was a close friend of the Nez Perce. The Craigs were also neighbors to the Spaldings. While living at Lapwai, William Craig helped the government work out treaties with the Nez Perce, Walla Walla, Flathead, and Blackfeet Indians. Later the government made him the first Indian agent for the Nez Perce at Lapwai.

Colonel William Craig became Idaho's first white homesteader. His farm was near Spaldings' Mission. OREGON HISTORICAL SOCIETY

Trouble At The Missions.

Not all Indians wanted the missionaries to be there. Some did not like the new religion. Many feared they would lose their land if more settlers came. By the 1840s, many immigrants had come west and were living on Indian land. The Indians could see their country being taken away from them. Many of the immigrants stopped at Whitman's mission at Walla Walla, and Whitman welcomed them.

The Spalding cabin was built in 1838. This is an artist's painting based on old writings and photographs. No photographs were taken until after the cabin had been partly destroyed.
C. M. DRURY (PAINTING BY ROWENA LUNG ALCORN)

The immigrants brought diseases with them. These diseases were new to the Indians, and many Indians died from them. Some Indians thought they were being poisoned. Smallpox was very bad at the time. Whole Indian villages died from it.

In great anger, a group of Cayuse and Nez Perce Indians attacked the Whitman mission in 1847. The Whitmans and several others were killed. Then one of the Nez Perce rode to Lapwai and got together a band of angry Nez Perce. They hoped to kill the Spaldings and get rid of the mission at Lapwai.

William Craig and some friendly Nez Perce protected the Spaldings. The Spaldings hid in the Craig home while the angry Indians wrecked the mission. Later the Spaldings, guarded by friendly Nez Perce, left for the safety of western Oregon. Many Nez Perce loved the Spaldings and were sad to see them go. This closed the missions. It would be many years before missionaries returned to Lapwai.

Today Lapwai is part of the Nez Perce Indian

Reservation. Many Nez Perce live there. The mission is gone, but in its place stands a beautiful park. The park reminds us of those brave people who came to live and work in an unknown country. It reminds us too of the warm and helpful Nez Perce people who welcomed the Spaldings and helped them with their work.

Ideas To Talk About

1. Why did some of the Indians not want the missionaries to be there?

2. Why did terrible things happen to the Whitmans?

3. What happened to the Spaldings at the Lapwai mission?

4. If you were a Nez Perce when the Spaldings lived at Lapwai, would you want them to be there or not? Explain your answer.

Father De Smet is seen here with chiefs of the Flathead, Coeur d'Alene, Kalispel, and Colville tribes. OREGON HISTORICAL SOCIETY

Father De Smet And The Catholic Missionaries.

The Flathead people wanted Catholic missionaries. The French-speaking people living among them had excited them about the Catholic religion. The Indians who journeyed to St. Louis to see William Clark had asked for "Black Robes". The Indians called Catholic priests Black Robes because of their black clothing.

Father De Smet became interested in working with the Indians of the Oregon Country. He had heard about the Nez Perce and Flathead coming to St. Louis. In 1840, he followed the Oregon Trail to the Green River (Wyoming) **rendezvous**. The Flathead heard of his coming, and a band of braves journeyed to meet him. Some of them came 800 miles. From Green River, the Flathead took him to Pierre's Hole. There he was met by 1,600 Flathead and Kalispel Indians who had come to see him. They were eager to see this Black Robe for whom they had waited so long.

The Indians wanted Father De Smet to preach and "pray the Great Prayer". This was the first Catholic service held in Idaho. Father De Smet was so warmly received, he decided he would like to work among these people. He asked the Flathead to find a valley where they could settle and he could build a mission. The Indians chose a valley in western Montana. In that valley, Father De Smet built his first Indian mission and church. The Indians were delighted to have a House of the Great Spirit among them.

Soon the Coeur d'Alene Indians asked Father De Smet to build a mission for them as well. A place was chosen on the St. Joe River near the present town of St. Maries. With the help of the

This photo shows an adobe wall inside the Sacred Heart Mission at Cataldo. How were the adobe walls made? GARRETT PHOTOGRAPHY

The Sacred Heart Mission was built at Cataldo in 1853. Today it is Idaho's oldest existing building. This photo shows the building after it was restored in 1976. It is still used as a Catholic church. IDAHO DEPARTMENT OF COMMERCE

Indians, work began in December 1842. By early spring, a new village was laid out. Roads and a church were built, and fields were planted. By October 1844, the little village had 100 families. However, the village had been built on low ground, and high water flooded the fields each spring. It was decided that the mission would have to be moved.

Sacred Heart Mission At Cataldo.

A new place was chosen near the present village of Cataldo. The spot was on soft rolling hills that rise from the Coeur d'Alene River to the mountains. Father Ravalli was sent to build the new mission. Father Ravalli was well-suited to mission work. While preparing to be a priest, he took extra studies. He studied medicine, math, science, art, and mechanics. The church he built at Cataldo still shows his outstanding work.

The new mission was called the **Sacred Heart Mission**. It was a beautiful building that still stands today. Every part was made from trees and other materials gathered nearby. There was no factory for thousands of miles around. Heavy pieces of wood were cut for the floor. The roof and walls were made with pine poles, woven with willows, and packed with grass and mud. Across the front of the church, outside, were six tall columns. These held up the roof of the porch. They were carved and rubbed smooth by hand.

The church building was begun in 1853. It took more than 20 years to finish. This is not surprising when you see the amount of wood carving inside the church. Father Ravalli and another priest carved pictures into the ceiling and walls, posts, and altars. Father Ravalli even carved two statues from wood blocks. The Coeur d'Alene were indeed proud of their House of the Great Spirit.

Review Questions

1. The Indians called Catholic priests ____________. [98]
2. The priest who met the Flathead and Kalispel at Pierre's Hole was ____________. [98]
3. The mission that was built for the Coeur d'Alene was called ____________. [99]
4. Father Ravalli built the new Sacred Heart Mission near the present village of ____________. [99]

Ideas To Talk About

1. Why were the Flathead and Kalispel so eager to meet Father De Smet?
2. Why was Father Ravalli very well-suited to work among the Indians?
3. Why were the Coeur d'Alene so proud of their church building?

Life At Sacred Heart Mission.

The mission at Cataldo soon became an important place. Everyone was welcome there. Its guests were Indians, soldiers, packers, hunters, and miners. Governor Stevens of Washington Territory was a guest there. Last but not least were the Indians. Children and families were taught there and given many kinds of help.

After visiting in 1853, Governor Stevens wrote that 500 people lived at the mission. It had a "fine church", several buildings, a dairy room, and a cook room. A "horse mill" was used for grinding flour. There were 12 log cabins for Indians to live in, and more were being built.

Governor Isaac Stevens was the first governor of Washington Territory. Northern Idaho was part of Washington Territory then. G. W. FULLER

Farming was going well. Two hundred acres of land were plowed for crops. The animals had plenty of pasture land. There were 100 hogs, 16 oxen, 30 cows, and many horses, mules, and young animals.

In 1877, the Coeur d'Alene Indian Reservation was moved to the south end of Lake Coeur d'Alene. The mission had to move also. A new mission was built near the Indian village of Tensed, where it remains today.

The "Old Mission Church" at Cataldo is Idaho's oldest public building. Time and weather have damaged the building over the years, and it has had major repairs twice. The last time was in 1975. In that year, the Catholic Church gave the building to the Coeur d'Alene tribe. Then the State of Idaho fixed up the building as part of the 1976 American Bicentennial Celebration. Once again it was made beautiful, and it still stands today to remind us of its exciting past.

What Did The Missionaries Do For Idaho?

The missionaries were neither all good nor all bad. On the good side, the Indians learned from them to farm and to raise animals. This allowed them to settle in one place. No longer did they have to journey through the mountains gathering wild roots, berries, and meat. Indian women learned to make wool into yarn and to weave or knit it into cloth. Now they could make clothing from cloth instead of animal skins.

On the bad side, the missionaries brought settlers, who took away the Indians' land. Though the missionaries taught peace, many settlers treated the Indians badly. They had one set of laws for Indians and another for themselves. The missionaries often sided with the settlers instead of with the Indians.

As the West filled with immigrants, the Indians were almost crowded out. Settlers' horses and cows ate the grass that once fed Indians' horses. They also ate many of the wild plants that Indians used for food. There were no longer enough buffalo, deer, and other wild animals for food.

The Indians were not happy with these changes. Many fought back. A number of people on both sides were killed. The missionaries worked hard to stop the fighting and killing. They also helped both groups understand each other.

Ideas To Talk About

1. Why did the Sacred Heart Mission become an important place?

2. If you had lived during Father De Smet's time, would you have wanted to work among the Indians as a missionary? Why or why not?

3. The missionaries changed the Indians' lives by teaching them farming and other ways of life. Do you think the missionaries should have done this?

The fine work inside the Sacred Heart Mission can be seen in this view of the front of the church. Carved pictures can still be seen on the walls, ceiling, posts, and altars. Who carved them?

GARRETT PHOTOGRAPHY

Thousands Of People Came West On The Oregon Trail.

As the fur trappers worked and lived in the Oregon Country, their stories were carried back to the United States. The missionaries wrote glowing reports back home. People heard that the land was good for farming. They heard that the weather was pleasant, and that it was a nice place to live. A lot of people wanted to move west. Americans began coming to "Oregon".

There were a lot of important problems for anyone coming to Oregon, however. It was awfully far from Missouri, and there were no roads to follow. Lewis and Clark had found a route, but it was too rough for wagons. The Astorians had found a better route through southern Idaho. There was as yet no road, however.

There were worse things. Several tribes, such as the Blackfeet, attacked and killed trappers and settlers. The Rocky Mountains towered into the sky like a wall to keep people out of the Oregon Country. There were only a few routes through the mountains. These were not easy routes.

West of the mountains were hundreds of miles of desert. A desert can be more deadly than unfriendly Indians. Worst of all, food for animals and people was hard to find in this huge land. A family couldn't carry enough food for a journey of several months. However, even in the face of these problems, people came to Oregon. The Oregon Trail was born.

John C. Fremont Maps the Oregon Trail.

You will remember that the United States wanted the Oregon Country. If a lot of Americans moved to "Oregon", the United States would have a good chance to take it. The government decided to do something to help Americans move west. In 1842, Captain **John C. Fremont** was sent to map the Oregon Trail. Fremont's maps could then be used by Americans wanting to go to Oregon.

In 1843, Fremont mapped the Oregon Trail across Idaho. His guide was the mountain man "Broken Hand" Fitzpatrick. The party was made up of about 40 people, many of them mountain men. They stopped at Bear Lake Valley, Fort Hall, and Fort Boise. At Glenns Ferry, they had to have Indians help them get their animals and carts across the Snake River.

Captain Fremont was a scientist as well as a soldier. He was brave, hardworking, and smart. He had studied math and science. As a young man, he had helped map railroad routes in wild country. He wanted to study plant and animal life in the West, along with the geography and trails. He was a fine person for the job.

Fremont brought instruments to tell the elevation, longitude, and latitude. He read these every day. He took the temperature several times a day. Each day, he wrote down everything he thought might be interesting or useful at a later time. He described how the country looked. He described the soil, the plants, and the animals living there. He even gave the scien-

Captain John C. Fremont mapped the Oregon Trail. Why would anyone be interested in a map of the Oregon Trail? G. W. FULLER

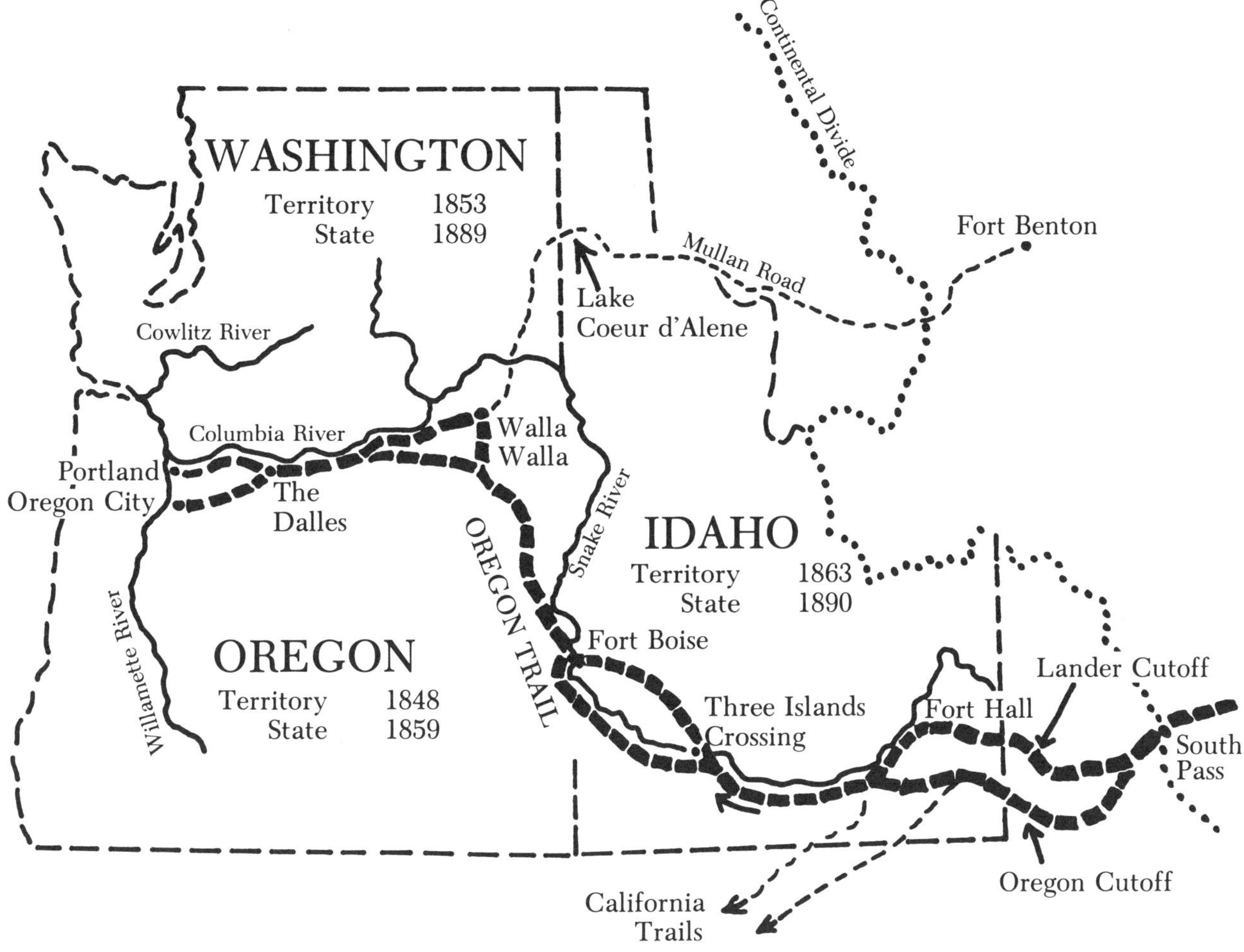

Many thousands of people rushed to Oregon over the Oregon Trail.

tific names of the plants! He described the Indians he saw, and their habits.

Each day, Fremont's party was up at daybreak. The horses were set to graze while everyone ate breakfast. Then the party marched all day, and camped an hour before sunset. This allowed time for the horses to graze while camp was set up for the night. Guards were always posted to watch the camp during the night. Fremont was often up at night studying instruments and writing reports.

Fremont's report on the Oregon Trail was widely read by the American people. It told Americans what they could expect. It proved a great help to people coming west in the years that followed.

Review Questions

1. The person sent to map the Oregon Trail was ______________. *[102]*
2. Captain Fremont was a ______________ as well as a soldier. *[102]*
3. Fremont's party had about 40 people, and many of them were ______________. *[102]*

Ideas To Talk About

1. What were some of the important problems faced by anyone coming to Oregon?
2. Why would Captain Fremont want to have mountain men in his party?
3. Captain Fremont carefully measured the elevation, longitude, and latitude. Why were these things important to him?
4. Why was it important to have a special route west, such as the Oregon Trail?

Many immigrants cut their names and the date on rocks where they camped. This is a picture of Register Rock along the Oregon Trail west of American Falls. Why would people want to leave their names along the trail? #6–84–3 U OF I LIBRARY

Americans Get Oregon Fever.

The missionaries proved that immigrant families could settle in the Oregon Country. Soon other families began to follow the missionaries. "Oregon Fever" took hold of America. The year 1842 was the first year that a large number of people came west on the Oregon Trail. In that year, a large group of farmers left the Midwest and journeyed to the **Willamette Valley** in western Oregon.

Each year, more and more people came west to Oregon. Farming was their main interest. A family could have 640 acres of free land in the Willamette Valley. Farmers in the Mississippi Basin were eager to leave that hot, damp valley of mosquitos and sickness. Almost all Oregon settlers were headed for the Willamette Valley and other western valleys. Very few thought of settling in Idaho. Idaho looked dry, and the settlers didn't think of irrigation.

Immigrants became a worry for the fur trading posts. The posts were kept open for trappers and Indians who sold furs. They didn't have enough food and goods for all the other people who stopped. Sometimes they refused to sell to the immigrants. One party took food and goods at gun point when they were refused at Fort Hall.

Prices were high at the trading posts. Jim Bridger quit trapping in 1842 and built Fort Bridger in Wyoming. This gave people another place to buy food and goods. Trading posts sometimes had herds of cattle, vegetable gardens, and grain. Fort Hall had a large herd of cattle in 1843 and grew some wheat and turnips. However, this still did not make enough food for the immigrants.

Following The Oregon Trail.

The Oregon Trail was the most important trail in western America. It began at Independence, Missouri, near Kansas City. It stretched 2,020 miles across America to the Willamette Valley town of Oregon City. It crossed three mountain ranges, many rivers, and the lands of ten Indian tribes. More than 64,500 people followed this trail to Oregon between 1840 and 1860.

The people entered Idaho near the town of Border, Wyoming. From there they went on to Fort Hall. Today this part of the trail passes through Montpelier, Soda Springs (then called Beer Springs), and the town of Fort Hall. The present town of Fort Hall is several miles east of old Fort Hall.

From Fort Hall they continued, passing through today's town of American Falls. Onward west the trail led them, passing near Declo, Burley, Twin Falls, and Filer. Further west they crossed the Snake River at Glenns Ferry. The crossing was called Three Island Crossing. A small state park marks that spot today.

From there, they followed the trail northwest. They passed north of Mountain Home and on to the Boise River. Along the Boise River, they passed through Boise, Garden City, Notus, and Parma. At the mouth of the Boise River, they arrived at the Snake River and old Fort Boise. Here they crossed the Snake again and pushed onward west across the present state of Oregon.

Ideas To Talk About

1. Why did so many people want to go to the Willamette Valley?

2. Why were prices so high along the Oregon Trail?

3. What was southern Idaho like when the immigrants passed through on the way to western Oregon?

Three-Island Crossing was one of the few places where immigrants could safely cross the Snake River. What present-day town is near this spot?
IDAHO HISTORICAL SOCIETY

Life On The Oregon Trail.

Most people on the Oregon Trail traveled in covered wagons. The wagon was the family's home during the trip. Family goods were packed tightly into the wagon. The trip was too dangerous for one family, so families gathered together into wagon trains.

The wagons were very heavy after they were loaded. They had no springs, so you can imagine the bumpy ride over the rough trail! A wagon was pulled by four or more oxen, horses, or mules. Riders on horseback rode beside the wagons, sometimes herding farm animals that were brought along. Hunters rode out to find wild animals for meat, and everyone kept an eye out for Indians.

Some wagon trains were very large. The first truly large wagon train came through Idaho in 1843. It had almost 1,000 people, many of them children. The people also brought horses and large herds of cattle. It should be remembered that they were going to farm in Oregon. They brought seeds, bulbs, small trees, and anything else they could carry to plant on their new land.

A giant wagon train crossed southern Idaho in 1844. It was perhaps the biggest one to make the journey. There were over 250 wagons and 1,475 people. The train stretched more than four miles along the trail.

The wagon trains crawled over the trail at about two miles an hour. You can walk faster than that. In dry weather, the air was filled with dust from wheels and many hoofs. In wet weather, the trail was a river of mud. Wagons got stuck in the mud, and other wagons would have to stop and pull them out. Wagons often broke down. Some were lost in rivers. Horses and oxen often became sick and died. Water was scarce for animals along the trail, and there were few plants for them to eat.

People, too, became sick and died. Thousands of people died on the way to Oregon. They were buried along the trail in unmarked graves. Sometimes they were buried under the wagon tracks so Indians would not find the graves. Though many did die, many more lived. For those who lived, the trip was an exciting adventure they would never forget.

The Sager Family

The giant train of 1844 had its share of bad fortune. One of the Missouri families in the train was that of Henry Sager, his wife Naomi, and seven children. A baby girl was born to the Sagers while they were coming through Kansas. Henry Sager died and was buried in western Wyoming. At Glenns Ferry, Naomi Sager got sick and died. The seven children went on west without a mother or father. When they reached the Whitman mission, the children were adopted by the Whitmans. Three years later, the Whitmans were killed by Indians, and the children were left homeless a second time.

This story is only one of thousands that happened along the Oregon Trail. The story of the Sager family is told in two fine books, *On To Oregon!* and *The Stout Hearted Seven*. The Sager story was also made into a movie, *Seven Alone*.

In 1852, the number of people on the Oregon Trail was greater than ever. By then, ferries had been built to cross several rivers. A wagon could be carried across the Portneuf River for a dollar. This was a great help. Many animals and wagons were lost in rivers. As time went on, the fur trading posts became immigrant stations. There weren't many furs to trade, but the fur companies could make money by doing business with the people going to Oregon. Fort Hall and Fort Boise had more goods for the people stopping by.

By 1846, so many Americans were living in the Oregon Country that England divided it with the United States. The southern half became Oregon Territory. England kept British Columbia and Vancouver Island, which are now part of Canada. One day, Oregon Territory would give us three new states: Oregon, Washington, and Idaho. A smaller part would go to Montana and Wyoming.

A wagon train is leaving St. Louis and starting west over the Oregon Trail. Instead of immigrants, these are mountain men on their way to trap furs. This is a painting by western artist W. H. Jackson. STATE HISTORICAL SOCIETY OF COLORADO

Ideas To Talk About

1. What was it like to travel west with a covered wagon?
2. In 1844, a wagon train came through southern Idaho with over 250 wagons and 1,475 people. Why would so many people be traveling together?
3. Why was travel easier on the Oregon Trail by 1852?
4. Why was it important to the United States that lots of Americans moved into the Oregon Country?

Mormons Settle In Eastern Idaho.

In 1847, the Great Basin of Utah began to fill with a new group of American immigrants. They were called Mormons. They were the people of the Church of Jesus Christ of Latter-Day Saints. These people were to play an important part in helping Idaho grow.

The Mormons had been driven out of Ohio, Missouri, and Illinois because of their religion. Led by **Brigham Young**, they came to Utah to be free to live as they believed. They wanted to build a Mormon state in the Great Basin. The Mormons began to build new towns and to irrigate the dry land for farming.

Many small valleys and streams run into the Great Basin. You will remember that Idaho's Bear River Basin is one of these. It was Young's plan to fill these small valleys with Mormon settlers. In 1855, Young decided to send some people north to settle beyond the Salt Lake Valley. He sent 27 men north into the Salmon River country of Idaho. On a tributary of the Salmon River, they built cabins and a **stockade**. They named the stream Limhi, and called their stockade **Fort Limhi**. (The name is now spelled **Lemhi**.)

The first tasks were to plant crops and to build an irrigation canal to water them. The land was planted to peas, potatoes, turnips, and corn. An early frost killed most of the crops. The people had to get food from Utah to live through the winter.

Brigham Young was president of the Mormon Church when the Mormons came to Utah. Why is Brigham Young important to Idaho history?
OREGON HISTORICAL SOCIETY

The next spring, 22 more people arrived. New crops were planted. This time they were destroyed by grasshoppers—millions came over the land and left the ground bare. Again the people had to go to Utah to get food for winter.

The settlers stayed until 1858. That year they were attacked by Bannock and Shoshoni Indians. Two settlers were killed, and five others wounded. Many of their cattle were taken by the Indians. Upon hearing of this latest bad fortune, Brigham Young called the settlers back to Utah. He decided that they were too far from the Salt Lake Valley.

Franklin: Idaho's First Permanent White Settlement.

In the spring of 1860, a new group of settlers was sent north from the Salt Lake Valley. Thirteen Mormon families came to Cache Valley to

The remains of Fort Lemhi looked like this in 1903. Notice the stone wall that forms a rectangle in the middle of the picture. Why did the settlers build the stone wall? #5-12-1A U OF I LIBRARY

farm and start a new settlement. They named the settlement Franklin, after one of their church leaders. Land was quickly cleared, ground plowed, and ditches dug for irrigation. This settlement did not fail. Though the first year's crops were small, the people stayed. Franklin, now a small town in southeast Idaho, became Idaho's first permanent white settlement.

Before a year had passed, Franklin had a Mormon church and a school. Hannah Comish started Idaho's first school for white children. Her cabin was the classroom. Idaho's settlers faced their first year bravely. They didn't know they were making Idaho history. No one thought about state lines. These first people of Franklin thought they were in Utah.

Review Questions

1. Mormon settlers came to Utah to ________________. [*107*]
2. The leader of the Mormons was __________. [*107*]
3. Mormon settlers came to Idaho from __________. [*107*]
4. The first Mormon settlers in Idaho tried to settle at __________ on a tributary of the Salmon River. [*107*]
5. Idaho's first permanent white settlement was __________, in southeast Idaho. [*107–108*]
6. Franklin was settled by __________ settlers in the year __________. [*107–108*]

The Mullan Road Opens Northern Idaho To Settlers.

The Whitman mission at Walla Walla brought more settlers into eastern Washington. Trouble between them and the Indians became very bad between 1855 and 1858. The government sent soldiers to protect the settlers.

The soldiers were kept at Fort Benton, on the Missouri River in Montana. The Oregon Trail was the only way to move soldiers west from Fort Benton. The soldiers had to go south to the Oregon Trail, then north through almost 400 miles of mountains. This was too slow. A shorter route was needed. A road was needed to connect the Missouri River with the Columbia River. Because of this need, the Mullan Road was begun.

The **Mullan Road** was built by a party of 100

men led by Captain **John Mullan**. Work began in 1858, and was finished in 1862. The road ran 624 miles from Fort Benton to Fort Walla Walla. It passed over high mountains and through thick forests. A path 25 feet wide was cut through the forest. Many bridges were built across the Coeur d'Alene River. There were no heavy machines to do the work. All the work was done by horses and by hand. The hardest work was building the road across the Idaho panhandle.

Northern Idaho's dream of a wagon road across the panhandle had to wait for several more years. Shortly after the Mullan Road was finished, part of it was destroyed by a great flood. The Coeur d'Alene River washed away the bridges and much of the road. For several years, this stretch of the road could be used only as a pack trail.

This is one of the few places that the Mullan Road can still be seen. The metal cage at the right protects the remains of the Mullan Tree. The photo was taken east of Coeur d'Alene. VIRGIL YOUNG

In 1866, however, at least 20,000 people used the Mullan Road going to and from Montana. The road saw freight and mining supplies, as well as mules, horses, and herds of cattle. Hunters, Indians, immigrants, miners, cowboys—all kinds of people—followed the Mullan Road. Last but not least, the Mullan Road helped open northern Idaho to mining in the years to come.

The Mullan Road of yesterday has become northern Idaho's "Main Street" of today. Along its route you will find Lake Coeur d'Alene and the towns of Coeur d'Alene, Kellogg, Wallace, and Mullan. The Mullan Road is now part of Highway 10 and Interstate 90. Railroads, too, follow this route. If you were to drive west from Chicago, you would drive through Idaho along the Mullan Road. Also you would drive through one of America's most beautiful places.

Fourth Of July Canyon

The builders of the Mullan Road left us a story to remember them by. On July 4, 1861, they were camped in northern Idaho. They decided to celebrate Independence Day by firing their guns and making lots of noise. There was so much noise, the Indians thought that the builders were fighting each other.

On a large tree beside the road, someone carved the date. That carved tree has stood beside the road for these many years since. Some years ago, the top of the tree broke off in a storm. The stump remains, and the date can still be seen: July 4, 1861. Since then the canyon has been called Fourth of July Canyon because of that lively Fourth of July celebration so many years ago. Today a stone marker nearby calls our attention to the Mullan Tree Memorial.

Idaho Was Returned To The Indians— For A Short Time.

Indians in all parts of the West became angry because their land was filling up with settlers. The Indians knew that if the immigrants didn't stop coming, they would be crowded out of their own country. In their early friendship with the whites, they hadn't known their land would become filled with them. Not only were a great many new people moving in, they were killing wild animals that Indians needed for food. Indians were dying from diseases brought by the settlers as well.

All across the West, Indians began fighting back. Bands of Indians would attack small groups of immigrants, often killing them. They hoped to kill or drive them from their land. There were many more Indian attacks during the 1850s.

Much of the Oregon Trail ran through Shoshoni land. However, nearly all of the thousands of immigrants passed on through. Only a few stayed in southern Idaho. The trappers and the fur trading posts had always been good friends with the Indians. This friendship lasted through much of the trouble. Finally, Indian anger fell on them, too.

Trouble for the trading posts started with an Indian attack on an immigrant party in August 1854. A party of 20 people, led by Alexander Ward, was headed for Oregon. It was attacked by Indians near the present town of Middleton. All the party was killed except the two young sons of Ward. The Indians were a band of Shoshoni living in the Boise Valley.

This attack brought soldiers. The soldiers found some Indians in the Boise Valley and killed them. They didn't bother to find out if these were the ones who attacked the Ward party. This made the Shoshoni so angry, that it was no longer safe for settlers to stay in southern Idaho. The fur trading posts at Fort Hall and Fort Boise had to be closed.

From 1855 to 1862, neither settlers nor traders lived in the Snake River country. Wagon trains kept coming, but those people were only passing through to Oregon. Mormons had tried to settle in Lemhi Valley in 1855. However, they were driven out by Indians in 1858. Not until 1860 did settlers come to southern Idaho to stay. These were the settlers of Franklin, in Cache Valley just over the line from Utah.

Idaho really belonged to the Indians during the late 1850s. The only settlers living in Idaho were in the north. William Craig was farming at Lapwai. The Catholic missionaries were still at Sacred Heart Mission at Cataldo. These people worked and lived among the Indians, so they kept the Indians' friendship.

Wagon trains filled with immigrants still poured across southern Idaho each summer. The Army sent some soldiers to a place near Fort Hall to protect the immigrants. Even the Army couldn't hold back the Indians, though. Large wagon trains could pass safely because of their large numbers of people. Smaller trains were very much in danger of Indian attack.

This was the shape of things when the first gold miners found their way into Idaho in 1860.

The old Mullan Road has become this modern freeway. On the right, we see the north end of Lake Coeur d'Alene. The Mullan Road ran 624 miles between two Army forts. What were the names of the forts? Where were they? IDAHO DEPARTMENT OF COMMERCE

Ideas To Talk About

1. Why did the government want a road between Fort Benton and Fort Walla Walla?
2. Why was the Mullan Road important to northern Idaho?
3. The immigrants going to western Oregon weren't settling on Shoshoni land. Why do you think the Shoshoni attacked the immigrants and their wagons?
4. Between 1855 and 1862, no settlers were living in the Snake River country. Why not?
5. While the Shoshoni were attacking trappers and wagon trains in southern Idaho, William Craig and the Catholic missionaries were living peacefully among the Indians in northern Idaho. Why do you think there was a difference?

This photo of the Mullan Tree was taken in 1921. Why is this tree of interest to us today? #5-14-1A U OF I LIBRARY

Idaho Becomes A Territory.

In 1863, President Abraham Lincoln signed a law that set up **Idaho Territory**. Why should this happen when there were almost no settlers in Idaho in 1860? The answer is GOLD. Gold was discovered in Idaho in 1860, and Americans began rushing to Idaho. In 1860, Idaho was part of Washington Territory. By 1863, there were more people in Idaho than in western Washington. This caused Idaho Territory to be cut off from Washington Territory. You will read about Idaho's exciting gold rush in Chapter 6.

How Did Idaho Get Its Name?

Many people believe that the name "Idaho" is a Shoshoni word. It has been said to mean "gem of the mountains" or "behold the sun coming down the mountain." There is no way to prove that the name came from an Indian word. It seems to have been thought up early in 1860 by a Colorado man. He wanted the name "Idaho" used for the territory that became Colorado. He said the name meant "gem of the mountains." Other people said that "Idaho" should not be used because it was not an Indian word. At the last minute, the name "Colorado" was used instead of "Idaho".

The name "Idaho" soon spread to the Oregon Country. In 1860, a Columbia River steamboat was built and named the Idaho. Later that year, gold was discovered in the Clearwater country. By 1862, the gold mines in the Clearwater and Salmon River country were called the Idaho mines. They were named for the steamboat that carried so many of the gold miners up the Columbia.

Soon the government had to form a new territory for the Idaho mines. It had been planned to call the new territory "Montana". Because of the Idaho mines, "Idaho" seemed more proper. At the last minute, the name "Idaho" was used instead of "Montana". Later, the name "Montana" was used for the large piece of land cut away from Idaho.

Idaho Was Not Called "Idaho" Until 1863. What was Idaho called before 1863? It had been called several things. When

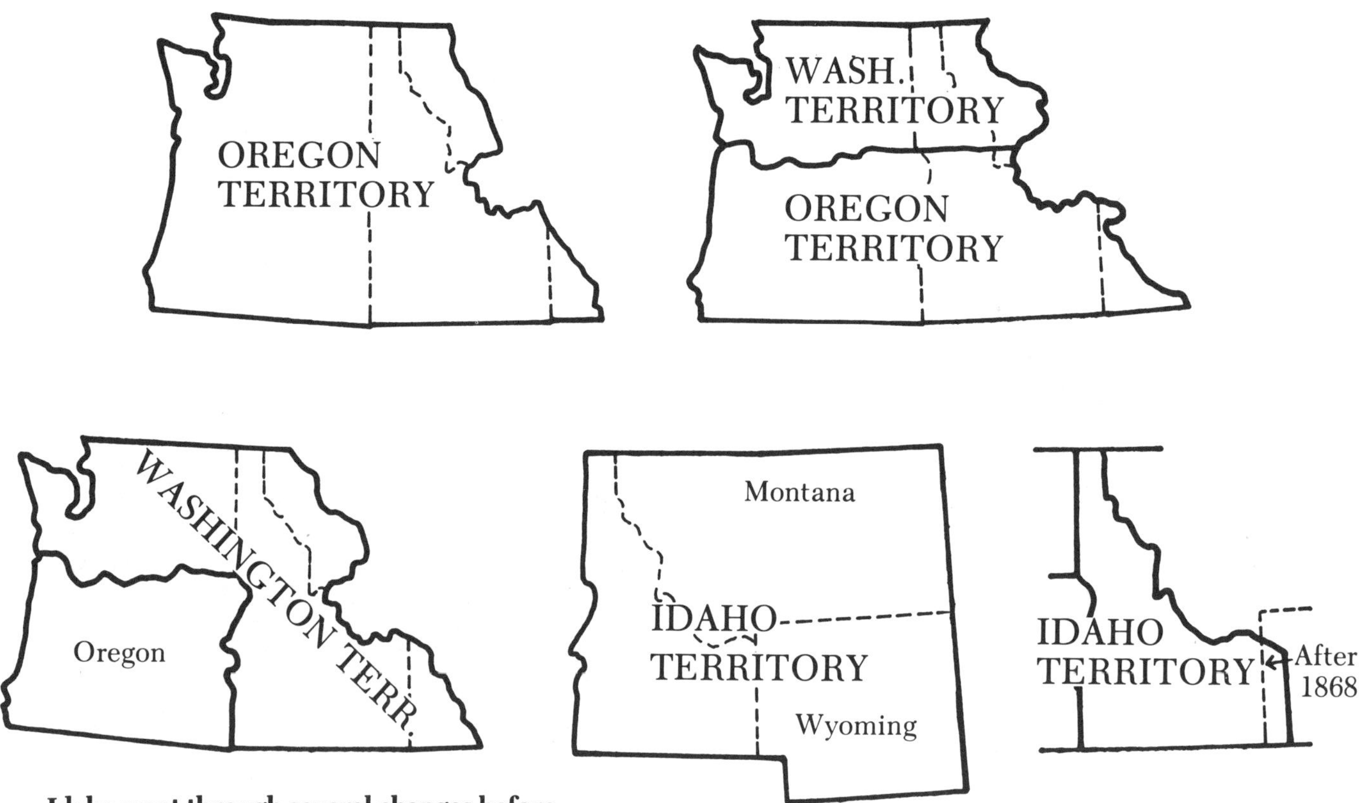

Idaho went through several changes before taking its present shape.

Lewis and Clark came west, Idaho was part of the Oregon Country. At that time, "Oregon" meant all the land between the Pacific and the Rockies, including a large piece in Canada. Later, settlers began to fill the empty land in western Oregon. This caused the Oregon Country to be divided into parts. The southern part became Oregon Territory in 1846.

As more Americans moved west, Oregon Territory was divided into two parts. The land north of the Columbia River became Washington Territory. The land south of the Columbia remained Oregon Territory. This left southern Idaho in Oregon Territory, but put northern Idaho in Washington Territory. When Governor Stevens visited Sacred Heart Mission at Cataldo, he was visiting an important part of Washington Territory.

Oregon became a state in 1859. Then all of Idaho was put into Washington Territory. From 1859 to 1863, Washington Territory was all of Washington and Idaho and parts of Montana and Wyoming.

When Idaho became Idaho Territory in 1863, Washington was given its present shape. However, the shape of Idaho would change twice more. In 1863, Idaho Territory included all of Montana and nearly all of Wyoming. Montana was separated from Idaho the next year. Idaho got its present shape when the Wyoming border was drawn in 1868.

Why So Many Changes? Why were there were so many changes? The changes came because immigrants kept filling up more empty land. As western Washington filled with farms and towns, Washington Territory was separated from Oregon Territory. Washington Territory was then divided when the eastern part began filling with miners and mining camps. The eastern part became Idaho Territory.

When Idaho Territory was created in 1863, it was a huge piece of land, and most of it was empty. The miners were mostly in northern Idaho and Boise Basin. However, in 1862 gold was discovered in western Montana. A new gold rush soon began around Virginia City. Gold strikes and new mining camps brought a flood of miners to Montana.

By late 1863, about one-third of Idaho's gold miners were around Montana's Virginia City.

Virginia City was separated from Lewiston by 300 miles of rough country, including the Bitterroot Mountains. There was no way for the government in Lewiston to serve the Montana miners. In winter, the trip could be made only by going around all of the mountains. Montana miners in the First Territorial Legislature at Lewiston had to go almost 2,000 miles to reach home. They went from Lewiston to Portland, to San Francisco, to Salt Lake City, then to Virginia City. They were very happy when Montana Territory was created in 1864.

Idaho's First Government. President Lincoln chose William H. Wallace to be Idaho's first governor. Wallace was a close friend of the President and was a pallbearer at his funeral.

Governor Wallace chose Lewiston to be Idaho's first **capital**. Lewiston was Idaho's only real city at that time. However, many people thought the capital should be closer to the mines. By this time, many of the miners had left northern Idaho. Over half of Idaho's miners were now in southern Idaho's Boise Basin. The Montana mines around Virginia City had about one-third of the miners. The northern Idaho mines had only about one-tenth of the people. Miners moved about so fast, that it was hard to guess where they might go next.

The First Territorial Legislature met in Lewiston during December 1863. Some people wanted to move the capital to Virginia City. Others wanted to move it to Boise City. Some wanted to leave it in Lewiston. The members went home without deciding what to do.

The Second Territorial Legislature met in Lewiston in December 1864. One of its first items of business was to decide to move the capital to Boise City. The move was made the following spring. Many people in northern Idaho were unhappy about losing the capital, and such feelings lasted many years. The panhandle remains today an important part of Idaho.

Review Questions

1. Idaho became a territory in the year ____________. [*111*]
2. The law that made Idaho a territory was signed by President ____________. [*111*]
3. The Clearwater and Salmon River mines were called the Idaho mines because of a Columbia River steamboat named the ____________. [*111*]
4. Idaho Territory got its name because of the ____________ mines. [*111*]
5. Before Idaho Territory was formed, Idaho was part of two other territories. They were (a) ____________ Territory and (b) ____________ Territory. [*112*]
6. Idaho Territory was separated from Washington Territory because ________________________. [*112*]
7. Montana Territory was separated from Idaho Territory because ________________________. [*112–113*]
8. Idaho Territory's first capital was ____________. [*113*]
9. In 1864, Idaho Territory's capital was moved to ____________. [*113*]

Chapter 5 Skill Activities

Words And Ideas

In Chapter 5, you will find a number of key words printed in **bold** print. Each key word stands for an important idea. Answering these questions will help you understand some of the key words.

You can find the key words in the Glossary at the back of the book. The number after each question is the page where the idea is found in the book. Answer each question with a complete sentence.

1. What is meant by **elevation**? [*102*]
2. What were Idaho Territory's two **capital** cities? [*113*]
3. Why did Idaho become **Idaho Territory** before it became a state? [*111–112*]
4. What is an **immigrant**? [*93*]
5. What went on at a **mission**? [*95–96, 100*]
6. Why did the **missionaries** come west? [*94*]
7. When did an immigrant become a **settler**? [*93*]
8. Why would the settlers at Fort Lemhi feel they needed a **stockade**? [*107*]
9. Why did people want to go to the **Willamette Valley**? [*104*]

Who Are These People?

Identify each of the following people. Write each answer in a complete sentence.

1. William Craig
2. Father De Smet
3. John C. Fremont
4. Abraham Lincoln
5. John Mullan
6. Eliza Spalding
7. Henry Spalding
8. Marcus Whitman
9. Narcissa Whitman
10. Brigham Young

Research Projects

1. **Wagons.** America moved west in wagons. What were they really like?

(a) Write a report about wagons. Look in an encyclopedia under "Conestoga Wagon," "Pioneer Life," and "Wagon."

(b) Draw a picture of a wagon and make a list of equipment needed for the trip west.

2. **Oregon Trail.** Draw a map of the Oregon Trail.

Where did the Oregon Trail come from, and where did it go? It stretched from Independence, Missouri, to Oregon City, Oregon. Be sure your map shows the present-day states that it passed through. Look in an encyclopedia under "Oregon Trail."

3. **Sacred Heart Mission.** Write a report on the Sacred Heart Mission at Cataldo. The beautiful mission church at Cataldo still stands. Draw a picture of the mission church to go with your report. You can use this book or other sources.

4. **John C. Fremont.** Write a report on Fremont, and give it to the class. Fremont was a famous American in his time. He was known for many things besides mapping the Oregon Trail. You can use information from this book and an encyclopedia.

5. **The Shapes of Idaho.** Draw maps of the different shapes of Idaho, and write a report about them. Idaho has had several different sizes and shapes before becoming its present self. You can use this book or another source.

Mapping The Way West

Trails were long, and places were far apart during this part of Idaho's history. Find the following places and draw them on a map. Begin with a plain outline map of Idaho. Idaho's Official Highway Map will have the information you need.

1. Boise
2. Fort Boise
3. Fort Hall
4. Fort Lemhi
5. Lapwai Mission
6. Lewiston
7. Mullan Road
8. Oregon Trail
9. Sacred Heart Mission
10. Three-Island Ford

Using Your Imagination

Writing a Diary. Pretend that you are a girl or boy coming west with your family on the Oregon Trail. Write a diary for one week of your journey. Tell about the following things: What have you have seen? What problems have you had? What kinds of things have happened along the trail? What are you thinking about, and how do you feel? What do you think your parents are thinking? What do you think will happen in the future?

Reviewing Chapter 5

Main Ideas In This Chapter

1. The Oregon Trail was a very important route from the United States to the Oregon Country.
2. Missionaries helped settle the Oregon Country.
3. Reverend Henry Spalding and his wife Eliza built Idaho's first mission among the Nez Perce at Lapwai.
4. The Spaldings taught the Nez Perce many new ways.
5. William Craig, mountain man, became Idaho's first homesteader when he settled at Lapwai.
6. Not all Indians wanted the missionaries to be there.
7. Father De Smet built Catholic missions among the Coeur d'Alene and other Indian tribes.
8. Sacred Heart Mission, built for the Coeur d'Alene tribe, became an important place in northern Idaho.
9. The missionaries were not all good and not all bad.

10. Travel was difficult and dangerous on the Oregon Trail.

11. John C. Fremont mapped the Oregon Trail so people could follow it to Oregon.

12. Most of the people who went west came for free farmland in western Oregon.

13. Mormons from Utah settled the valley of southeast Idaho.

14. In 1860, Mormons settled Franklin, Idaho's first permanent white settlement.

15. The Mullan Road was built to carry soldiers from Fort Benton to eastern Washington. It became an important road for northern Idaho.

16. Indians drove out all of the trappers and settlers in southern Idaho between 1855 and 1862.

17. Gold brought many new people into Idaho beginning in 1860.

18. Idaho Territory was formed in 1863.

19. Idaho was named for the Idaho mines in northern Idaho, which were named for a steamboat that brought miners up the Columbia River.

20. Idaho's first capital was Lewiston. It was moved to Boise City the following year.

Further Reading For Children

Alter, Judy. *Extraordinary Women of the American West.* New York: Children's Press, 1999.

Horn, Huston. *The Pioneers.* (Time-Life Series of the Old West) New York: Time-Life Books, 1974. [Excellent photographs.]

Lake, A. I. *Women of the West.* (The Wild West in American History Series) Vero Beach, Florida: Rourke Publications, Inc., 1990.

Morrow, Honore. *On To Oregon.* (A Beech Tree Paperback Book) William Morrow & Company, 1991. [The story of the Sager family. Earlier editions in 1926, 1946, and 1954.]

Reef, Catherine. *Buffalo Soldiers.* New York: Twenty-first Century Books, Henry Holt & Company, 1993. [Story of African-American soldiers.]

Sakuri, Gail. *Asian-Americans in the Old West.* (Cornerstones of Freedom Series) New York: Children's Press, 2000.

Stefoff, Rebecca. *Children of the Westward Trail.* Brookfield, Connecticut: Millbrook Press, 1996.

Stefoff, Rebecca. *The Oregon Trail in American History.* Springfield, New Jersey: Enslow Publishers, Inc., 1997.

Wright, Courtni C. *Wagon Train: A Family Goes West in 1865.* New York: Holiday House, 1995.

Technology Resources

Internet Web Site:

Idaho Compass Web Site
http://education.boisestate.edu/compass
This colorful web site contains interesting information and learning activities for students and classroom ideas for teachers.

Computer Programs:

Oregon Trail 5th Edition, The Learning Company.

Media: CD-ROM. Platform: Mac OS, Windows 95 / 98 / Me / XP / 2000. [Game for children nine and older. Players work against all the hazards of a wagon-train voyage.]

Oregon Trail 2, The Learning Company. Media: CD-ROM. Platform: Windows 95/98/Me. Students in grades 5–12 experience history firsthand as they travel the Oregon, California, and Mormon trails. Set in the mid 1800s, this educational simulation portrays the dangers of crossing the continent in a covered wagon. Students must equip their wagons with the necessary supplies, including food, clothing, and livestock, and make their decisions wisely or suffer the consequences.

Elementary Advantage 2002, Encore software, Inc. Media: 6-CD set. Platform: Windows 95/98/Me. Requires 100 MB hard drive space. For grades 3–5, this program contains 10 school subjects, including grammar, spelling, writing, basic math, and geography. The social studies segment focuses on the Oregon Trail.

Time Line

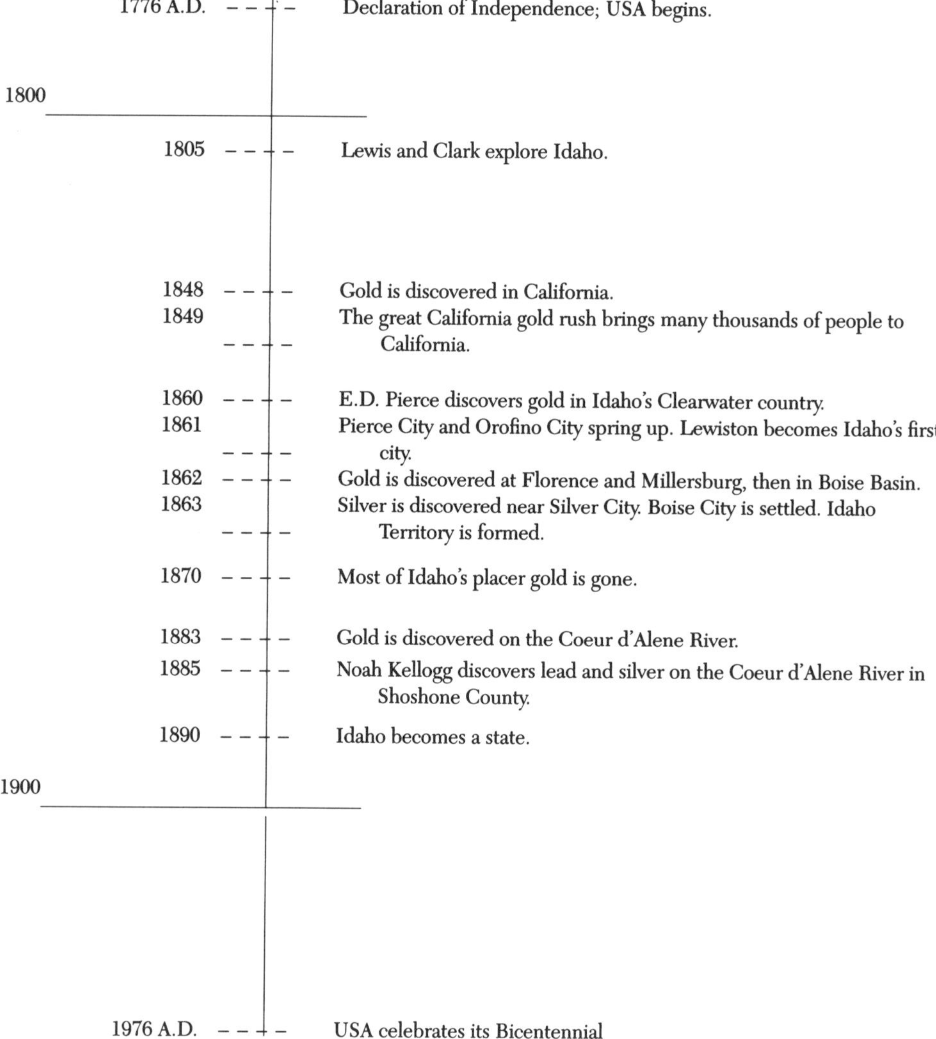

1776 A.D. — Declaration of Independence; USA begins.

1800

1805 — Lewis and Clark explore Idaho.

1848 — Gold is discovered in California.

1849 — The great California gold rush brings many thousands of people to California.

1860 — E.D. Pierce discovers gold in Idaho's Clearwater country.

1861 — Pierce City and Orofino City spring up. Lewiston becomes Idaho's first city.

1862 — Gold is discovered at Florence and Millersburg, then in Boise Basin.

1863 — Silver is discovered near Silver City. Boise City is settled. Idaho Territory is formed.

1870 — Most of Idaho's placer gold is gone.

1883 — Gold is discovered on the Coeur d'Alene River.

1885 — Noah Kellogg discovers lead and silver on the Coeur d'Alene River in Shoshone County.

1890 — Idaho becomes a state.

1900

1976 A.D. — USA celebrates its Bicentennial

1990 — Idaho Centennial

Chapter 6
The Great Idaho Gold Rush

Gold Brings Miners To Idaho.

Idaho's gold rush began in 1860. It started because of the California gold rush of 1849. Gold had been discovered in the gravel at Sutter's mill near the present city of Sacramento. The California gold find excited people around the world. In 1849, tens of thousands of people rushed to California to search and dig for the yellow metal. These people became known as the "forty-niners." Searching for gold, they were called **prospectors**.

Not everyone found gold in California. Not all prospectors stayed in California. They went looking for gold in all directions. Some spread southeast into Arizona and New Mexico. Some spread east into Nevada. Others spread north into Oregon and Washington, and even into Canada.

Indians kept prospectors out of Idaho for several years. Few men were willing to risk their lives to search for gold in Shoshoni and Bannock country. For a while, the Indians in northern Idaho were able to keep prospectors out. However, the Army defeated several northern tribes in 1858. Among these were the Coeur d'Alene living at Cataldo. After that, those Indians could do nothing to stop the immigrants. Only the Nez Perce still protected their land. They used guards to watch their trails.

Review Questions

1. Idaho's gold rush began in the year ____________. [*117*]

2. People searching for gold were called ____________. [*117*]

3. Prospectors stayed out of Idaho for many years because of ____________. [*117*]

Gold Is Discovered In The Clearwater Country.

In the spring of 1860, **Elias Pierce** found gold on a tributary of the Clearwater River. His first pan of dirt had only about three cents worth of gold in it. It was not a rich pan. However, it proved there was gold in the Clearwater country.

In 1860, Elias Pierce discovered gold and started the Idaho gold rush. Where did he discover gold?
IDAHO HISTORICAL SOCIETY

This tiny bit of gold was enough to start a new rush of people into Idaho.

Pierce had discovered gold on Nez Perce land. The Clearwater country was part of the Nez Perce Reservation set aside by the Treaty of 1855. When Pierce had started up the Clearwater, he was stopped near the present city of Lewiston by a band of Nez Perce. The band was led by Chief Timothy. Timothy was a peace-loving Nez Perce who had accepted the Christian religion. Pierce talked him into letting the party look for gold on the Clearwater.

Pierce came as a friend of the Nez Perce. He spoke Nez Perce and had traded with them for several years before. After finding the gold, he told them he would bring others to search for more gold. The Indians were interested in the gold, but didn't want any more people to come. They didn't want to lose any more of their land.

There were also settlers who wanted Pierce to stay away from the Nez Perce land. They thought it was dangerous, as well as against the law. Farmers in eastern Washington were afraid gold miners might start a new Indian war.

Pierce returned in the fall of 1860 with a party of miners. They spent six weeks keeping away from the Nez Perce guards. If they had been caught, the Nez Perce probably would not have harmed them. The Nez Perce were still peaceful. Shoshoni or Bannock Indians might have killed them.

On a tributary of the Clearwater, the Pierce party found placer gold all about them. They named the stream Orofino Creek. ("Oro fino" is Spanish for "fine gold.") Soon they had mined more than 100 dollars in gold.

Winter was coming, and they had to prepare for it. Pierce and his party took their gold to Walla Walla, where they bought supplies and equipment. The gold caused much excitement in Walla Walla. Some of the miners returned to Orofino Creek for the winter. Arriving in December, they built eight log cabins. The next spring, the cabins would be part of Pierce City, Idaho's first mining camp. Today it is the town of Pierce.

The winter snow was deep, but they kept on working. They cut lumber, built wooden mining tools, and staked **claims**. **Staking a claim** was very easy. A miner chose a piece of ground and drove a wooden stake at each corner. A sign was then fastened to one of the stakes, telling the

This is probably the first picture of Lewiston, taken in 1863. What river do you see? U OF I LIBRARY

miner's name and what the claim was for. With that done, digging could begin!

In January, the snow melted enough to do some mining. In February, one miner took $800 in gold to Walla Walla. Idaho was now set for a gold rush!

Review Questions

1. In 1860, ____________ found gold on a tributary of the ____________ River. [*117*]
2. This gold was found on land that belonged to the ____________ Indians. [*118*]
3. The place where this first gold was discovered is now the town of ____________. [*118*]

The News Of Gold Spreads Like Fire!

The news of gold in the Clearwater country spread like fire. In no time at all, hundreds, then thousands were pouring into the Clearwater country. The Nez Perce had decided to let the miners dig gold on their land. They didn't care about the gravel in a few mountain streams. However, they would protect their good farm land.

During February 1861, Chief Reuben, a young Nez Perce chief, built a warehouse where the Clearwater meets the Snake. In only a few more months, the town of Lewiston would spring up there. Reuben and William Craig (of Lapwai) built terry boats to carry miners across the Snake and Clearwater rivers. These ferries were soon making thousands of dollars a week. That was more than most of the miners would ever make from gold mining.

Before long, a settlement appeared at the mouth of the Clearwater. Stores were set up, and other businesses soon followed. The new settlement was named Lewiston, in honor of Meriwether Lewis. Northern Idaho's first town was born, and it grew rapidly. Lewiston instantly became a supply center for people headed for the mines.

Gold Fever. Gold fever seemed to strike everyone. Farmers from western Oregon and Walla Walla left their fields. Storekeepers left their shops. Blacksmiths left their fires. Lawyers,

This advertisement appeared in the East during the Idaho gold rush. Why would people want to come west by steamboat? How would they get to the mines from Fort Benton? VIRGIL YOUNG

Luna House was an important hotel in Lewiston for many years. This photo was taken in 1868. Why would Lewiston need a hotel during the 1860s? IDAHO HISTORICAL SOCIETY

pony express riders, and poets came searching for gold. Miners from far-off California poured into the Clearwater country.

The easiest way to come from the Pacific coast was by steamboat up the Columbia and Snake rivers. The first of these "steamers" reached Lewiston in 1861. Soon several steamboats were making the trip, loaded with miners and other people looking for adventure and wealth. The boats also brought mining tools and supplies, goods, food, and whisky. News of gold kept more and more people pouring into Idaho. Lewiston was soon an important business center.

Lewiston was not the only town to spring up. Wherever gold was found, a new camp would suddenly appear. It is hard to think of these early camps as towns. Often they had "city" in their names. Pierce City was the first. Orofino City sprang up close to Pierce City. It was reported in August 1861 that Orofino City had 400 tents and houses, and 24 stores. It was the usual mining camp, filled with people seeking their fortunes.

A few months later, however, Orofino City was empty. News of other gold strikes took the miners elsewhere. With no people, there was no town. The present town of Orofino is not the old mining camp. The present town is more than 35 miles away, where Orofino Creek flows into the Clearwater.

In June, Pierce City had between 2,000 and 3,000 people. There were countless others in nearby mountains. New stories of wealth kept more and more people pouring into Idaho. Early reports said there was enough gold for 20,000. A story said eight miners on Rhodes Creek were digging $2,000 a week. Some of the stories might have been true, but soon there were more miners than there was gold.

Many other mining camps appeared as the miners spread out from Orofino Creek. Gold was found at the mouth of Elk Creek, and Elk City began to fill with people. Three weeks later Elk City had nearly 1,000 people and 25 finished buildings. Moose City grew up quickly high in the Bitterroot Mountains. As many as 9,000 lived there. Today it is hard to find a trace of this once roaring town.

Review Questions

1. Lewiston became an important town because ____________________. *[119]*

2. Name at least three of the mining camps that sprang up in the Clearwater country:
(a) __________ (b) __________
(c) __________. *[120]*

Ideas To Talk About

1. Why did mining camps fill up suddenly with people, then quickly empty out again?
2. Why did some people get gold fever, dropping everything to join the gold rush? Remember, not everyone did.

Gold Is Found In The Salmon River Country.

Fabulous Florence. A new, richer gold strike soon made many of the miners forget about Orofino Creek. Gold was found further south, in the Salmon River country near the head of Slate Creek. The "towns" of **Florence** and Millersburg quickly appeared. Millersburg was named for a young pony express rider, **Joaquin Miller**. He was one of the first people to the arrive at the new gold field. Joaquin Miller later became famous as the "Poet of the Sierras." Much of what we know about the gold rush and Millersburg comes from his writings.

Florence was the name on everyone's lips. Florence was perhaps the richest placer gold strike ever made in the United States—for the short time it lasted. Exciting stories came from the Salmon River country. It was said Jacob Weiser had taken $6,600 in gold in just four days. Nearby another miner took $600 from just one pan of dirt. With this kind of news, there was no stopping the rush of miners into the Salmon River country.

The rush to "Fabulous Florence" emptied the miners out of Orofino City and Elk City. Others began arriving from Oregon, California, and other faraway places. In April 1862, there were 5,000 miners at Florence. A month later, there were 10,000 there. One wrote home that he counted 600 to 1,000 people a day passing along the road between Lewiston and Florence. Of course, most were going to the mines, not away from them. Before long, the Salmon River and many of its tributaries were swarming with miners.

Miners and the Nez Perce Indians. The miners swarming into the Salmon River country made the Nez Perce angry. In the beginning, the miners had promised to stay north of the Clearwater. Soon it was clear there was no way to keep them there. The Salmon River mines were in the heart of the Nez Perce reservation. The Nez Perce chiefs didn't like having the miners so close to their villages. Even so, they kept the young men from making war on them. Groups of miners would promise bands of Indians to honor their rights. The Indians would agree to allow further illegal use of their land.

Gold Is Discovered In Boise Basin.

In 1862, gold was discovered in southern Idaho in the Boise Basin. Soon the gold mines in southern Idaho were more important than those further north. Not only were the gold strikes in southern Idaho just as rich, but there was much more gold. There was enough gold for many, many miners—more miners than all the northern mines. These new gold strikes promised enough gold to last for many years. Many years of gold mining would bring permanent settle-

As a young man, Joaquin Miller was one of the first to get to the newly-found gold at Florence. Later Miller become famous. Why? MAJOR LEE MOORHOUSE, #7-3-1 U OF I LIBRARY

ments and towns. In the years to come, millions of dollars in gold would be mined in the Boise Basin alone.

Boise Basin is the mountain area of the Boise River and its tributaries. Much of it lies in Boise County. The city of Boise is on the lower Boise River in the Snake River Valley. It is in Ada County.

This new rush began when a miner named Moses Splawn in the northern Idaho camp of Elk City became friends with a Bannock Indian. The Bannock told Splawn of a place further south where there was much of the "shiny metal." In 1862, Splawn went with George Grimes and several other miners to search for the place. In August, Splawn and his party found gold on a small tributary of the Boise River. The stream is now called Grimes Creek. The village of Centerville now stands near the spot where they discovered gold.

While mining, they were attacked by Indians. Grimes was killed. The other miners had to flee for their lives. This was Shoshoni and Bannock country, and the danger was great. Danger from Indians could not stop Idaho's gold fever, however. In 1863, a large group of miners drove the Indians out of Boise Basin.

Idaho City soon became the most important mining camp in Boise Basin. The country around Idaho City had over 15,000 people in 1863. Other important camps were Pioneerville and Placerville. Nearby, Centerville was named because it was halfway between Idaho City and Placerville.

Review Questions

1. One of the richest placer gold strikes in the United States was at ____________, in the Salmon River country. [*121*]

2. Much of what we know about Florence and Millersburg comes from the writings of a young pony express rider who later became famous as a poet. His name was ____________. [*121*]

3. A large amount of gold, enough to last for many years, was discovered in southern Idaho in the ____________. [*121*]

4. The most important mining town in the Boise Basin was ____________. [*122*]

Miners poured into Florence to "get rich quick." This photo was taken after the gold rush was over. Today there are no buildings left, and the forest is growing over the area. Why did everyone leave Florence? IDAHO DEPARTMENT OF COMMERCE

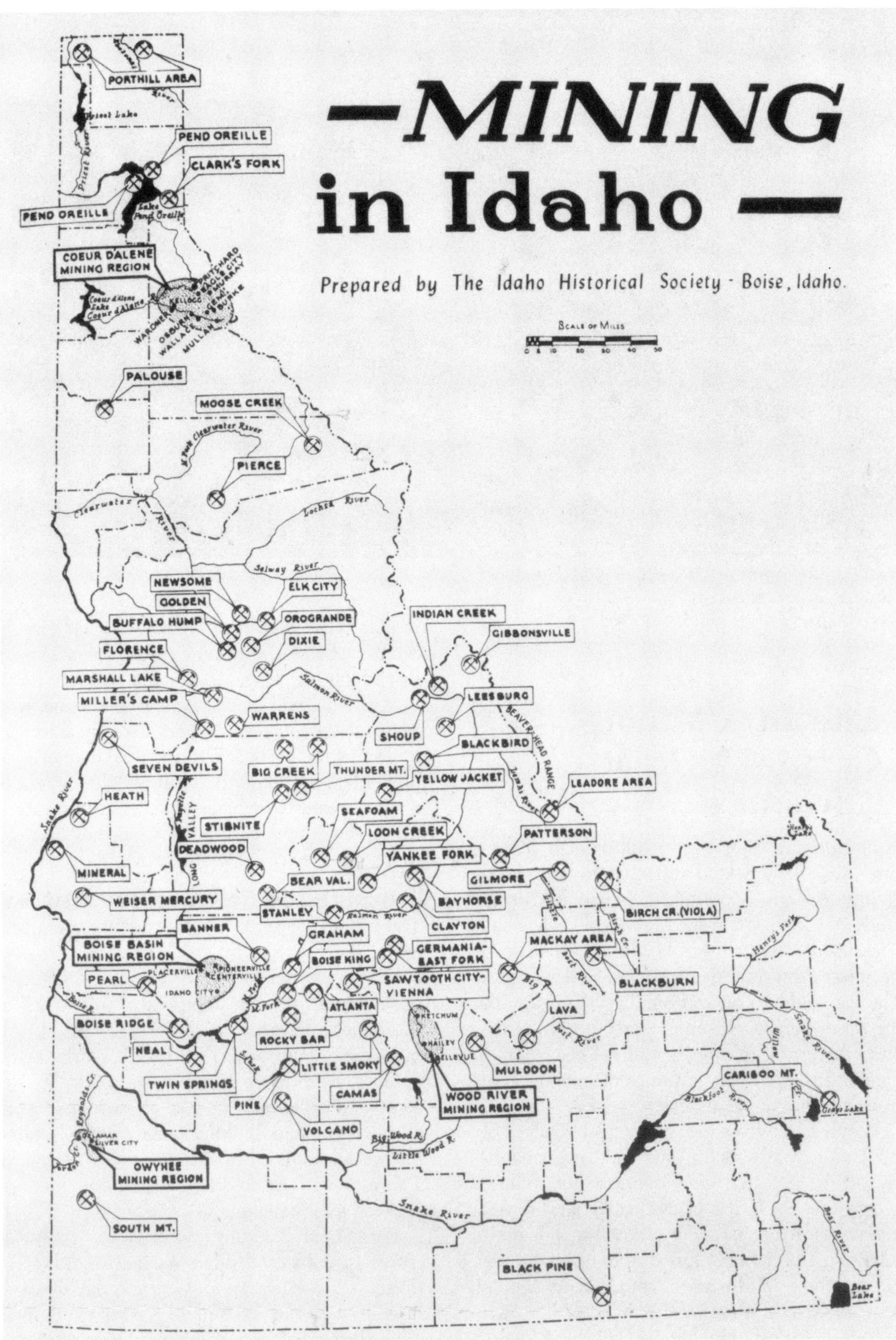

This map shows Idaho's many mining areas.

IDAHO HISTORICAL SOCIETY

Most mining camps began as "tent cities," such as this one. #6-138-1 U OF I LIBRARY

Life In A Mining Camp—A Great Adventure.

The mining camps were full of high adventure. Almost every kind of person under the sun gathered there. Most of them had left other kinds of work to come and dig for gold. They had been farmers, carpenters, blacksmiths, teachers, preachers, lawyers, dentists, and mill workers. The list could go on and on. They all came for the same things—adventure and wealth. It excited them to think they could get gold by just digging it out of the ground. Fortunes in gold were quickly gained and lost.

People came from every state and territory of the United States, and from almost every country on earth. Their skins were white, yellow, brown, and black. It is likely that 95 of every 100 people were honest. The other five, however, might well be looking for ways to cheat people out of their hard-earned gold. Many people were robbed or murdered for gold.

Camps sprang up wherever gold was found. Some camps became towns. Others disappeared as soon as the gold was gone. In most camps, buildings were started right away. They were built of whatever was handy. Most "houses" were just rough log cabins. If a cabin had any furniture, it was built by the people who lived in it. Many lived in tents. Others lived in caves or holes dug in hillsides. Cooking was done over an open fire built outdoors. Most people thought of a mining camp as a place to stay for only a short time. They didn't care much what they lived in, as long as they could keep warm and dry.

Businesses Followed the Miners. The miners were followed by other people who didn't come to dig for gold. They came to get gold by doing business with the miners. Trains of pack animals brought food and goods to sell to the miners. Stores and saloons were set up. Almost every kind of job paid well. Workers and animals were needed to haul freight to the camps. Carpenters and mill workers were needed to build buildings. As camps became bigger, all kinds of businesses could be found. There were blacksmiths, carpenters, doctors, lawyers, and preachers.

Permanent buildings were soon built for stores, saloons, and other businesses. Many of these were made from logs and hand-sawed lumber. A few of the buildings were made from adobe brick. Saloon owners spent a lot of money to bring in fine furniture and beautiful things for their businesses. Often saloons had hardwood

Soon tents were replaced by log cabins and other wooden buildings. Why did many people use logs instead of lumber to build their houses? #12–7 U OF I LIBRARY

This was a restaurant at Thunder Mountain. What kind of building is it in? IDAHO HISTORICAL SOCIETY

This was a miner's cabin on Moore's Flat. What has happened to most of the old miners' cabins? IDAHO HISTORICAL SOCIETY

furniture, mirrors, lamps, and drapes to make them inviting to the miners.

The price of everything in camp was high—food, clothing, boots, kettles, tobacco, and tools. Everything in camp had to be carried in on the backs of horses and mules. This cost money. The miners brought what they could with them. However, this wasn't much. Many had to go on foot. They had to carry tools and food on their own backs. A few were lucky enough to have horses. Even with a horse, no one could carry much food. In camp, flour sold for $27 to $150 for a 100-pound sack, depending on how easy it was to get. It sometimes cost $1.50 to send a letter home.

Gold flowed freely in the mining camps. This helped make prices high. A miner's gold was money. It was called "dust." Miners carried their "dust" in a small leather sack with a string at the top. The smallest amount of money or gold used in many camps was "two bits," or 25 cents.

Food in the Mining Camps. The miners' food was often poor and hard to get, and they had to pay high prices for it. They ate mainly flour, bacon, beans, lard, and salt. These were things that were easy to carry and didn't spoil quickly. During the winter, they ate little else. You know from what you have learned in school that this was a bad diet. You shouldn't be surprised to learn that many miners became sick. They came down with scurvy and other diseases caused by not having enough vitamins and minerals.

You might think they would have eaten meat and fish they could catch near their camps. They ate very little of these, though, because they were too busy trying to get rich. They didn't want to spend time hunting and fishing. Besides, Indians were a danger for anyone who got too far away from camp.

Better trails were soon cleared to the main mining camps. Pack trains then brought food, goods, and people. They brought food such as butter, eggs, dried fruit, onions, rice, sugar, and syrup. Fresh fruit and vegetables couldn't be brought all the way from western Oregon. In 1863, just eight months after gold was discovered in Boise Basin, vegetables were being grown in the Payette and Boise valleys. The miners in nearby camps paid a dollar a dozen for fresh onions, and two dollars a dozen for fresh ears of corn. When a load of fresh food came into camp, it was cause for a celebration!

The Miners' Fun. Though the miners worked long and hard, they had to rest and have fun sometimes. The camps had plenty of ways for them to spend their gold. Every mining camp had its saloons, sometimes a dozen in one camp! In a saloon, miners could drink whiskey and gamble. Larger camps had dance halls and women to dance with. The miners would also have foot races, wrestling, horse races, and shooting matches. Plays were sometimes put on by groups of miners, and sometimes actors came into the camp. Most miners spent their gold almost as soon as they got it. Most of the gold

Two miners are using a "diamond hitch" to tie the load on their pack mule. VIRGIL YOUNG

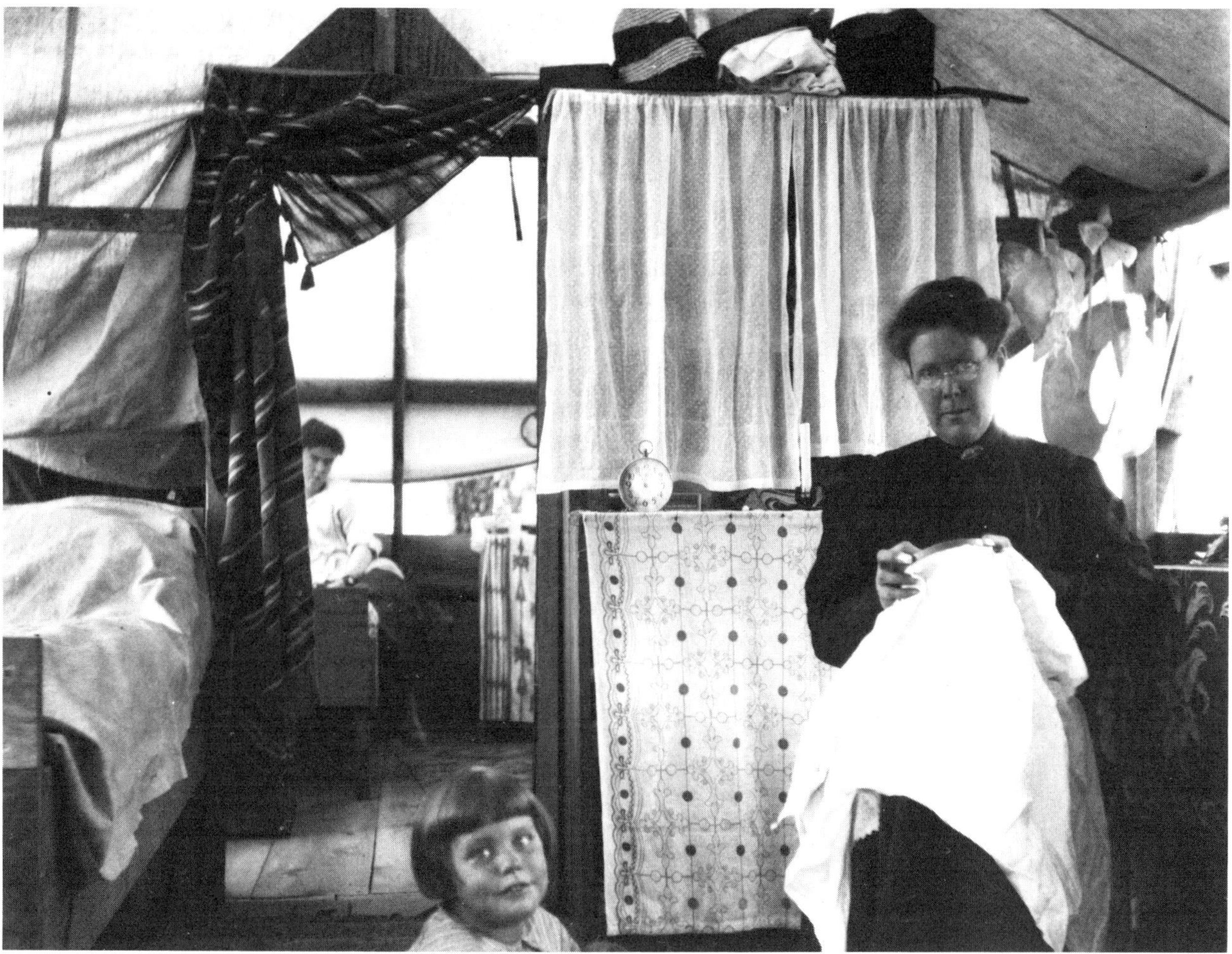

An Idaho miner's family is shown here in their tent house. Do you think it would be fun to live this way? IDAHO HISTORICAL SOCIETY

ended up in the hands of gamblers, saloon owners, and others who kept stores or hauled freight.

Women and Children. Many men poured into the mining camps. The younger men often were not yet married. Those with wives and children most often left them home while going off to seek their fortunes. As a camp grew, however, women and children would begin to appear. Some were the families of miners, others those of storekeepers, lawyers, and doctors.

When women and children came to camp, schools and churches were built. A camp then became a real town with homes and businesses, not just a place to make a quick fortune. When there seemed to be enough gold for several years of mining, homes of adobe brick and painted wood replaced the tents. Silver City grew into a city of beautiful homes and fine mansions for some of the wealthy mine owners. Newspapers were started in several of the mining camps.

In 1864, the "town" of Florence had six children. A school was built, and a teacher was hired. In 1865, it was reported that there were 1,239 children of school age in Idaho Territory. There were, however, only three school houses.

Ideas To Talk About

1. What kinds of people could be found in a mining camp?
2. Why was a mining camp a good place to set up a business?
3. Why did saloon owners spend a lot of money on fine furniture and other beautiful things for their businesses?
4. (a) Why didn't the miners eat good food? (b) What did they eat?
5. Most miners spent their gold almost as soon as they got it. How did they spend it?

This stone cabin was probably built by Chinese gold miners. It can be seen across the Salmon River a few miles north of Riggins. The cabin looked this way in 1988. VIRGIL YOUNG

Chinese Miners Come To Idaho.

The first Chinese came to America from China during the 1849 California gold rush. Between 1853 and 1882, they arrived in America by the boat load. In the West, they worked as miners, helped build the railroads, and did other kinds of heavy work. Some set up laundries and other businesses.

In 1865, Chinese men began to arrive in Lewiston by steamboat, and they quickly spread into Idaho's gold mines. Others went to Idaho City and other camps in the Boise Basin. A large number settled in Boise City. By 1870, Idaho had more Chinese miners than any others.

The Chinese first began working along the Snake and Clearwater rivers and at the Orofino mines. Some worked for themselves, and some worked for other miners. There were more than 500 Chinese miners in the Pierce and Orofino mines in March 1865. As those mines were worked out, most of the other miners left. By the end of 1865, nearly all of the 120 miners at Orofino City were Chinese.

Other miners often disliked the Chinese and treated them badly. Of all the different people who came to the camps, only the Chinese were thought of as "foreigners." The Chinese looked different from the other people and stayed mostly in their own groups. They wore different clothes, spoke their own language, and had many strange customs. For these reasons, and perhaps others, other miners often thought of them as inferior. Many Chinese were robbed, beaten, and even murdered in mining camps.

At first, some miners would not allow the Chinese in their camps. Later, miners would vote whether or not the Chinese could stay. If they could stay, the Chinese had to buy whatever claims could be bought. Mostly they could get only worked-over mines that other miners no longer wanted. For a while, Chinese miners were taxed $5.00 a month to work their mines. As time went on, more and more miners were happy to sell their "wornout" mines to the Chinese. Chinese miners might pay from $100 to $500 for an old mine.

In spite of these things, Chinese often reaped rich rewards with these "wornout" mines. They were hardworking and didn't waste their gold like most others did. Many of them intended to save up a lot of money in America, then return to China to live in wealth. Often they took more gold from a mine than did the miners before them.

Idaho City became a Chinese center when "easy" gold became harder to find in Boise Basin. More and more miners sold their mines to Chinese miners. After the gold rush was finished at Florence, Chinese miners worked those

A Chinese man is selling vegetables in Idaho City. Where do you think he got vegetables to sell?
IDAHO HISTORICAL SOCIETY

Sam Lee, a Chinese man, is shown in front of his laundry at Challis around 1900 or 1910. Why do you think Sam Lee stayed in Challis after the gold rush was over? #5–104–29 U OF I LIBRARY

mines for many years. From about 1870 until about 1884, most of the people living at Florence were Chinese.

In 1870, Idaho had 17,804 people, and 4,272 of them were Chinese. Lewiston, Idaho City, and Boise were large Chinese centers. Lewiston had 1,500 Chinese in 1870. During the 1870s, Boise had only 2,500 people, and 1,000 of them were Chinese. There were fewer Chinese in Idaho after the 1870s. Only 400 remained in Lewiston by 1885. Most of Idaho's Chinese were men. There were very few women and children.

Many of the Chinese returned to China or moved to the large Chinatown in San Francisco. Some stayed in Idaho and mined for many years. Others quit and opened laundries and cafes, or found other kinds of work. A few stayed and lived in small mountain towns until old age. The number of Chinese in Idaho slowly grew smaller, but they remained an important part of Idaho for many years.

Ideas To Talk About

1. Why did large numbers of Chinese come to America?
2. What were some of the problems that Chinese miners had?
3. Why do you think the other miners treated the Chinese so badly?
4. Why do you think the Chinese stayed in the gold mines long after most others had left?
5. As the years went by, what happened to most of Idaho's Chinese people?

Mining Gold Was Hard Work.

Gold is a very heavy metal. It is one of many things that make up the earth's crust. In the beginning, gold is locked into certain kinds of rock. As wind and water wear down the rock, the rock breaks into gravel and sand. When gold is present in the rock, it falls out and mixes with the

Miners were working on Granite Creek in Boise Basin in 1905. The man with his boots off is sitting on a large water pipe. What do you think the pipe was used for? IDAHO HISTORICAL SOCIETY

sand and gravel. In nature, most gold is found in tiny pieces from the size of a grain of wheat to the size of sand and dust. The easiest place to find gold is in a mountain stream, or in gravel and soil where a stream once flowed. Gold found in such places is called **placer gold**.

Placer Mining. During the gold rush, miners dug for gold in stream beds and in the soil nearby. This kind of mining is called **placer mining**. With the right tools, small pieces of gold could be washed out—or rather the sand and soil were washed away from the gold. The simplest tools were a pick, a shovel, and a metal pan.

The miner used the pan to look for gold. Some soil or gravel would be scooped into the pan. With water, the miner would wash the gravel, sand, and dirt over the side of the pan. The pieces of gold were heavier than the rock. After much washing, the gold was the last thing left in the bottom of the pan. This was called "panning for gold."

A miner who found gold would stake a claim and begin mining. Panning gold is slow, hard work. Gold near the surface is the easiest to get. However, gold works its way down through the gravel, so the richest pockets of gold are buried deep. For this reason, the miner needed better tools and lots of water to wash away the soil and gravel.

Placer mining was something that could be done alone. However, a miner often worked with one or more partners to share the hard work. With enough work and water, the dirt and gravel could be washed away from the gold. Miners often used ditches and wooden **flumes** to carry water to their mines. They used **rockers** and **sluice boxes** to wash away the soil and gravel from the gold. With lots of water and hard work, a group of miners could dig and wash their way down to the bottom of the gravel and get lots of gold.

Some groups of miners rigged up large pipes that shot powerful streams of water, like a fire hose. These powerful streams of water could wash away entire river banks and hillsides. This was called **hydraulic mining.** It was much easier than digging to the bottom of the gravel. Gold mining was never easy. Even with partners, flumes, sluice boxes and water pipes, it was very hard work. The miners had to shovel wet soil and gravel all day. Often they had to carry the soil and gravel to water so they could wash it. Their hands and feet were in icy water much of the time. Like the fur trappers, they could work only during the warmer months of the year. Most gold is found in the mountains where the warm season is short. When the weather allowed, the miners worked from daybreak until dark. They worked at top speed, knowing that the faster they worked, the richer they might become.

Sometimes a miner would find a **nugget**. This was a piece of almost pure gold. It might be the size of a grain of wheat, or a pea, or a walnut, or an egg. It could be worth several dollars or several thousand dollars. Large ones were rare. Finding a nugget caused great excitement, and finding several might cause a new gold rush. It was nugget gold that set off the rush to "Fabulous Florence." Joaquin Miller described the gold at Florence and Millersburg as "wheat-like grains . . . in such heaps as had never been found in California."

Few People Got Rich. The fact is, however, that only a few people became rich from gold. Most of those who found gold spent it freely and saved very little. Some miners would dig a few hundred dollars in "easy" gold from near the surface, then be off looking for a better mine. For every miner who "struck it rich," thousands barely made a living. Most mines soon ran out of gold. Many went home "broke."

"Gold fever" fired the dream of "getting rich quick." Most miners wanted to find the richest mine possible. Many good mines were left by miners who set off looking for something better. A few miners were known to leave a million dollars in the ground because they didn't know the value of the mine they were leaving. Often those who "struck it rich" would sell out cheaply and go looking for something richer. Many of the miners who made rich gold discoveries were broke after a few years.

This was called hydraulic mining. Miners rigged up pipes that shot powerful streams of water. The water could wash away an entire river bank or hillside in the search for gold. The picture was taken in Boise Basin in 1898. IDAHO HISTORICAL SOCIETY

Searching Idaho for Gold. Before the gold rush ended, miners searched every part of Idaho for gold. As they spread through the mountains, they found gold in many places. Gold was found in Lemhi County in 1866, causing Leesburg to spring up. In 1869, gold was found on Loon Creek on the Middle Fork of the Salmon. In 1870, the mountains east of Gray's Lake in eastern Idaho had two mining towns, Caribou City and Keenan. Today all of these are ghost towns.

As late as 1883 and 1884, placer gold was found on the Coeur d'Alene River. A new rush of miners went to the Idaho panhandle, and new mining camps quickly appeared. The Coeur d'Alene gold rush didn't last very long. However, it led to something much more important. Miners looking for gold discovered silver, lead, and zinc. Soon these metals were bringing wealth far greater than the early miners ever dreamed of. Today the world-famous Coeur d'Alene mines of Silver Valley produce almost half of the silver mined in the United States. Three of those early camps—Mullan, Kellogg, and Wallace—are now important silver mining centers. You will read about silver mining in Chapter 10.

Review Questions

1. Washing small pieces of gold out of soil and gravel was called ____________ mining. [*130*]
2. A large piece of almost pure gold was called a ____________. [*131*]
3. The simplest tools that a miner used were the (a) ____________, (b) ____________, and (c) ____________. [*130*]
4. Miners often used ditches and ____________ to carry water to their mines. [*130*]
5. Miners used ____________ and ____________ to wash the sand and gravel away from the gold. [*130*]

Ideas To Talk About

1. What made mining such hard work?
2. Why did few people get rich during the gold rush?

Chapter 6 Skill Activities

Words And Ideas In Chapter 6, you will find a number of key words printed in **bold** print. Each key word stands for an important idea. Answering these questions will help you understand some of the key words.

You can find the key words in the Glossary at the back of the book. The number after each question is the page where the idea is found in the book. Answer each question with a complete sentence.

1. How did a miner **stake a claim**? [*118–119*]
2. What was a **flume** used for? [*130*]
3. How large was a **nugget**? [*131*]
4. What is **placer gold**? [*130*]
5. What were the simplest tools used for **placer mining**? [*130*]
6. What did a miner do when **prospecting**? [*117*]
7. What did miners use **rockers** and **sluice boxes** for? [*130*]

Using Your Imagination

1. **Joining the Gold Rush.** You are 20 years old, living in Portland, Oregon. The year is 1861. You have heard about the gold strikes in Florence, and you decide to try to find your fortune.

To get to Florence, you must travel up the Columbia and Snake rivers to Lewiston. At Lewiston, you will buy a burro to carry your supplies to Florence. Also you will have to buy all of your supplies in Lewiston. There are no supply stores in Florence, and you can't get out during the winter.

(a) Make a list of everything you will need for six months. Remember, you must plan for you and your burro.

(b) Share and discuss your list with other students. Watch for things that weren't invented in 1861.

2. **Writing a Letter Home.** You have been living in the gold camps for six months. Finally you find time to write a letter home to your family.

Tell them some of the following things: Where are you? Are you all right? What have you been doing? What is life like in a gold camp? Your family will want to know all of these things—and many more.

Searching For Gold

Below is a list of Idaho mining camps. Like a miner searching for gold, you may have to search for these camps. On a plain outline map of Idaho, mark as many as you can find. You may use this book, an Official Highway Map, or other sources. For some, you may need to use clues given in this book.

1. Caribou City
2. Elk City
3. Florence
4. Idaho City
5. Kellogg
6. Leesburg
7. Moose City
8. Mullan
9. Orofino City
10. Pierce City
11. Pioneerville
12. Placerville
13. Silver City
14. Wallace

Research Projects

1. *Where Does Gold Come From?* How does gold get into the rocks? What is gold used for? Read the encyclopedia under "Gold" to answer these questions—and others. Write a report on what you have learned about gold.

2. *How Do We Get Gold Out of the Rocks?* How is gold removed from ore? Your encyclopedia may have a picture that shows how. Make a poster that shows how gold is removed from the rocks and made into gold bars.

Reviewing Chapter 6

Main Ideas In This Chapter

1. Beginning in 1860, a gold rush brought many new people into Idaho.
2. Idaho's first gold was discovered in the Clearwater country at Pierce.
3. Gold miners invaded Nez Perce land.
4. The gold rush brought many kinds of people from many different places.
5. Florence was a very rich gold strike in the Salmon River country.
6. There was enough gold in Boise Basin to last for many years.
7. Most gold rush mining was placer mining.
8. Very few families came to the mining camps.
9. Life in a mining camp was an adventure.
10. Many Chinese miners worked in Idaho's gold mines.
11. Few people got rich from mining gold.
12. A gold rush along the Coeur d'Alene River led to the discovery of rich silver, lead, and zinc ore.

Further Reading For Children

Hart, Patricia, and Ivar Nelson. *Mining Town.* Seattle: University of Washington Press, 1984. [Photographic record of Silver Valley in northern Idaho. Excellent photographs.]

Johnson, William Weber. *The Forty-Niners.* (Time-Life Series of the Old West) New York: Time-Life Books, 1974. [Excellent photographs of miners and other people; descriptions of camp life; drawings and explanations of mining equipment.]

Miller, Donald C. *Ghost Towns of Idaho.* Boulder, Colorado: Pruett Publishing Company, 1976. [Excellent photographs and descriptions of dozens of Idaho ghost towns.]

Sparling, Wayne. *Southern Idaho Ghost Towns.* Caldwell, Idaho: Caxton Printers, Ltd., 1974. [Excellent photographs and descriptions of southern Idaho ghost towns.]

Weis, Norman D. *Ghost Towns of the Northwest.* Caldwell, Idaho: Caxton Printers, Ltd., 1971. [Interesting photographs of several Idaho ghost towns.]

Welch, Julia Conway. *Gold Town to Ghost Town.* Moscow, Idaho: University of Idaho Press, 1982. [Story of Silver City, Idaho. Excellent photographs.]

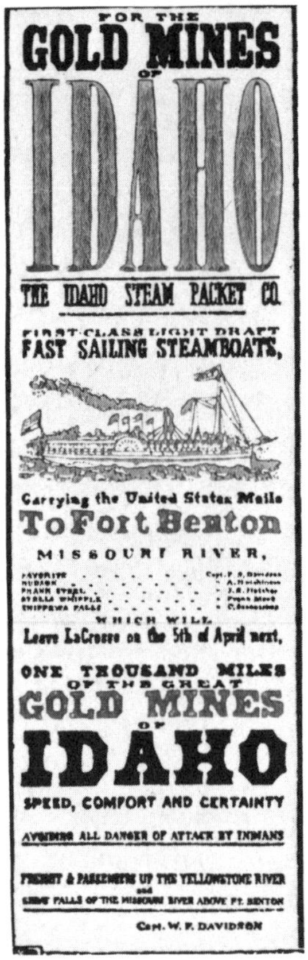

FOR THE
GOLD MINES
OF
IDAHO
THE IDAHO STEAM PACKET CO.
FIRST-CLASS LIGHT DRAFT
FAST SAILING STEAMBOATS,
Carrying the United States Mails
To Fort Benton
MISSOURI RIVER,
WHICH WILL
Leave LaCrosse on the 5th of April next,
ONE THOUSAND MILES
OF THE GREAT
GOLD MINES
OF
IDAHO
SPEED, COMFORT AND CERTAINTY
AVOIDING ALL DANGER OF ATTACK BY INDIANS
COM. W. F. DAVIDSON

Time Line

1776 A.D.	Declaration of Independence; USA begins.
1800	
1805	Lewis and Clark explore Idaho.
1831	Nez Perce and Flathead Indians travel to St. Louis to ask for missionaries.
1834	First missionaries come to Idaho.
1836	Spaldings build mission at Lapwai; Whitmans build mission near Walla Walla, Washington.
1839	White settlers begin coming to Oregon on the Oregon Trail.
1840	William Craig settles on homestead near Lapwai; Father De Smet holds religious service. Indians at Pierre's Hole.
1846	Oregon Country becomes part of the United States.
1847	Mormons begin to settle the Great Basin of Utah.
1848	Gold is discovered in California.
1853	The Sacred Heart Mission is begun at Cataldo.
1855	Mormon settlers move to Idaho and build Fort Lemhi; Fort Hall and Fort Boise are closed.
1858	Mormons abandon Fort Lemhi and return to Utah.
1860	Franklin becomes Idaho's first permanent white settlement. Gold is discovered in northern Idaho; Gold rush begins.
1862	Mullan Road is completed in northern Idaho; Great flood destroys much of it.
1863	Idaho Territory is formed.
1890	Idaho becomes a state.
1900	
1976 A.D.	USA celebrates its Bicentennial
1990	Idaho Centennial

Chapter 7
Taming The Land

Farmers And Ranchers Follow The Miners.

When the miners came to Idaho in great numbers, they needed food. At first, nearly all the food came from western Oregon and Washington. Fresh food could not be sent that far, however. Soon people in Idaho began growing food to sell to the miners.

Vegetables were planted in places as close as possible to the mines. Gardens and farms were started near Lewiston, and in the Boise, Payette, and Weiser valleys. Vegetables were growing in Payette Valley just eight months after gold was found in Boise Basin. The crop brought a good price. Green onions brought a dollar a dozen at nearby mining camps. Fresh ears of corn brought two dollars a dozen. These prices were really much higher than they might sound today. At that time, cowboys worked for 20 to 40 dollars a month! Before long, farmers were also selling badly-needed horses to the miners.

This is Julia Davis Park in Boise. In 1864, Thomas Davis started an apple orchard on this land. Who do you think bought most of Thomas Davis's apples? VIRGIL YOUNG

An apple orchard was started near Lewiston in 1863. Soon its apples were being sold in mining camps along the Salmon River and in Montana. In 1864, Thomas Davis started a large apple orchard at Boise. It was where Julia Davis Park now stands. Farming, fruit growing and **ranching** grew steadily in Idaho Territory during the 1860s and 1870s. Southwest Idaho had many orchards.

Farming, fruit growing and ranching soon brought more people to Idaho than did the mines. During the 1860s, farmers and ranchers settled on the Clearwater Plateau and the lower Salmon River. Mount Idaho started in 1861 as a station on the way from Lewiston to the mines. Ranchers began settling on Camas Prairie (Idaho County) in 1863. Grangeville was started in 1876 when a farmers' meeting hall was built there. Settlers came to Weippe Prairie in 1875.

North of the Clearwater, the first farmers settled around Moscow and Genesee. They began arriving in 1869, and more came each year. Much further north, Rathdrum began as a log cabin on Rathdrum Prairie in 1861. Settlers came to Coeur d'Alene in 1877. Sandpoint began as a store and trading post in 1880.

Review Questions

1. The first gardens and farms in Idaho were started to ____________________. [*135*]

2. Soon farming, fruit growing, and ranching brought more people to Idaho than ____________. [*135*]

Ranches And Cowboys Bring The "Old West" To Idaho.

Towns and farms grew up quickly in certain choice places. However, Idaho Territory was a huge land, and it took a long time to fill up. Great stretches of land were well suited for grazing **livestock**: cattle, horses, and sheep. A growing number of ranchers began to take advantage of this fine **range land**.

Ranchers were slower coming to Idaho than to Texas, Wyoming, and Montana. However, after several years the range land in those places began to suffer from heavy grazing. Ranchers began looking for new grazing land. Many found Idaho to be good cattle country. Idaho's best range land was in eastern Idaho, the Salmon River country, and Hagerman Valley. The grass was good, and the winters were not as cold as on the open plains farther east. Other places became important, too. Cattle ranches soon dotted the Snake River country from Raft River to Oregon.

Western artist Frederic Remington left us this picture of a cowboy. *HARPER'S MONTHLY*, JULY 1891

The Snake River country became part of the "Old West." Texas longhorn cattle came to Idaho through Utah and Oregon. Cattle roamed the open country nearly everywhere. These were the times of **open range**—there were almost no wire fences. Grass was free for the taking. Hard-riding, gun-toting cowboys, sometimes called buckaroos, became part of Idaho.

During summer, the cattle grazed on mountainsides and in the higher mountain valleys. For winter, they were driven down into the valleys where they could find plenty of dry bunch grass. The cattle business was ideal during the early years. Cattle could graze the year around, and there seemed to be no end to the grass. Ranch work was easy and cheap. Calves were branded and turned loose. Later, they were rounded up as fat cattle. Mining camps paid well for the beef. Ranchers became as wealthy as some of the mine owners.

Trouble For Ranchers: Hard Winters And Homesteaders.

Things began to change for the ranchers, however. After several years of grazing, there was less bunch grass. Then nature brought several cruel winters. Blizzards and deep snow buried the bunch grass, and the cattle had no winter feed. No hay had been raised for winter feeding. During the winter of 1886–1887, many thousands of cattle starved and froze to death.

A different kind of problem would change the cattle business forever—farmers. Farms began to appear on the open range. In 1862, the government began giving families 160 acres of open land to begin farming. These farms were called **homesteads**. The farmers put up wire fences to keep the cattle from destroying their crops. Then the cattle could no longer roam freely. Often they were cut off from their watering places. During cold weather, cattle sometimes piled up against the fences and died.

The ranchers were very angry about the farmers. They called the farmers "nesters." Sometimes ranchers and farmers fought over the land. In the end, however, much of the open range became farm land. Idaho had plenty of other

Range cattle in the Old West were "longhorn" cattle. Many had longer horns than these.
VIRGIL YOUNG

land for grazing. The range cattle were moved to forest lands and desert lands not well suited for farming.

The 1880s were the last years of the "old West" as Americans think of it. By now, the cattle business had changed. Many ranchers "went broke" after the bad weather killed most of their cattle. Now there were more fences and less open range. Ranchers began raising hay for winter feed. Railroads took the cattle to market. No longer did cowboys drive the herds hundreds of miles.

Today Idaho is one of those western states that still have great stretches of grazing land. During the summer, you can see fat cattle grazing in the mountains and meadows. During winter, you will see animals grazing on the open desert land of southern Idaho. You may also see cowboys riding among their herds of cattle. Range cattle are raised much the same way now as they were during the exciting days of the old West.

Ideas To Talk About

1. Why did towns spring up quickly in some places and not in others?
2. The cattle business was ideal for a number of years. Why was this?
3. Why was open range such a good thing for ranchers?
4. Cruel winters killed many thousands of cattle. How could the ranchers have prevented many of these deaths?
5. Why should there be trouble between the ranchers and the homesteaders?

The Cowboy.

Of all the figures from the old West, the best loved is the cowboy, in Idaho sometimes called a buckaroo. You have seen them many times in movies, on television, and in books. Most often the buckaroo is shown as a man with a six-gun and powerful fists. He is either looking for trouble, or helping someone else out of trouble. Though this picture makes for exciting stories, it is not a true picture of most cowboys.

You know how the cowboy looked. He wore a broad-rimmed hat, chaps, Levis, and high-heeled boots. With his horse, he herded cattle, rounded them up, or drove them to market. Of course, he rode his horse everywhere, including into town.

The cowboy might call his horse a **bronco**, from the Spanish word meaning "wild." In Idaho, the cowboy often called his horse a **cayuse**. He had to buy his own saddle and bedding. However, his horse most likely belonged to the owner of the cattle.

The cowboy's life was full of hard work and hardship, but it was a free life. His pay was low—from 20 to 40 dollars a month. Sometimes he worked for a share of the calf crop. In this way, he could build up a herd of his own.

A cowboy might look after as many as 1,000 cattle. It was his job to keep the herd on the right

This picture shows some of the equipment a cowboy carried with him. Name as many of these items as you can. JOHN A. TAYE (DRAWING)

part of the range. He had to keep the cattle where there was plenty of grass, and make sure they always had salt.

The Roundup. The cowboy worked two **roundups** each year. The first was in June. This was to round up strays and to brand the calves. The brand was a mark burned into the skin of the animal to show who owned it. No two brands were alike. When cattle grazed on the open range, animals from different herds often would mix together. Cowboys from the different outfits had to sort out their own animals. The brands also helped the owners find their cattle if rustlers stole them.

When an animal grew up without a brand, it was called a **maverick**. Ranchers agreed these would be branded with "M" when taken to market. When they were sold, the money was divided among all the ranchers who shared the range. Mavericks were favorites for cattle rustlers. They were easy to steal because they were not branded.

The second roundup was in the fall. This was to gather up fat cattle for market. At a roundup, there was a boss and several cowboys. Each cowboy had four or five horses. For the spring roundup, there was also a cook and a chuck wagon. In the fall, there was no chuck wagon. Everyone had to carry his own food and bedding on a pack animal.

In early times, Idaho cattle were taken to market by herding them along a trail to the east. This was a "cattle drive." Cowboys would drive large herds hundreds or even thousands of miles. One herd might have several thousand animals. Some early Idaho herds were driven as far east as Omaha, Nebraska. Later, when the railroads were built, cattle were hauled east by train.

Review Questions

1. A cowboy might call his horse a ____________ or a ____________. [*137*]

2. Gathering cattle together for branding or for market was called a ____________. [*138*]

3. A calf was branded to ________________________. [*138*]

Ideas To Talk About

1. How would you describe a cowboy's life?

2. What do you think would be the best part and the worst part of being a cowboy?

Cattle still graze on range land in many parts of Idaho. These are Herefords, known for their reddish coat and white markings. IDAHO DEPARTMENT OF COMMERCE

The Overland Hotel was an important meeting place in Boise. It was built in 1863 and torn down in 1903. Why do you think it was torn down? #5-8-2 U OF I LIBRARY

Farms And Towns Spread Through Southwest Idaho.

Boise City and a new Fort Boise began almost together. In 1863, the government built a fort near a spot that would soon become Boise City. This new Fort Boise was a station for soldiers who would protect the settlers from Indians. Today the "new" Fort Boise can be seen near Fort Street and Fifth in Boise.

When word got around that a fort was going to be built, a group of settlers began planning a new town. Boise City was laid out in 1863 between Fort Boise and the Boise River. The new town quickly became a trading center for the nearby Boise Basin mines. In 1864, Boise City became the capital of Idaho Territory. By 1870, there were more than 400 buildings and about 1,000 people.

You already learned that vegetables and fruit trees were planted around Boise soon after the town was started. Within two years, all the best farm land in Boise Valley had been taken by settlers. Star and Middleton became villages. Notus and Riverside began as trading posts near old Fort Boise, which had closed in 1855.

Payette Valley was settled about the same time. Picket Corral, Martinsville, and Falk's Store were settlements that grew up there. Martinsville later became Emmettsville, and then Emmett. In 1866, Bluff's Ferry began carrying people across the river near the present town of Payette. When the railroad came through in 1883, a new town, Boomerang, was built along the railroad. Later Boomerang was named Payette, after François Payette.

François Payette had been a fur trapper for many years along the Payette River, which was also named for him. He quit trapping in 1834 and became manager of Fort Boise until he retired in 1844. Immigrants on the Oregon Trail remembered him as a "merry, fat old gentleman" who was very kind and polite to them.

Boise's main street is shown in this picture painted in 1864. #5-8-7A U OF I LIBRARY

Horses, buggies, and livery stables were important to the early farmers and town people of Idaho. This livery stable stood on Main Street in Moscow. Why did people need livery stables?
#5-1-13A U OF I LIBRARY

Abbott's fruit orchard was located northwest of Boise. What kind of fruit are these men picking?
IDAHO HISTORICAL SOCIETY

In 1863, a settlement was built at the present town of Weiser. In the early 1870s, a bridge was built across the Weiser River, and later a town was laid out. The town was first called Weiser Bridge, but later shortened to Weiser. Other settlers began farming along the upper Weiser River. Midvale, Cambridge, and Council soon appeared there.

In 1883, a new railroad was finished across southern Idaho. It was called the Oregon Short Line. It was, and still is, part of the Union Pacific Railroad. As the railroad stretched west across Idaho, settlements and towns sprang up beside it. In 1883, Caldwell was laid out along the new railroad. At first it was called Hamburg or Bugtown. Nampa began as a settlement called New Jerusalem. After the town was laid out, it was named Nampa, according to legend, after a Shoshoni Chief Nampah.

King Hill and Mountain Home began as stage stations on the way to the mines. Mountain Home began about ten miles east of the present town, and was sometimes called Rattlesnake Station. It sat on Rattlesnake Creek, where the road to the gold mines crossed the Oregon Trail.

Freighters, wagons, and mules posed for a picture on Mountain Home's main street. The year was 1884. What special name was given to freighters who drove mules? IDAHO HISTORICAL SOCIETY

When the railroad came through in 1883, a tent town began near the tracks. At first it was called Tuttville for a stage driver. Later it was given the name of the old stage station, Mountain Home.

Glenns Ferry began as early as 1865, when the Glenn brothers built a ferry across the Snake River. When the railroad came through in 1883, the town was laid out a short distance away. The village of Bruneau was settled in 1869. It soon became a farming, business, and social center for the nearby farmers.

The O'Farrell cabin was Boise's first home and place of worship. It was built of logs in 1863. The cabin now stands for visitors to see on Fort Street at the edge of Fort Boise. The large roof was added later to protect it from the weather. #5-8-8 U OF I LIBRARY

Ideas To Talk About

1. Settlements grew up around several ferries. Why would people settle near a ferry?
2. Notice that the first settlements in southwest Idaho were in river valleys. Why would people choose to settle in river valleys?
3. The early settlements at Payette and Mountain Home were moved when the railroad came through. Why would people want to move to the railroad?

Mormon Settlers Spread Through Eastern Idaho.

The story of eastern Idaho is mostly the story of Mormon settlers. Franklin was the first permanent settlement in 1860. In less than ten years, upper Cache Valley was dotted with Mormon settlements. Today Preston is the largest of these. Settlers also spread into Bear River Valley.

This was the railroad bridge at Eagle Rock in 1889. Taylor's wagon road bridge is seen in the background. Eagle Rock later became Idaho Falls. IDAHO HISTORICAL SOCIETY

Paris was settled in 1863, followed by Montpelier, Bloomington, and St. Charles.

To the north and west, Grace, Malad City, Soda Springs, and other settlements grew up. You will remember that Soda Springs was a point on the Oregon Trail. West of the present town were two bubbling springs, Steamboat Spring and Beer Springs. These springs have since been covered by Soda Point Reservoir.

Farms in this corner of Idaho grew food for the Montana gold miners. Gold was discovered in western Montana in 1862. A freight and stage road soon ran from Salt Lake City to Montana through eastern Idaho. The road carried freight and food from Utah and the farms of eastern Idaho.

Several settlements grew up along this road. The most important of these became Idaho Falls. In 1863, a ferry was built on the Snake River a few miles north. Two years later, a bridge was built where Idaho Falls now stands. A settlement began there and was named Eagle Rock. The name Eagle Rock was changed later to Idaho Falls. Eagle Rock was the earliest settlement in the upper Snake River Valley.

There were a few earlier settlers before the wave of Mormons. These were ranchers with herds of cattle and horses. They were followed by rustlers, who lived by stealing cattle from the ranchers. Well into the 1870s, Pierre's Hole and the upper forks of the Snake were favorite hideouts for rustlers.

Fort Hall was started when the Fort Hall Indian Reservation was set aside in 1868. The town of Fort Hall began as Fort Hall Post, east of the present town of Blackfoot. It was the home of a few traders and others who lived there and worked with the Indians.

The Utah and Northern Railroad was built through eastern Idaho between 1877 and 1879. This brought new towns almost overnight. Railroad settlements grew up at Eagle Rock, Blackfoot, Pocatello, and the present Fort Hall. Blackfoot was laid out in 1878, Rexburg in 1883, and Rigby in 1884. St. Anthony, Pocatello, and Driggs followed in 1889.

These were the most important towns in eastern Idaho before Idaho became a state.

Settlers Come To Magic Valley.

Farming came late to Magic Valley. The first settlements were stage stations and river crossings. The best known of these was Rock Creek Station, built in 1863 near the present city of Twin Falls.

The next settlers in Magic Valley were ranchers in the late 1860s. Several large ranches were started in the Raft River country south of the Snake River. Later, sheep growers began building up large flocks of sheep north and south of the Snake River.

In 1883, the Oregon Short Line brought railroad stations to Magic Valley. Minidoka, Naples, and Toponis were settled as railroad stations. Later, Naples became Shoshone, and Toponis became Gooding. Farming in Magic Valley could not begin until water was brought to the thirsty land. This had to wait until 1903, when Milner Dam was built on the Snake River.

Review Questions

1. Pierres Hole (Teton Valley) was a favorite hiding place for ____________. *[142]*
2. Rustlers lived by ________________________. *[142]*
3. Eastern Idaho was settled mostly by ____________ settlers. *[141–142]*
4. Farms in eastern Idaho grew food for the Montana ____________. *[142]*
5. Farming could not begin in Magic Valley until ________________________. *[143]*

Idaho's Indians Settle On Reservations.

If settlers were filling up the Indians' land, what would happen to the Indians? What would they do? How could they live? These were important questions for the Indians. Idaho's Indians had always lived by hunting and gathering food. The settlers did not leave the Indians enough land for that way of life. The government knew that this was a problem for the Indians. Therefore, it set up a system to set aside certain lands for the Indians. Such lands are called **reservations.**

A reservation is land set aside as a place for Indians to live. Most reservations were formed by treaties with tribes or separate bands. An Indian **treaty** is an agreement between the U. S. government and a group of Indians. The government promised to protect the Indians' reservation lands, and protect the Indians from attack. The Indians promised not to attack settlers. Often the government promised to pay the Indians a certain amount in food or other goods each year.

In moving to reservations, the Indians traded freedom for safety. It was hard to learn a new way of life. They had to set up tribal governments suited to reservation life. The old kinds of Indian government didn't work well when so many people lived so close together. Food was another problem. Indians had to grow their own food on the reservation. It took time to learn how to farm.

Sometimes settlers and the government did not honor the treaties. Settlers would sometimes move onto reservation land. Later they would force the Indians to sign new treaties that left them less land. The Shoshoni and the Nez Perce lost much land in this way.

Reservations may seem like a good idea. However, they didn't stop all the trouble. For one thing, many Indians didn't want to live on a reservation. Often it meant that they had to move to a new place. Once they had moved, they didn't want to stay there all the time. Indians had always been free to move about as they wished. They wanted to leave the reservation to hunt, just as they had for thousands of years. The reservations were too small for there to be enough wild food.

Idaho's Five Reservations. The Nez Perce signed a treaty in 1855 that gave them a huge reservation. It stretched from the Blue Mountains of Oregon to the Bitterroot Mountains of Idaho. In 1863, the government forced the Nez Perce to sign a different treaty that gave them much less land. The smaller reservation lies around Lapwai.

The Fort Hall Reservation was set up by a treaty signed in 1868. The Bannock and several bands of Shoshoni settled there.

In 1873, the Coeur d'Alene Reservation was placed at the south end of Lake Coeur d'Alene. The present Sacred Heart Mission is at DeSmet and the old Indian village of Tensed.

The Duck Valley Reservation was set aside in 1877. It lies around the town of Owyhee, Nevada, on both sides of the Idaho-Nevada border. Western Shoshoni and Northern Paiute both settled there.

The Kutenai Reservation was the smallest and last Idaho reservation. Most of Idaho's Kutenai went to live on the Flathead Reservation in Montana. However, a small group stayed in northern Idaho. They were given a very small piece of land near Bonners Ferry in 1894.

Reservations Divided the Tribes.

Reservations served to divide the tribes instead of bringing them together. Most of the Kutenai tribe settled in Montana and Canada. Only a small group remained in Idaho. The Kalispel were settled in Montana and Washington, but not in Idaho. Not all Nez Perce settled at Lapwai. Chief Joseph and his band were settled in Washington State. Some Shoshoni were settled at Fort Hall Reservation, and others went to the Duck Valley Reservation. The Northern Paiute were divided between Nevada and Oregon. Of Idaho's tribes, only the Coeur d'Alene and the Bannock remain undivided.

Ideas To Talk About

1. Why were reservations set aside for the Indians?

After the Indians settled on reservations, they began living in log cabins and other wooden houses. This Nez Perce family is seen at their home at Kamiah in 1887. IDAHO HISTORICAL SOCIETY

2. Many Indians didn't like living on a reservation. Why not?

3. What were some of the problems that Indians had with their reservations?

War With Idaho's Indians.

At first, Idaho's Indians were peaceful. They were helpful to Lewis and Clark, and to others who followed. When trappers and settlers came onto Indian land, however, the Indians became less friendly. There was scattered fighting between trappers and small bands of Indians. During the 1850s, Bannock and Shoshoni bands attacked wagon trains on the Oregon Trail. The trading posts, Fort Hall and Fort Boise, had to be closed in 1855.

The flood of settlers into Idaho after 1860 upset Idaho's Indians. Some decided to fight. They hoped to keep settlers off the land. During the next several years, there was scattered fighting between the Indians and the miners and settlers. Both Indians and whites were killed in this fighting.

Soldiers were sent to trouble spots to stop the fighting. In Idaho, soldiers fought battles with bands of Coeur d'Alene, Nez Perce, Shoshoni, Bannock, and Northern Paiute. When the soldiers defeated a band, those Indians were settled on reservation land. Once the Indians were on reservations, Idaho was free to grow as the settlers wished.

J. E. Rees ran this trading post (store) on the Lemhi Reservation from 1892 to 1907. In 1909, the Lemhi Reservation was closed. Those Indians went to live on the Fort Hall Reservation. #6-73-1 U OF I LIBRARY

The fighting between Indians and others has been called "Indian Wars." Mostly these were small battles between soldiers and Indian bands. In Idaho, only the Nez Perce fighting could really be called a war.

The Nez Perce War.

The Nez Perce War is an important part of American history. Chief Joseph and his people fought and defeated the U. S. Army for 11 weeks and 1,600 miles. His "people" were a band of hundreds of women, children, old people, and about 250 warriors. After much suffering, Joseph and his people surrendered at Bear Paw Mountain in Montana. Today Chief Joseph is thought to be one of the truly great military leaders of all time.

The Treaties. The Nez Perce were always among the settlers' best Indian friends. You will remember that they helped Lewis and Clark, the Spaldings, and others who came to Idaho.

In 1855, the Nez Perce signed a treaty that gave them a large reservation. The 1855 treaty left them most of the land they had always lived on. It stretched from the Blue Mountains of Oregon to the Bitterroots of Idaho. Soon, however, settlers began moving into the Wallowa Valley in eastern Oregon. This was the home of Old Joseph and his band. Old Joseph begged the government to remove the settlers. Nothing happened, except that more people kept coming.

Then gold was found on the Clearwater. The gold rush brought another flood of people onto Nez Perce land. Instead of protecting the Indian land, the government let settlers take more of it. For some reason, the government (Congress) had never voted to accept the 1855 treaty. In 1863, the government made the Nez Perce sign a treaty for a much smaller reservation.

Old Joseph, father of Chief Joseph, refused to sign the 1863 treaty. His home, Wallowa Valley, would not be part of the smaller reservation. The 1863 treaty was signed by Chief Lawyer and several other chiefs.

The Battle of White Bird Canyon took place in the canyon shown in the picture. The zig-zag mark on the hill at the top center is an old highway that was added many years later. What town is seen at the bottom of the picture? IDAHO DEPARTMENT OF COMMERCE

More settlers came into Wallowa Valley. They put up fences and brought in cattle and horses. The Indians' horses began to starve, because the settlers took up all the pasture. Old Joseph died in 1872. His son, young Joseph, became Chief Joseph.

War Begins. In 1877, the government ordered the Wallowa Nez Perce to settle on the Nez Perce Reservation at Lapwai. Soon afterward, some bands of young Nez Perce killed several settlers on the lower Salmon River. General Howard sent soldiers to protect the settlers. Near the present village of White Bird, the soldiers met about 300 Nez Perce warriors. The Indians were led by Chief White Bird. The soldiers were defeated in the fierce battle that followed. Only a few Indians were killed, while one-third of the soldiers died in the battle. The Battle of White Bird Canyon was the first battle in the Nez Perce War.

Chief Joseph took over a band of the Nez Perce after this battle. It was his duty to take care of the people who were too young, too old, or too weak to fight. The band began to flee to the east. They decided to leave their land rather than be punished and made to go to the reservation.

Joseph met soldiers at the Clearwater near Kamiah. The Battle of Clearwater lasted for two days, and many Indians and soldiers were left dead. Joseph's 300 warriors held off General Howard's 400 soldiers.

From Kamiah, Chief Joseph began a retreat over the Lolo Trail. His band was made up of women, children, and old people. They pushed over high mountains, through deep canyons, across wild rivers, and through thick brush.

The Nez Perce had plenty of horses and rode them hard. Many animals were worn out and left dead along the trail. In only 11 days, Joseph had led and driven his people from Kamiah, over the Lolo Trail, and through Lolo Pass into Montana. He did not lose a single person on this part of the retreat. Most surprising, they outran General Howard and his soldiers.

Joseph followed the rugged Bitterroots south into the Lemhi Valley. From there, he turned east through Yellowstone Park. Then he turned toward Canada. General Howard knew his soldiers could never catch the Nez Perce. He wired east for other soldiers to cut off Joseph's flight. Joseph's men defeated the soldiers sent to stop them, then moved on toward Canada.

Surrender. Finally, soldiers trapped Joseph and his band at Bear Paw Mountain in Montana. It was a cruel battle, and the Indians suffered greatly. When Joseph saw that his people could fight no more, he knew they must surrender. He sent a message to General Howard. His words were sad, and they have since become famous. His message ended with the words, "From where the sun now stands, I will fight no more forever." The Nez Perce War had ended.

Today Chief Joseph is a hero to many people. General Howard and others who fought against him praised him as a great leader. For 1,600 miles, Joseph and his men fought off company after company of the Army's best soldiers. He led and drove his small band over some of America's roughest country. Time after time, his battle plans were more clever than those of the soldiers who chased him. Chief Joseph and his band were stopped only a few miles from Canada and freedom.

This is Chief Lawyer. He and several other Nez Perce chiefs signed the 1863 treaty for a smaller reservation. Old Chief Joseph and some others refused to sign. G. W. FULLER

Ideas To Talk About

1. Why was there fighting between the Indians and settlers?
2. What was the trouble with the Nez Perce Reservation?
3. Why do you think Old Joseph didn't sign the 1863 treaty?
4. Do you think Chief White Bird and Chief Joseph were right in fighting the soldiers instead of going peacefully to Lapwai? Defend your answer.

Chapter 7 Skill Activities

Words And Ideas

In Chapter 7, you will find a number of key words printed in **bold** print. Each key word stands for an important idea. Answering these questions will help you understand some of the key words.

You can find the key words in the Glossary at

the back of the book. The number after each question is the page where the idea is found in the book. Answer each question with a complete sentence.

1. **Bronco** is a popular word in Idaho. What does it mean? [*137*]
2. What was a **cayuse**? [*137*]
3. What was a **homestead**? [*136*]
4. What are **livestock**? [*136*]
5. What was done with **mavericks**? [*138*]
6. What is meant by **open range**? [*136*]
7. What is the difference between a **ranch** and a farm? [*136–137*]
8. What is **range land**? [*136*]
9. What is a **reservation**? [*143*]
10. Why did ranchers have **roundups**? [*138*]
11. What was an Indian **treaty**? [*143*]

Research Projects

1. **Cattle.** Write a report about cattle. You might want to make your report into a booklet.

Why do people raise cattle? What are cattle used for? What is the difference between beef cattle and dairy cattle? Your encyclopedia should have the answers to these questions and many others. It should also have a lot of beautiful pictures of cattle.

2. **Sheep.** Write a report about sheep.

Why do people raise sheep? What are sheep used for? Use your encyclopedia to find out.

3. **Cowboy Life.** Write a report about cowboy life.

There are still cowboys working today. Look in an encyclopedia under "Cowboy" and "Western Frontier Life." The book *The Cowboys* is full of information about cowboys in the old West. The book *Buckaroo* tells about cowboys today. Both books are listed at the end of this chapter.

4. **Cattle Brands.** Some cattle brands are quite interesting to look at and think about. Many brands will be found on page 133 of *The Cowboys*, which is listed at the end of this chapter.

(a) Write a report on cattle brands.

(b) Design your own brand. Pretend you are a rancher and you want a brand for your cattle. Keep in mind that a brand must be drawn so it can't be changed into a different brand. You can test your brand by letting someone else try to change it. If you don't have any cattle (and most of us don't), what else could your brand be used for?

5. **Ranching.** Write a report on ranching. Ranching in the old West was a lot different from farming. You can look in an encyclopedia under "Ranching." Much more information will be found in the book *The Cowboys*, listed at the end of this chapter.

6. **Nez Perce War.** Study the map of Chief Joseph's long journey across the mountains with his band of people. Draw the map, then write a report explaining the journey.

Mapping Idaho's Settlers

A. In this unit, we saw settlers spreading out across Idaho. Make a map that shows where people were settling in Idaho. Begin with a plain outline map of Idaho.

This book and the Idaho Official Highway Map should have the information you need. Below is a list of places to put on your map. Why not add your town to the list?

1. Bear River Valley—1863
2. Boise—1863
3. Boise Valley—1863
4. Cache Valley—1860
5. Caldwell—1883
6. Coeur d'Alene—1877
7. Emmett—1864
8. Franklin—1860
9. Fort Hall (town)—1868
10. Glenns Ferry—1865
11. Grangeville—1876
12. Idaho Falls (Eagle Rock)—1865
13. Lewiston—1861
14. Moscow—1871
15. Mountain Home—1883
16. Nampa—1885
17. Payette—1883
18. Payette Valley—1862
19. Preston—1866
20. Sandpoint—1880
21. Soda Springs—1863
22. Teton Valley—1882
23. Weiser—1863

B. Idaho's Indians became settlers, too. They settled on Indian reservations. To the map above, add Idaho's Indian reservations: Coeur d'Alene, Duck Valley, Fort Hall, Kutenai, and Nez Perce.

Reviewing Chapter 7

Main Ideas In This Chapter

1. The first farms and orchards in Idaho were started to sell food to the mining camps.
2. Farming, fruit growing, and ranching soon brought more people to Idaho than did mining.
3. Southern Idaho was part of the "Old West" with cowboys and great herds of longhorn cattle.
4. In the beginning, ranching was easy and profitable. Mining camps paid well for the beef. Ranchers became as wealthy as some of the mine owners.
5. Homesteaders put an end to the open range for ranchers.
6. Cruel winters and fences changed the nature of ranching.
7. Cowboys lived an interesting life, but with hard work and low pay.
8. Farms and farming towns quickly spread along the river valleys of southwest Idaho.
9. The coming of the railroads to Idaho caused a number of settlements to spring up along the tracks.
10. Mormon farmers settled the valleys of eastern Idaho.
11. Magic Valley had early settlements at stage stations and river crossings, and later there were railroad settlements. However, farming did not begin in Magic Valley until after 1903, when Milner Dam brought water to the land.
12. As settlers filled the land, the Indians were settled on Indian reservations.
13. Living on a reservation meant learning a new way of life. It took time for the Indians to make the change.
14. There was fighting between some settlers and some Indians. People were killed on both sides.
15. "Wars" were fought between soldiers and some of the Indians.
16. Not all of Idaho's Indians fought the settlers. Some went peacefully to live on their reservations.
17. The Nez Perce War was an important part of American history. The fighting caused much suffering among the Nez Perce, and many Indians and soldiers died.
18. Chief Joseph fought brilliantly. Today he is a hero to many people.

Picture Books of Cowboy Life

Markus, Kurt. *Buckaroo.* (A New York Graphic Society Book) Boston: Little, Brown & Company, 1987. [A breath-taking book on present-day ranch and cowboy life in Idaho and the Great Basin.]

Stoecklein, David R. *The Idaho Cowboy: A Photographic Portrayal*. Ketchum, Idaho: Stoecklein Publishing, 1991. [Wonderful pictures of real cowboys, ranches, and animals.]

Further Reading For Children

Forbis, William H. *The Cowboys*. (Time-Life Series of the Old West) New York: Time-Life Books, 1973. [Excellent photographs and descriptions.]

Granfield, Linda. *Cowboy: An Album*. New York: Ticknor & Fields, 1994.

Hanley, Mike, and Ellis Lucia. *Owyhee Trails, The West's Forgotten Corner*. Caldwell, Idaho: Caxton Press, 1973. [Author Mike Hanley ranches near Jordan Valley, Oregon, in the shadow of the Owyhee Mountains. With Ellis Lucia, he tells interesting tales of the past and the present of this wild and rugged corner of the west. This unique book continues to stay in print.]

McCall, Edith. *Adventures of Cowboys on Cattle Drives*. New York: Royal Fireworks Press, 2001.

Sanford, William. *Bill Pickett: African American Rodeo Star*. Berkeley Heights, New Jersey: Enslow Publications, 1997.

Movie

I Will Fight No More Forever. VHS 109 minutes. Starring James Whitmore and Sam Elliot. Recommended by the National Education Association. Available from Questar at www.questar1.com. [This film is recommended over other versions.]

Time Line

1776 A.D.	Declaration of Independence; USA begins.
1800	
1805	Lewis and Clark explore Idaho. Indians welcome white men.
1855	First Nez Perce Treaty. Large reservation is formed.
1858	War between U.S. Army and northern Indian tribes.
1860	E.D. Pierce discovers gold in the Clearwater country.
1863	Battle of Bear River. Second Nez Perce Treaty; the large Nez Perce reservation is made smaller. Idaho Territory is formed.
1866–68	Snake Indian War.
1869	Fort Hall Indian Reservation is formed.
1872	Old Chief Joseph dies; Young Joseph becomes chief.
1873	Coeur d'Alene Indian Reservation is formed.
1875	Lemhi Indian Reservation is formed.
1877	Nez Perce Indian War. Duck Valley Indian Reservation is formed.
1878	Bannock Indian War.
1879	Sheepeater Indian War.
1890	Idaho becomes a state.
1894	Kutenai Indian Reservation is formed.
1900	
1909	Lemhi Indian Reservation is closed.
1976 A.D.	USA celebrates its Bicentennial
1990	Idaho Centennial

Chapter 8
Pioneer Life In Idaho Territory

Pioneer Life Was Hard In Early Idaho.

You have grown up seeing machines do every kind of work. You see machines every day at home and at school, and in factories. It may be hard to think of living *without machines!* Yet, many of Idaho's first settlers did just that. Most of them were quite poor. They brought almost nothing with them. At first many of them had no money to buy or build a house. They couldn't buy farm machines and had a hard time getting farm animals.

Early settlers are often called **pioneers**. A pioneer is the first person to do something. Idaho's pioneers were the first people to come and settle, and they opened the way for others to follow. Life was very hard during those first years. Often there were barely enough crops to feed the family and the farm animals. The family had to wait to buy things it needed until there were extra crops to sell. A family might farm for several years before getting a log house.

Log houses were drafty because of the cracks between the logs. The pioneers tried to keep the cracks sealed with mud, but cold air came through anyway. This pioneer cabin near Potlatch may have been built in the 1860s or 1870s. IDAHO HISTORICAL SOCIETY

Teton Valley pioneers "picked" potatoes by hand in the early days. Horses were used to plow them out of the ground. #5–2–15 U OF I LIBRARY

A few pioneers wrote about their life in Idaho. Much of what we know about Idaho's pioneers comes from those who wrote about it.

Pioneer Life In Cache Valley.

Lars Frederickson was eight years old when he walked across the plains from Omaha, Nebraska. The year was 1865. He was going to Salt Lake City with his mother and brother. In 1868, Lars and his family moved to Weston, Idaho. Weston is in Cache Valley near Franklin and Preston. That year he was 11, and he began doing grown-up work on his family's new farm. The story of Lars and the people of Weston is the story of thousands of other **pioneers**. These brave people came to make a new life in this great new land.

Weston was started in 1865 when seven Mormon families settled along Weston Creek. Their first homes were dugouts. A dugout was a hole dug in the ground with a dirt roof built over the top. It had an open fireplace with a chimney. Wood was burned for both cooking and heating. None of these crude houses had stoves. People had to kneel on the dirt floor to do the cooking.

Wheat was the main crop the first year, planted by hand. Each family had a little strip of land divided by a small ditch. After the crops were planted, a large irrigation ditch was built. The large ditch fed the small ditches, and the small ditches watered the grain. They built a dam across the creek so the ditches would fill with water. The dam was made of willow sticks, sod, and dirt. They carried the dirt in large baskets made from willows and hung between two poles.

Lars tells us that beavers helped the Weston pioneers to build the dam. When the beavers saw that a dam was being built, they worked on it at night. The beavers would cut willows into pieces three or four feet long, and weave them together in the water. Then they would pack the sticks with mud. "The beavers ran the night shift, so they were a great help to the first settlers." In about four weeks, the dam had water flowing into the ditches.

When the grain was ripe, it was cut by hand. The cutting tool was a **scythe**, with a rack to catch the stems of grain. It was called a "cradle" or a "strong-arm reaper." There were no threshing machines, so the grain was tramped out by horses and oxen. The whole family shook the straw and removed it from the grain. The chaff was removed by throwing the grain up into the wind with a shovel. The wind would blow away the chaff and dirt, and leave the grain. The wheat had to be taken to Utah to be ground into flour.

The next year several farmers went together and bought an old threshing machine that was nearly worn out. Someone built a mill to grind the grain into flour. The flour mill was run by a water wheel placed in the creek. The water wheel turned large grinding stones that ground the wheat into flour.

It was 1869 before the pioneers of Weston built log houses to live in. They lived in their dugouts for four years. The log houses were much nicer. Each one had a large open fireplace at one end for cooking and heating. One of the houses had a cooking stove—the only stove in Weston.

Every year, crickets ate many of the crops. In 1871, some farmers built a machine to kill the insects. It had a **water wheel** on one end, and a pair of rollers on the other. The machine was put in the ditch. When the crickets came floating down the stream, they were crushed by the rollers. The water turned as brown as tobacco juice, but the machine couldn't kill all the insects. Many of the crops were lost anyway. Even so, 1871 was a good year for the families of Weston. They grew enough extra oats that year to buy cooking stoves.

Behind the mules is a large steam-powered tractor. The steam tractor was used to help with threshing grain and other hard farm work. However, horses or mules had to haul tanks of water to the steam tractor. The animals also hauled the grain out of the field. IDAHO HISTORICAL SOCIETY

After the horse-drawn mower cut the grain, the stalks of grain were gathered by hand and tied into bundles. The bundles were leaned together into a shock. Why do you think the grain was piled this way? BISBEE - TWIN FALLS PUBLIC LIBRARY

Review Questions

1. Many early pioneers had to farm without using ____________. [*151*]
2. Lars had to live in a ____________ when the family moved to Weston. [*152*]
3. The Weston farmers had to build ditches and a dam so that ________________________. [*152*]

Ideas To Talk About

1. Why were the people of Weston so poor at first?
2. Why do you think the people of Weston lived in dugouts at first, instead of building log houses right away?
3. What was some of the hard work that the Weston farmers had to do?

Pioneer Life In Boise Valley.

Lida Johnson was born in a cabin with a dirt floor and a dirt roof. The year was 1864, and the place was Eagle Island near Boise City. The log cabin was one of the first in the valley. The following year the family moved to a place near Caldwell. Later she wrote about her early life.

"Mother cooked in a fireplace in the wintertime, and at an outdoor campfire in the summer. We baked potatoes in hot ashes covered with hot coals, and they were more delicious than when baked in an oven. As worms were unknown in those days, we left the roasting ears [corn] in the husk, and these were placed in the hot ashes to roast. . . . Chickens and wild game were roasted in the same manner. . . . Other foods were cooked in a big iron kettle hung on a tripod over the fire."

"For winter use, Mother dried apples, gooseberries, pumpkin and squash, which were our main fruits and vegetables for winter use. About 1880 we first used canning as a method of preserving fruit and vegetables. Tin cans were used, and the tops were soldered on with a soldering iron. . . . Our brooms were made with broomcorn stock. Our tools were crude but satisfactory."

"It was my job during the summer months to make enough lye for Mother to make soap. This, of course, was done after hog killing in the fall. . . . Father made an ash hopper, and I would fill it with wood ashes from our fire. I would keep putting water on the ashes, and the lye would drip through into a pan beneath the hopper. Our washing was done in a large barrel with a big chugstick that was flat at one end."

"It was 1886 before we used glass jars for canning. I was a girl in my teens before Mother had her first cookstove, and I was nearly grown before we had our first chairs."

"Father did all his plowing, hauling wood, and stacking hay and grain with ox teams until the early '70s, when he got his first team of horses from immigrants." (Mrs. Lida M. Johnson Isham, "Reminiscences," *The Idaho Statesman*, July 24, 1932.)

Cooking And Heating.

Pioneers didn't have an easy time cooking. Cooking over a fireplace was better than kneeling on a dirt floor. However, cooking with a fire-

Washing clothes with this 1888 model washing machine was much easier than washing clothes by hand. How do you think the water got into the tub? #6–93–1A U OF I LIBRARY

place was not easy. It was very exciting when a family could afford to buy a cooking stove. The fireplace or cooking stove was used both for cooking and for heating the house. The stoves burned wood, though in later times some people burned coal.

Log houses were drafty because of the many cracks between the logs. The people tried to keep the cracks sealed with mud, but a lot of cold air came through anyway. Because of this, log houses were hard to keep warm. Of course, the house was warm only while the fire was burning. At night the fire went out, and the house got cold. Someone always had to get up in the cold house the next morning and build the fire. There were no warm floors to walk on. The whole family might shiver into their clothes before the house was warm. The family was up at daybreak. The animals had to be fed, and there were dozens of household jobs to do. In Idaho, men, women, and children often shared the field work.

You could cook up almost any kind of delicious food in this 1905 kitchen. What kind of fuel do you think the stove burned? IDAHO HISTORICAL SOCIETY

Hot water had to be heated in a kettle or tub over the fire. Every fireplace or stove had a kettle of hot water for general use. Bathing was done in a metal or wooden tub set up near the fire. Extra water had to be heated for bath water. Several people might bathe in the same water before it was thrown out. It was so much trouble to take a bath, people didn't bathe very often.

Schools and churches were also drafty and hard to heat. They were heated with big, wood-burning stoves. A big **potbellied stove** was part of every schoolroom. In winter, the sides of the stove might glow red-hot. People complained that they roasted on one side and froze on the other.

What did your great-grandparents use these kitchen tools for? Study the picture and make some guesses. This picture was taken in an antique store. VIRGIL YOUNG

Running water and indoor toilets were unknown in Idaho Territory. Water didn't come from a faucet. It had to be carried by hand from a stream or a well. Later there were hand pumps that pumped water from under the ground. Water for washing hands and faces was poured into a basin, then dumped out when it was dirty. Most people had to wash in cold water.

Bathrooms were unknown on farms and in most small towns until well into the 1900s. "Outhouses" or "privies" served the people until they got running water in their houses. Like other things, running water and toilets came to the larger towns first. Farms were the last places to get them.

The home of Dr. Thayer appeared this way in 1898. Wooden homes were comfortable, but didn't last as long as homes made of brick or stone. IDAHO HISTORICAL SOCIETY

This fine home was built in Boise in 1905. How many years do you think homes like this will last? IDAHO HISTORICAL SOCIETY

The Hatch home in Franklin was built in the 1870s. It was built of cut stones. IDAHO DEPARTMENT OF COMMERCE

Pot-bellied stoves were used to heat offices, stores, schools, and homes. Notice that the office has electric lights. In what year do you think this picture was taken? #12–193 U OF I LIBRARY

Review Questions

1. Lida Johnson was born in a cabin that had a __________ and a __________. [*154*]
2. What kind of foods did Lida's family dry for winter? (a) __________ (b) __________ (c) __________ (d) __________ [*154*]
3. Soap was made from hog fat and __________. [*154*]
4. Most pioneers burned __________ for cooking and heating. [*155*]
5. Log cabins were cold because __________. [*155*]
6. Running water and indoor toilets were __________ in Idaho Territory. [*155*]

Ideas To Talk About

1. If pioneer life was so hard, why do you think people lived that way?
2. What do you think would have been the hardest thing about pioneer life?
3. What do you think would have been the best thing about pioneer life?

Lighting The Home.

Light was a problem for the pioneers. Candles and lamps were used indoors. Candles could be bought, but people often made them at home using animal fat. Lamps burned kerosene, whale oil, lard, beef fat, and other such things. There were a few gasoline lamps by 1871. Lamps gave off a dim, smoking, flickering light. The light was so poor that few people could read much by lamp light without getting sleepy. If young Abe Lincoln read by firelight, he must have had tired eyes. Lamps were not very safe, either. Broken and exploding lamps were known to burn down many a house. Most people got up at daybreak, and went to bed shortly after dark.

Electricity was first used in Idaho in 1882. A mining company near Ketchum built a dam that made electricity for their mine. Hailey was the first town to have electric lights. The lights were turned on May 19, 1887. Boise had wanted to be

Pioneers used these items for lighting. All of them burn kerosene except the candle. A glass lamp was used to light a room. The lantern with the handle could be carried outside to light a path or barn at night. Breaking a kerosene lamp could set the house on fire. VIRGIL YOUNG

first, but its lights weren't turned on until July 4, 1887.

Boise's electricity came from a power plant run by water in an irrigation canal. The power plant stood along Boise Avenue south of the present Boise State University. In 1887, it was reported that Boise had 275 electric "lamps" in use. By 1889, Boise had put up 40 electric street lights. The same year, at least two of Boise's hotels put in electric lights.

Idaho Was A Good Place To Be A Pioneer.

Even though pioneer life was hard, Idaho was a good place to begin farming. The gold and silver mines brought large numbers of people who needed to buy food. People in the mining camps and early towns bought food and horses raised on Idaho farms. In this way, farmers got money needed for their families and homes. They could also buy farm machinery and build farm buildings.

The mines brought a flow of money into Idaho. Because of this, Idaho Territory was a

Members of this pioneer farm family lived near Moscow for many years. This picture was taken around 1905. VIRGIL YOUNG

good place to make a living. In many parts of the United States, there were no nearby markets for farm goods. Farmers in those places remained poor for a long time.

Review Questions

1. Lamps that burned kerosene and animal fat gave off a ____________ light. [*156*]
2. Electricity first came to Idaho in the year ____________ at a mine near Hailey. [*157*]
3. In 1887, ____________ became the first Idaho town to have electric lights. [*157*]
4. Idaho was a good place to begin farming because ________________________. [*157*]
5. The mines brought a flow of ____________ into Idaho Territory. [*158*]

The first school in St. Maries was in this log school building. The picture was taken in 1885 or 1886. #5-69-1 U OF I LIBRARY

Pioneer Schools.

School at Florence. Idaho pioneers wanted schools for their children. The first public school in Idaho opened in the mining town of Florence during the winter of 1864–1865. Statira Robinson came from Ohio to Idaho to teach that school. Her husband had come to seek gold, and he had left his family in Ohio. The miners and businessmen "passed the hat" for enough money to bring Mrs. Robinson to Florence.

To get to Florence, Statira Robinson and her two children went down the Atlantic coast by boat to Panama. They crossed Panama on land, then took a boat to San Francisco. From there they came by boat to Portland and then to Lewiston. They came from Lewiston to Mount Idaho by wagon, then by saddle horse to Florence. It was a long, hard trip for Mrs. Robinson and her two small children.

The Florence school was a good building for that time and place. It was 12 feet wide and 14 feet long, with walls eight feet high. It was built of logs. The floor was made of hand-sawed boards, and the roof had handmade shingles. The furniture was simple but strong. The one desk for the whole school was a heavy log ripped down the center and set on four strong legs. The top was planed and sanded until it was smooth. Everyone sat on a bench made in the same way.

The blackboard was a piece of wood about 18 inches wide and three feet long. It was made black with lamp black. A carpenter gave the children some chunks of chalk to write with. The books were any that the parents happened to have. In those days, parents bought their children's books. They took the books from school to school as they moved. It is likely that no two children in Florence had the same books.

There were only six children in the Florence school, and one of them was the son of the Robinsons. These six children were Idaho's only "public school" children that year. There was no school in Florence the next year, for most of the people had moved away by then.

Review Questions

1. The first public school in Idaho was at ____________ in the winter of ____________. [*158*]
2. The school at Florence lasted only ____________ school year(s). [*158*]

Ideas To Talk About

1. Why do you think the people of Florence went to so much trouble to have a school?
2. Describe the school at Florence.

School at Franklin. The Florence school was not Idaho's first school for white children, however. That honor belongs to the 13 families who settled Franklin. During their first fall in Franklin (1860), the settlers started a school. It began in the home of its teacher, Hanna Comish. The school had 20 children.

Later that fall, the men of Franklin built a one-room schoolhouse. It was made of logs, and had a dirt floor and a dirt roof. Because the roof leaked, the children went home when it rained. The school term lasted three months. The Franklin school was started before Idaho Territory was formed in 1863. It wasn't a "public school," because there were no school laws and no school taxes.

School at Weston. A school was built in Weston in 1869. Lars Frederickson went to the Weston school when he was a boy. The farmers of Cache Valley had less money to spend than did the miners at Florence. Because of this, the Franklin and Weston school buildings were not as good as the one at Florence.

The Weston school was a log building 18 feet by 30 feet. The school had no furniture except benches to sit on. The benches had no backs and no desk tops. The children used their knees for desks. They had no notebooks; they wrote on slates. When the slates were filled and the teacher had seen them, they were rubbed off and used again. The school lasted only three months during the winter. There was no school during the summer, because all the children worked on the farms.

Moscow's first public school (Russell School) was built in 1884. This picture, taken around 1886, shows a "fine two-story building." #5-1-4A U OF I LIBRARY

The Buhl High School girls' basketball team was Idaho State Champion in 1925, 1926, and 1927. They were also Northwest Champions in 1925 and 1926. The girls went to Kansas for the national play-off games. Before they could play, they had to shovel snow off the outdoor court. The Buhl team lost but had a great trip.
VIRGIL YOUNG

Ideas To Talk About

1. How were the schools in Cache Valley (Franklin and Weston) different from the school at Florence?

2. Why were these schools different from the school at Florence?

Other Schools. Some schoolhouses were better than the one at Weston, and some were worse. In 1865–1866, one of the worst was at Dixie in Boise Valley. The school was a log house measuring 12 feet by 14 feet. It had a dirt floor and a low roof covered with dirt. The roof was made of logs, then covered with grass and dirt. It had plenty of fresh air, for the windows and doors were just openings. There was no way to close them. The children did not go to school in cold weather.

The pioneers built whatever kind of schools they could afford. When the people were poor, the schools were poor. As the people earned more money, the schools became better. In the 1880s, there was a great interest in building better schools in Idaho. Emmettsville boasted of a new two-story school with "modern furnishings." Lewiston built a six-room three-story school with "modern furnishings." Many Idaho towns built new and better schools during this time.

In 1882, Boise City built the finest school in Idaho. It was a four-story building with 16 rooms. The school and grounds took up a whole city block. The school had about 700 students in 13 grades, from primary through high school. This was the only public high school in Idaho Territory. The building stood where the Idaho capitol building now stands. "Old Central School" was torn down in 1919 to make room for one wing of the state capitol.

Schools were built wherever people lived. Since most people lived on farms, most schools were in the country. A country school was most often a one-room school. Children of all grades were taught together in the same classroom. The children walked to school, or sometimes rode horses. Since horses were generally needed at home for farm work, not many children rode horses to school.

One-room and two-room schools were used in Idaho until modern times. It was not until 1947 that most of Idaho's country schools were closed. After that, the farm children were bused to schools in town. Today you can still see some old country schoolhouses. Watch for them when you are driving on Idaho's country roads.

These children are doing their lessons at Moscow's Whitworth School in 1936 or 1937. How is this classroom different from yours? VIRGIL YOUNG

Review Questions

1. Idaho's first school for white children was built at ____________ in the year ____________. [*159*]
2. The only public high school in Idaho Territory was built at ____________ in the year ____________. [*160*]
3. Most schools in Idaho Territory were built in the ____________ for farm children. [*160*]
4. Country schools most often had only ____________ schoolroom(s), where children of all grades were taught together. [*160*]
5. Schools in Idaho Territory became better when ________________________. [*160*]

This 1912 photo shows children waiting in horse-drawn school buses (wagons). The school is Bickel School in Twin Falls. BISBEE - TWIN FALLS PUBLIC LIBRARY

Stagecoaches were used in Idaho until cars replaced them. Notice that the street is not paved. BISBEE - TWIN FALLS PUBLIC LIBRARY

Transportation Was Slow And Difficult.

You already know that many of the miners had to walk to the mines. The miners joked about it, calling it "Foot and Walker's Transportation Line." In the spring of 1863, a saddle train began to carry miners to the Boise Basin mines from the Columbia River. This was a string of about 20 horses or mules. Sixteen animals carried passengers, and the other four carried goods and baggage.

Stagecoaches began to replace saddle trains in 1864 as soon as wagon roads were built. A stagecoach was pulled by a team of four or six horses. It carried passengers, mail, and "fast" freight. Much of the gold and silver from the mines was shipped by stage. The stagecoach was the most important means of transportation in the West until railroads were built.

Riding a stage was not much fun. The ride was noisy and bumpy, and the passengers were jammed together inside. The rest stops were few and very poor. Stage stations were almost always dirty and smelly, and often the food was bad. Passengers suffered from dust and heat in the summer. In the spring and fall there was mud, and in winter there was snow and cold weather. You could depend on mosquitoes and rattlesnakes in warm weather. Sometimes a stagecoach was held up by bandits. They would rob the passengers and steal the mail and gold if any was aboard.

Idaho was served by two important stage lines. One ran 675 miles from Salt Lake City to The Dalles, Oregon. It made three trips a week. The route passed through the Malad and Raft River valleys, through the Snake River Valley, then west to the Columbia River. The other stage line ran from Salt Lake City to Virginia City, Montana. It passed through eastern Idaho and crossed the river at Eagle Rock (Idaho Falls).

Today very few old stage stations are left standing. This station was on the stage road between Poison Creek and Jordan Valley. Why do you think this building has lasted longer than some of the others? IDAHO HISTORICAL SOCIETY

Before wagon roads were built, food and goods were carried to the mines by **pack trains**. These were strings of pack horses or mules loaded with as much as they could carry. A mule could carry as much as 450 pounds. A pack train might have as many as 40 or 50, or more, animals. During 1860 and 1861, every single thing used by the 12,000 people living around Pierce City and Orofino City was carried there by pack

Branco Station was a stage station about five miles below Silver City. Standing on the hub of the stage is James Hawley, who later became Idaho's governor in 1910. IDAHO HISTORICAL SOCIETY

Pack trains carried loads over trails where wagons and coaches couldn't go. Mr. Dittman's pack horses are seen here at Ferrel between 1895 and 1905. What kind of goods do you think these horses carried? #5–3–2G U OF I LIBRARY

animals! The ever-suffering animals even packed huge pieces of heavy mining machinery into the high mountain country.

Toll Roads, Bridges, and Ferries.

Wagon roads and bridges were badly needed. Idaho's government had no money to build roads and bridges in those early years. Instead, someone would build a road, bridge, or **ferry**, then charge people a **toll** to use it. Idaho had at least 40 ferries on the Snake River alone, and at least 13 on other rivers. Later, counties took over the job of building roads. Even so, there were still toll bridges and ferries in use after Idaho became a state.

Toll roads and toll bridges were used for heavy **freight wagons**. Freight wagons were heavy and slow moving, but could carry very heavy loads. A single wagon might haul as much as five tons. However, they could go only 12 or 15 miles a day. The large loads made the cost of hauling goods cheaper. In turn, this made the prices of goods in mining camps cheaper.

A freight wagon was pulled by several teams of horses, mules, or oxen. There were from 12 to

This ox team is pulling a very heavy piece of machinery near Hailey. The animals are hitched together in pairs. How many oxen are in this team? IDAHO HISTORICAL SOCIETY

20 animals, two to a team. The rough and tough drivers of those teams had interesting names. A **mule skinner** drove mule teams, and a **bull whacker** drove ox teams. They would crack their long whips and swear their animals over steep mountains, through roaring streams, and through all kinds of weather. Freighting was a way of life in the early West, just as trucking is today.

Review Questions

1. A string of horses or mules that carried passengers was called a ____________. *[161]*

Hawkins toll gate was on the road between Placerville and Horseshoe Bend. What was a toll gate used for? IDAHO HISTORICAL SOCIETY

2. Before the railroads were built, the ____________ was the most important means of transportation in the West. [*161*]

3. A string of horses or mules that carried freight was called a ____________. [*161*]

4. Teams of horses, mules, or oxen pulled wagons with very heavy loads. These slow-moving wagons were called ____________. [*162*]

5. People had to pay money to use roads, bridges, and ferries. This money was called a ____________. [*162*]

Freight wagons were sturdy and could carry very heavy loads. Try to find the brakes on these wagons. #6–46–1A U OF I LIBRARY

Ideas To Talk About

1. Why were stage lines, pack trains, and freight wagons important to Idaho Territory?

2. Why were toll roads, toll bridges, and toll ferries important to Idaho Territory?

In 1916, Buhll's freight wagon hauled freight from Calder to Mica Creek. What kind of animals are these? #6–46-A U OF I LIBRARY

Ferries carried people, horses, wagons, stagecoaches, and other things across rivers. The ferry at Peck is seen here in August 1910. What river did this ferry cross? #5-4-3H U OF I LIBRARY

Steamboats In Idaho.

It may be strange to think of **steamboats** in a country of mountains and desert. Idaho has a great deal of water, though. Over the years, dozens of steamboats worked up and down the Columbia and Snake rivers. The first steamboat to reach Lewiston was the **Colonel Wright**. The steamboat **Idaho** brought many miners to Lewiston, and gave its name to the Idaho mines. Steamboats carried large loads of passengers and freight.

Steamboats also ran on Lake Coeur d'Alene and Lake Pend Oreille. Shallow boats carried freight up the Coeur d'Alene River to Cataldo. At Cataldo, the freight was unloaded and hauled to the Coeur d'Alene mines in wagons. Steamboats became less important and finally disappeared as railroads were built to all parts of Idaho.

It is interesting that Lewiston is once again

The steamboat *Coeur d'Alene* met the train to trade loads at the Old Mission Landing (Cataldo) on the Coeur d'Alene River. Why do you think the boat didn't go any further up the Coeur d'Alene River? #6-38-2 U OF I LIBRARY

The Union Pacific Railroad did not bring its tracks to Boise until 1925. This huge crowd is celebrating the first cross-country passenger train to come to Boise. The sign in the crowd says "We have waited 40 years for this train." #5-8-5K U OF I LIBRARY

Idaho's "seaport" city. Modern tugboats now haul barges loaded with logs, lumber, grain, and other products from Lewiston to the Pacific coast.

The Iron Horse Comes To Idaho.

Pioneers liked to call trains the "iron horse." Idaho's first railroad was built from Utah to Franklin in 1874. The Utah and Northern Railroad later connected Ogden, Utah, with the Montana mining country. It could haul passengers and freight faster and easier than anything else in Idaho. This iron horse could go as fast as 40 miles an hour! It averaged 20 miles an hour between Ogden and Franklin, even with stops for other towns.

Between 1880 and 1882, the Northern Pacific Railroad brought its line through the Idaho panhandle. This connected northern Idaho with far-off markets. Idaho's forest and mining products could then be shipped to the eastern United States.

These two railroads built the farming country of northern and eastern Idaho. They made it possible to sell farm crops to outside markets. Before long, settlers had filled the rest of the rich farmland in these places.

Huge railroad trestles were built in northern Idaho because of the rough hilly country. Wooden trestles such as this one are still used in northern Idaho. #6-47-1 U OF I LIBRARY

Between 1882 and 1884, the Union Pacific Railroad built the Oregon Short Line across southern Idaho. This railroad made southern Idaho grow. Towns sprang up along the tracks, and people moved to those towns for jobs. Idaho

Roads weren't the only problems suffered by automobile travelers. This photo was taken on the road between Lowman and Idaho City. What are these people doing? IDAHO HISTORICAL SOCIETY

Early automobile travel was much better than horse and stagecoach. However, it was many years before Idaho roads caught up with the automobile age. Notice the narrow rutted road in this 1930 picture. #12–177 U OF I LIBRARY

cattle and sheep could then be shipped to market more easily. Perhaps most important, the railroad speeded the settling of the rich farmland in southern Idaho. It brought new farms, new towns, new jobs, and new businesses.

Newspapers Keep Idaho In Touch With The Outside World.

It may be hard to think of newspapers in those rough and tough mining camps. The fact is, many miners and settlers were eager for news. At first, newspapers in the camps came from places like Walla Walla and The Dalles. There were also papers from far-off cities like San Francisco or New York. The papers could be weeks or months old, traveling slowly and passing through many hands. Miners might pay as much as $2.50 for a single copy of such a paper.

The desire for news caused newspapers to be printed in Idaho Territory. Idaho's first newspaper was *The Golden Age*. It began in Lewiston in 1862 and was printed until 1865. The *Boise News* began in Idaho City (then Bannack City) in 1863. Later its name was changed to the *Idaho World*, and it remained an important newspaper for more than 50 years.

The Idaho Statesman started in Boise City in 1864 as *The Idaho Tri-Weekly Statesman*. It became a daily paper in 1888, and is now Idaho's largest newspaper. The *Owyhee Avalanche* started in Silver City in 1865. It was printed until 1932. Several other papers started in Idaho Territory are still in business.

Most of Idaho's early papers were printed only once a week, not every day like many papers today. *The Golden Age* was a small, four-page paper with six columns to the page. Such papers took most of their news out of larger newspapers printed in larger cities. Because of this, news was quite old by the time it appeared in an Idaho newspaper.

This is a Fourth of July celebration at Orofino in 1900. What are these people celebrating on the Fourth of July? A. B. CURTIS #13-X33 U OF I LIBRARY

The Telegraph And Telephone Come To Idaho.

Telegraph. When **telegraph** wires reached Idaho, they connected Idaho with other parts of the United States. People could then send and receive messages by **telegram**. Idaho's newspapers could receive news as quickly as papers in other places. Idaho's first telegraph station was built in Franklin in 1869. A line connected Franklin with Salt Lake City.

Silver City was the first town in Idaho to receive world news by "lightning." It happened in 1874 over a wire from Winnemucca, Nevada. The wire was run from Silver City to Boise City in 1875.

Telephone. Idaho's first telephone line reached Franklin from Utah in 1868. In the next several years, telephone service spread slowly among Idaho's larger towns. In 1884, Idaho's largest city, Boise, had fewer than three dozen telephones. However, by 1887, the number had grown to at least 50 for calls within the city. There were several others for making long-distance calls.

Most of Idaho had to wait for telephone and telegraph service. The railroads needed telegraph and telephone service, so railroad towns got them first. After the railroad towns had service, it was only a matter of time until wires were run to other towns.

Idaho is a long way from the large California cities—San Francisco, Sacramento, and Los Angeles. We are much farther from the large cities of the East. The telegraph and the telephone, together with the railroad, brought Idaho into touch with those distant places. These were the beginnings of the instant communication that we enjoy today.

Review Questions

1. Idaho's first newspaper was printed in the town of ____________ in the year ____________. [*166*]

Many early telephones looked like this. When the phone rang, you heard the two bells at the top. You spoke into the mouthpiece on the front and listened with the receiver that hangs on the left side. The handle on the right was used to ring the telephone operator. VIRGIL YOUNG

2. Idaho's largest newspaper today is *The Idaho Statesman*. It was started in the town of ____________ in the year ____________. [*166*]
3. Most Idaho towns could thank the ____________ for bringing them telegraph and telephone service. [*167*]

Ideas To Talk About

1. Why do you think the miners and settlers were eager for news from other places?
2. Why do you think most of Idaho's newspapers were printed only once a week?
3. Why was it important for Idaho to be connected to the rest of the United States by railroad, telegraph, and telephone?
4. How do boats get from Lewiston to the Pacific Ocean?

Chapter 8 Skill Activities

Words And Ideas

In Chapter 8, you will find a number of key words printed in **bold** print. Each key word stands for an important idea. Answering these questions will help you understand some of the key words.

You can find the key words in the Glossary at the back of the book. The number after each question is the page where the idea is found in the book. Answer each question with a complete sentence.

1. What was the difference between a **bull whacker** and a **mule skinner?** [*162*]
2. Why did some pioneer families live in **dugouts**? [*151–152*]
3. Why were **ferries** needed during pioneer times? [*162*]
4. Why were **freight wagons** better than **pack trains** for hauling goods? [*162*]
5. Who is a **pioneer**? [*151*]
6. What kind of fuel was burned in a **potbellied stove**? [*155*]
7. Why were **saddle trains** used instead of stagecoaches? [*161*]
8. What was a **scythe** used for? [*152*]
9. Where were **steamboats** used in Idaho? [*164*]
10. What is a **telegram**? [*166*]
11. What is a **toll**? [*162*]

Research Projects

1. **Telegraph.** Why did Idaho pioneers get so excited when the telegraph arrived? What did the telegraph do? Why was it important? How does it work? An encyclopedia will help you answer these questions.

Write a report about the telegraph. You might also want to build a simple telegraph set.

2. **Transportation.** Traveling was slow and difficult during pioneer times. There were no cars, trucks, or airplanes.

Write a report about pioneer transportation. You can use information in this book.

3. **Artifacts.** Many families have some pioneer items that they keep and treasure. These might be clothing, tools, kitchen items, toys, or other things. Ask people to share their artifacts with the class.

Have a one-day display of pioneer artifacts. Be very careful in handling such items. They are very old, and if anything happens to them, they cannot be replaced.

Grandparent's Day

Have a special Grandparents' Day to invite your grandparents and other senior citizens to school. Ask them to tell any pioneer stories that they may have learned as children. Your grandparents didn't live in pioneer times, but their parents or grandparents did.

Pioneer School Day

Did you know that pioneer school children were expected to sit up straight? That they answered their teacher with "yes, ma'am" or "yes, sir"? That they stood up when they recited?

Have a special Pioneer School Day. The following are some things to do that day:

(a) **Reading Class.** There is only one reading book for each grade. Everybody takes turns reading aloud. When it is your turn, you stand in front of the teacher's desk, line up your toes on the crack in the floor, and begin. The teacher will tell you when to stop.

(b) **Spelling Bee.** Everybody lines up across the front of the room. The teacher calls out words, and the students take turns spelling them aloud. Anyone who misses a word sits down. The last one standing is the champion.

(c) **Cipher Down.** Two students go to the blackboard to add or subtract. All other students practice the same problems at their seats. They must practice, because each of them will go to the board later.

The teacher calls out numbers, such as 124, 367, 423, 244. The students write them in a column. Finally, the teacher says "add." When they hear this, the students quickly draw a line across the bottom and work as fast as they can to get the right answer.

The first one to get the right answer wins that round. The loser sits down, and someone else comes up to compete with the winner. The last student left at the board is the winner.

(d) **Manners.** Don't forget to sit up straight, say "yes, ma'am" or "yes, sir," and stand up to recite.

Using Your Imagination

1. **Stagecoach Line.** Make a poster to advertise your own stagecoach line. It should point out the advantages of traveling on your stage line. Be sure to tell the cities that you serve, the distances between them, and the time schedule.

2. **Advertising Idaho.** Make a poster that advertises Idaho as a good place to settle. Idaho was a good place to be a pioneer. Why? What could you say to people to make them want to come to Idaho to live?

3. **Paint a Mural.** Paint a mural that shows the main activities of a pioneer family from sunrise until sunset.

4. **Model Pioneer Town.** Build a model pioneer town. Begin by studying pictures of real pioneer towns.

Your town should have houses, stores, a bank, a restaurant, and a livery stable. Larger towns will have a hotel and some saloons. Horses are tied to hitching rails and posts in front of the businesses. Main Street should be only two or three blocks long.

Buildings should be no more than three inches long. You can make them out of cardboard, clay, play dough, sugar cubes, or whatever you like. Most buildings were made of rough boards and had false fronts. Some houses were made of logs. Try to make your buildings look like those in pictures.

Reviewing Chapter 8

Main Ideas In This Chapter

1. Life was hard for Idaho's pioneers.
2. Pioneer children began doing adult work as soon as they were able.
3. The first pioneer homes were crude and uncomfortable, and all housework was done by hand.
4. Much farm work had to be done with hand tools.
5. Wood was burned to do the cooking and heat the home.
6. At first there was no electricity. Light came from candles, lamps, and fireplaces.
7. Electricity was first used in Idaho in 1882, and it was 1887 before the first two towns had electric lights. The electricity was made using water wheels placed in streams.
8. Idaho was a good place to be a pioneer.
9. Idaho's first school for white children was built in Franklin in 1860. The first **public** school was built in Florence in 1864.
10. Idaho pioneers went to great effort to have schools for their children.
11. The quality of the pioneer school depended on how much money people had to spend.
12. For transportation, early pioneers used saddle trains, stagecoaches, and freight wagons pulled by animals.
13. To travel from place to place, people used toll roads, toll bridges, and toll ferries.
14. Steamboats were used to bring people and supplies up the Columbia and Snake rivers to Lewiston and the northern Idaho mines. Steamboats were also used on Lake Coeur d'Alene, Lake Pend Oreille, and the larger rivers of northern Idaho.
15. Railroads helped fill Idaho Territory with settlers, because Idaho products could be shipped to far-off markets.
16. Idaho newspapers were started because miners and settlers were eager for news from the outside world.
17. Newspapers, the telegraph, and the telephone brought Idaho into touch with other parts of the United States.

Further Reading For Children

Brink, Carol Ryrie. *Caddie Woodlawn.* New York: Aladdin Paperbacks, Simon & Schuster, 1990. [A Newberry winner. Mrs. Brink was born in Moscow and wrote about her grandmother's life as a pioneer girl.]

Gregory, Kristiana. *Jimmy Spoon and the Pony Express.* (An Apple Paperback) New York: Scholastic, Inc., 1994.

Nevin, David. *The Expressmen.* (Time-Life Series of the Old West) New York: Time-Life Books, 1974. [Excellent photographs and drawings of transportation in the old west.]

Nevin, David. *The Soldiers.* (Time-Life Series of the Old West) New York: Time-Life Books, 1973–74. [Interesting pictures of soldiers who were sent to protect the western settlers and the Indians that they fought. Maps and art work.]

Tunnell, Michael O. *Mailing May.* (A Greenwillow Book) New York: HarperCollins, 1997. [Award-winning book. Little May longs to visit her grandmother. May's parents cannot afford a railway ticket for the 75-mile trip. By a strange circumstance, her parents are able to send her on the mail train as mail (a "baby chick") for 53 cents. Based on a true 1914 Idaho story.]

Wheeler, Keith. *The Railroaders.* (Time-Life Series of the Old West) New York: Time-Life Books, 1973. [Interesting and startling pictures of the railroads as they were built across America.]

Wheeler, Keith. *The Townsmen.* (Time-Life Series of the Old West) New York: Time-Life Books, 1975. [Interesting photographs of pioneer settlements and towns. Lots of excellent pictures of pioneer people.]

Wilder, Laura I. *Growing Up in the Little House.* (A Puffin Book Paperback) New York: Viking Penguin, Inc, 1996. [A biography of Laura I. Wilder. Her story offers an excellent glimpse of pioneer life.]

Wilder, Laura I. *Little House on the Prairie.* New York: HarperCollins Publishers, 2000. [Story of growing up in pioneer times. A television series was based on this book. Earlier editions may be available.]

Life in Idaho.

Sarah Easterday

Can you picture living in a family with one brother, four sisters, thirteen kittens, five cats, two dogs, ten cows, and my parents?

My family and I live across Balanced Rock canyon. Every day, I ride the school bus twelve miles to Castleford Elementary School. Some people travel far to see the famous Balanced Rock, but I see it twice a day as I travel to and from school.

Most of the farms around us are large, and we all irrigate with sprinklers.

There are no telephone lines where I live, so my dad put a mobile phone in our home. It is powered by a battery.

I am a modern-day pioneer.

Amy Kinyon

After school I feed my calf and horses, and help my dad feed. I started driving a truck to help feed when I was about five years old. In the summertime, I sit on the tractor while my dad and granddad plant beans. I watch to see if anything goes wrong.

I like to ride my horse in the desert and help brand calves. My favorite times are playing with my kitten and 4-H steer. I like 4-H very much. Someday I wish to win grand champion.

Krista Brown

When I wake up at 6:30 A.M., I feed my rabbits hay and sometimes pellets. After school I feed the rabbits, cows, and chickens. We have 35 rabbits. They are my favorite, but I like all of the animals. I take 4-H and my project is rabbits.

We have 14 laying hens that I feed. They are really funny looking right now because they are molting. This means they are losing their feathers.

I help my dad in the summer during irrigation season. I set tubes and get blisters on my hands, but it's fun to help.

I love living on a farm, because I learn a lot about animals of all kinds, and we don't have the worries of living in a city.

Karen Hudson

My brother and I feed our goats out of our hands. We have nine big goats and 19 little ones.

In the spring I help plant our garden, and when the vegetables come up, I help weed the garden. One thing our family plants is Indian corn.

Chapter 9
Farming: Idaho's Soil And Water

Farming Is Huge In Idaho.

Farming is one of Idaho's biggest businesses. About half of Idaho's people depend on farming for their living. Many are farmers, but many others work in businesses that depend on farming. Some businesses sell and ship the farmers' crops. Others process farm crops into the food we see in stores. Still others sell things that farmers need to buy. Idaho's farm crops are sold all across the United States, and many are sold to other countries.

Idaho's Rich Soil. Our **soil** is lasting wealth. With careful use, soil can grow crops year after year. Gold and silver mines may come and go. Forests may disappear when someone cuts down all the trees. New trees may take a person's lifetime to grow a new forest. The soil, however, will always be there. If we take good care of it, it can be farmed almost forever.

Idaho's settlers found that Idaho was blessed with rich soil. Valleys and prairies proved to grow fine crops. When the first farmers grew extra food, they sold it to other people. These were mostly miners and people living in the few small towns.

Irrigation canals carry life-giving water to farms in many parts of Idaho. Where does the water come from? IDAHO HISTORICAL SOCIETY

These cattle are grazing on a farm near Castleford. VIRGIL YOUNG

In the beginning, there were only a few towns, and the miners kept moving about. Fresh food could not be shipped very far. There was no way to keep it cold, and transportation was slow and hard. Roads were poor, and there were no cars or trucks. These things limited the amount of food that farmers could sell.

Railroads and Irrigation. Two things changed Idaho's farming—railroads and irrigation. Railroads could move heavy loads clear across America. Large amounts of grain and other crops could be shipped to far-off markets. Cattle and other animals could be hauled instead of being driven to market. Railroads made farming promising to those people who wanted to follow the pioneers. Idaho's empty lands invited people to come and begin farming. Many did.

Water was more important than the railroads. Without water, Idaho's desert land was suited only for grazing cattle, horses, and sheep. The desert soil was rich, however. Water could make crops grow and the land bloom. In southern Idaho, the story of farming is the story of **irrigation**.

Review Questions

1. About half of Idaho's people depend on ____________ to make their living. [*171*]
2. ______________ made it possible to sell farm crops and animals in far-off markets. [*172*]
3. ______________ made it possible to farm southern Idaho's desert land. [*172*]

Soil Conservation. **Soil conservation** means protecting our soil and using it wisely. We should all care about protecting our soil. Our soil is important to each and every one of us. Most of the food we eat comes from the soil, and without soil the human race would starve and die.

The most valuable soil is the **topsoil**. Topsoil is the rich top layer of soil that plants grow in. In most places, the layer of topsoil is less than a foot deep. Most plants must have this soil to grow. They can't live in the poor soil below it. It takes nature several hundred years to make just one inch of topsoil. On the other hand, careless use can destroy this inch of soil in just a few weeks.

Soil is destroyed in many ways. **Erosion** is the most important way. When water washes soil away, it is called **water erosion**. At other times, the wind blows soil away. This is called **wind erosion**. When plants cover the soil, they help prevent the wind and water erosion. In the forests, the trees help keep the soil in place. On farms, certain crops keep the soil from washing or blowing away. America has lost millions of acres of soil because of poor farming and tree-cutting methods.

Soil is wasted in other ways, too. Bad farming methods can make the soil grow poor crops. Much farm land is lost because our cities grow and take more and more land. Other soil is lost by **pollution**. Soil is sometimes poisoned by chemicals and other kinds of waste.

Soil conservation isn't just a farm and forest problem. People in towns and cities need to take good care of the soil in their yards and gardens. Soil must not be harmed or wasted. When soil is lost, it is lost forever. Nature will not replace it in our lifetimes.

Ideas To Talk About

1. How is soil wasted or destroyed?
2. Why is our soil important to us?
3. Why is soil conservation a problem for city people just as much as it is for farm people?

Water comes from the canals to the fields in small ditches. In this picture, siphon tubes lift the water out of the ditch onto the field. Water runs across the field in small ditches called corrugations. What crop do you see here?
U. S. BUREAU OF RECLAMATION

Farming Depends On Water.

It takes a surprising amount of water to raise crops. In the states of Iowa and Missouri, there are about four inches of rain each month during the summer. This is plenty of water to raise fine crops. The Idaho panhandle receives from 22 to 32 inches of **rainfall** each year. This is plenty of water for growing grain, peas, hay, and other crops. Southern Idaho's desert soil gets almost no rainfall during the summer months.

A southern Idaho farmer waters his crops every eight to ten days during the summer. The crops must be watered from five to ten times, depending on the crop and the weather. Each watering puts four or more inches of water on the land. As much as 36 inches of water may be put on the land by the end of the summer.

Cattle and chickens eat grain that they turn into meat, milk, and eggs. It takes 1,800 gallons of water to grow enough grain to make **one pound of beef**. It takes 40 gallons of water to grow enough grain to make **one egg**. These amounts show how important irrigation is to southern Idaho.

Irrigation Tamed Idaho's Desert Land.

The dry lands of the American West are within sight of high mountains that store great amounts of water. The water is stored in the form of winter snow and summer rain. Special

These men are stacking hay by hand. The hay was cut by a horse-drawn mower. BISBEE - TWIN FALLS PUBLIC LIBRARY

Horses were an important source of power for farmers for many years. These men and horses have been picking up hay in the field and putting it on this stack. Try to find out the names of these machines. IDAHO HISTORICAL SOCIETY

ways are needed to bring this mountain water to the soil where it is needed. The Mormon pioneers of Utah and Idaho were America's pioneers in the science of irrigation.

Mormons began irrigating in Salt Lake City on July 24, 1847. Water from City Creek was turned into a small ditch and spread over a piece of dry ground. This idea worked well, and soon Mormon farmers spread through the Salt Lake Valley and the Great Basin. Mormon farmers arrived in Idaho's Lemhi Valley in 1855, bringing their ideas for watering the land. They built a small ditch that summer on Pattee Creek. Though Indian trouble forced them to leave for a while in 1858, this ditch is still being used today.

You will remember that Mormons began Idaho's first permanent white settlement at Franklin in 1860. Bear Lake Valley was settled in 1863 and Malad Valley in 1864. In the years to follow, more and more Mormon farmers spread into the rich valleys of eastern Idaho. The farmers at Preston built a **canal** 15 miles long in 1871. It carried water to 15,000 acres and cost $30,000.

The Utah and Northern Railroad was built to Franklin in 1873. This invited people to come to eastern Idaho and fill up the empty land. The railroads and irrigation kept a flow of farmers, mostly Mormon, coming into eastern Idaho long after Idaho became a state.

Irrigation quickly spread from the Bear River Basin to the Snake River Valley. More and more canals were built, and more and more land was farmed. By 1907, there were 264 canals along the Snake River.

Water was claimed from the streams in the

Steam-powered tractors were used through the 1920s. They made it possible to thresh large amounts of grain. Why do you think steam-powered tractors went out of use? IDAHO HISTORICAL SOCIETY

Today potatoes are harvested with modern equipment. One machine digs them and loads them into the truck. ORE-IDA FOODS, INC.

same way that gold was claimed from the ground. A person posted a notice beside the stream where the water was to be taken out. The claim was then recorded with the office of the County Recorder. The recorded water claim gave that person a **water right**. This gave the person the right to use a certain amount of water from the stream.

The farmers at Weston built a dam (with the help of beavers) and a canal by hand. A few could do the work when the stream was small. Early farms were watered by farmers working alone or by neighbors working together. This was true of the farms in the Boise, Payette, Weiser, and Cache valleys and around Lewiston. Ditches and canals were built with simple tools—picks and shovels. Perhaps a team of horses might pull a small scraper.

Bigger Dams And Ditches Are Needed. Soon all the easy places for building small dams and ditches were taken. To build more farms, bigger dams and bigger ditches were needed. This meant more money was

This photo, taken before 1919, shows the King Hill irrigation canal being built. This part, built above the ground, is called a flume. It was made of poured concrete with steel rods inside to make it strong. Canals were often built across rough, dry land such as this. KING HILL IRRIGATION DISTRICT

needed. People and machines had to be hired to do this kind of work.

In the 1880s, the railroad brought thousands of people who wanted desert land. Of course, more dams and canals were needed before the land could be farmed. This job was too large for neighbors working together. In 1894 and 1902, the government made new land and water laws. These laws helped bring water to more than two million acres of southern Idaho desert land.

Review Questions

1. What part of Idaho gets enough rainfall to grow crops without irrigation? ____________ [*173*]

2. What part of Idaho gets almost no rainfall during the summer months? ____________ [*173*]

3. It takes ____________ gallons of water to grow enough grain to make one egg. [*173*]

4. The ____________ were the first people to irrigate land in southern Idaho. [*174*]

Ideas To Talk About

1. Why did the first Idaho Mormon pioneers settle in southeast Idaho instead of some other part of Idaho?

Ira B. Perrine can be called the "Father of Magic Valley." Why? H. T. FRENCH

2. Soon bigger dams and bigger ditches were needed. Why couldn't neighbors get together to build them?

Ira Perrine Builds Magic Valley.

The government gave Idaho a million acres of desert land under a law called the Carey Act. Idaho then had to find ways to have dams and canals built. Also the land had to be divided and

Milner Dam brought farms and towns to Magic Valley. Where is this dam located? When was it built? VIRGIL YOUNG

A homestead family had to live on the land and farm it for five years. After that, the land became theirs. Many lived in small shacks such as this until they could afford a better house. This homestead was located in the Kuna area.

IDAHO HISTORICAL SOCIETY

sold for farming. The State of Idaho didn't have enough money to build the dams and canals. Instead, the state called on business people to do the work and sell the land to farmers.

Ira Perrine was the one who went to work to bring water to what is now Magic Valley. For many years, Perrine dreamed of the desert blooming like a giant garden. He had dreamed of using the mighty Snake River to water this garden. He tried to interest other people in his idea. However, the idea of putting a dam across the Snake River seemed crazy to most people. It made sense to dam a smaller stream, but who would be crazy enough to try to dam the Snake?

On October 11, 1900, Perrine posted claim notices on the north and south sides of the Snake River Canyon. Then he went to the County Recorder and paid the $2.00 filing fee. He had just claimed all the water in the Snake River!

Later, Perrine was able to find people and money to get the work started. In 1903, **Milner Dam** was built on the Snake River between Burley and Twin Falls. The dam was just a few miles above the spot where one of the Astorians had drowned in the boiling, rocky canyon in 1811. This was a bold attack on the mighty Snake. It was the beginning of a group of large dams that now tame the once wild river.

In 1903, a family could buy 160 acres of land for 50 cents an acre. The water right cost $25.00 an acre. Families bought the land and began clearing away sagebrush and planting crops.

A pioneer in Magic Valley is clearing his new land by grubbing out the sagebrush. The sagebrush had to be removed before the land could be farmed. The photo was taken about 1904.

BISBEE - TWIN FALLS PUBLIC LIBRARY

The blacksmith was important in any early American town. This blacksmith is putting a metal shoe on a horse. How is the shoe fastened to the horse's hoof? Why does the horse need a metal shoe? U OF I LIBRARY

The livery stable was an important business in early Idaho towns. This 1913 photo was taken in Craigmont, then known as Vollmer. #5-98-1A U OF I LIBRARY

This 1904 photo shows the first building in Twin Falls. A new town was just beginning. TWIN FALLS PUBLIC LIBRARY

By 1910, Twin Falls had several fine brick buildings on Main Street. BISBEE - TWIN FALLS PUBLIC LIBRARY

Their water came from large canals reaching out from Milner Dam. These carried water for many miles over thirsty land on both sides of the Snake River Canyon.

Magic Valley Grows. Towns sprang up. The towns grew as the farms grew rich crops. New wealth flowed into Idaho became of these new farms. Flour mills were built. Blacksmith shops, livery stables, hotels, hardware stores, and dry goods stores appeared in each new town. As the towns grew more, doctors, dentists, and lawyers arrived. Perrine's dream had more than come true.

The town of Twin Falls was begun in 1904. From the beginning, Twin Falls was the center of business for the new farming area. It remains so today. Other towns appeared: Buhl, Kimberly,

Ira B. Perrine farmed Blue Lakes Ranch in the Snake River Canyon for years before Milner Dam was built. If you look closely, you will see Blue Lakes Bridge and fruit orchards. BISBEE - TWIN FALLS PUBLIC LIBRARY

Hansen, Jerome, Wendell, Hazelton, Eden, and Murtaugh.

Some of the towns grew up on the south side of the canyon, and some grew up on the north side. Today we hardly notice this. We simply drive the highway from one town to another. However, the Snake River Canyon is nearly 500 feet deep between Twin Falls and Jerome. Its walls drop almost straight down from the desert floor.

For many years, the only way people could get from Twin Falls to Jerome was through the canyon. They had to go down a steep, winding road to the bottom of the canyon. There they had to cross the river on a ferry, then climb another

In 1927, the rim-to-rim steel bridge was built across the Snake River Canyon. People no longer had to use the Blue Lakes Bridge. Why was the rim-to-rim bridge better? VIRGIL YOUNG

This was King Hill in the early 1920s. How is this street different from most town streets today?
GLENN MILLS

berry bushes, and an orchard. There was also a ferry for crossing the river.

That sight must have seemed like magic to people looking down into the canyon from the desert above. The name Magic Valley, however, didn't come into use until 1937. Today it is the name for the 10,000 square miles of rich farm land. Magic Valley stretches from Rupert on the east to King Hill on the west. Do you believe in magic? Even if you don't, Magic Valley is a great name for this rich farming valley.

steep, winding road out of the canyon. In 1911, a bridge was built at the bottom of the canyon to replace the ferry. Still it was a terrible trip for horses and wagons, and for early gasoline cars.

In 1927, a steel bridge—stretching 1,400 feet from rim to rim—was built across the canyon near Twin Falls. How exciting it was not to have to make the terrible trip down into the canyon and back up again! There was a big celebration when the bridge opened. A crowd of 5,000 people gathered to hear Governor Baldridge speak. Mrs. Perrine christened the bridge with a bottle of sweet cider. Thousands of people gathered for barbecues, football games, dancing, and fireworks.

The Twin Falls bridge was built by business people, and it was a toll bridge for the first ten years. In 1937, the state bought it from its owners and removed the toll. The free bridge was then named Perrine Memorial Bridge. By the 1970s, the bridge was not able to carry the heavy trucks that travel most of America's highways. In 1976, the 1927 bridge was replaced by a newer and stronger Perrine Memorial Bridge.

Next time you cross the Perrine Memorial Bridge at Twin Falls, look down into the deep canyon. It is almost 500 feet down into the water. Looking west, you will see the Blue Lakes Country Club, named for the beautiful lakes on the canyon bottom. In the 1870s and 1880s, there was a post office, a stage station, and a ferry at the edge of the lower lake.

In 1884, Ira Perrine started Blue Lakes Ranch on this land. Soon several hundred acres were blooming with green pasture, cattle, hay, grain,

The Blue Lakes Bridge replaced the ferry between Twin Falls and Jerome. People still had to use the steep road in and out of the canyon. Notice the stagecoach crossing the bridge.
BISBEE - TWIN FALLS PUBLIC LIBRARY

A young cowboy is moving cattle on a present-day Magic Valley farm. VIRGIL YOUNG

Magic Valley farms now raise sheep and other farm animals. VIRGIL YOUNG

Review Questions

1. The man who brought water to Magic Valley was ____________. [*176–177*]

2. Magic Valley was irrigated only after the mighty ____________ River was tamed by ____________ Dam. [*177*]

Ideas To Talk About

1. Why did people think it was a crazy idea to try to put a dam across the Snake River?

2. Why did towns spring up as soon as irrigation water came to the dry lands of Magic Valley?

3. Why were the people of Magic Valley so excited when the steel rim-to-rim bridge was built across the Snake River Canyon at Twin Falls?

4. Why is Magic Valley a good name for this part of Idaho?

The City Of American Falls Is Moved.

Can you imagine moving a whole city, buildings and all? That happened to American Falls between 1923 and 1927. The town was moved to save the farms of Magic Valley.

Southern Idaho farmers suffered from bad **droughts** in 1905, 1919, and 1924. A drought is a time when there isn't enough water. In those years, the water in the Snake River was too low to fill all the irrigation canals. There were also other years when there wasn't enough water for all the farmers who needed it. Many farmers lost their crops from lack of water.

The first dams didn't store much water. Like Milner Dam, they were built mostly to force water into canals. This worked well as long as the river had enough water to fill the canals. However, more and more canals were being built,

American Falls Dam and Reservoir store water for Magic Valley. The tower standing in the water is an old grain elevator. Why do you think it is standing in the water? IDAHO HISTORICAL SOCIETY

and there wasn't always enough water to fill them all.

A river does not always have the same amount of water in it. Some winters bring more snow to the mountains than other winters. A heavy snow makes a heavy flow of water the next spring and summer. A light snow may leave farmers short of water the next summer. Also there is much more water in the spring than later in the summer. When warm weather comes and the snow begins to melt, water in the rivers can get very high. Later in the summer, there is much less water in the rivers.

In 1923, a study was done to find out what could be done about water for the farmers. It was decided that water needed to be stored for summer irrigation. Water can be stored by building a **storage dam** on a river. A large storage dam was needed on the Snake River above Magic Valley. This dam would catch much of the heavy spring flow and store it in a **reservoir**. Later, in the summer, water would be let out as the farmers needed it. The best place for the dam was at American Falls.

Problems. There were many problems with putting a dam at American Falls. To begin with, the town of American Falls and its 1,100 people sat right where the lake would be! Besides that, many farms would be flooded out.

To build the dam, several major things would have to be done. All of them cost a lot of money! First, the town would have to be moved to higher ground. Idaho Power Company would have to build a new electric power plant. Union Pacific Railroad would have to move three miles of track. The Snake River bridge would have to be raised 21 feet. The Fort Hall Indians would have to agree to give up more of their land. The U. S. government would have to agree to pay part of the cost. However, without the dam, the whole system of irrigation in Magic Valley might fail.

The Dam is Built. The American Falls Dam made history. All these problems were solved, and the dam was finished in 1927. It took 400 people working around the clock for two years and two months to do the job. As water filled up behind the dam, it made American Falls Reservoir. This man-made lake covers 88 square miles of land. The lake is 25 miles long and three and one-half miles wide.

The dam served well for many years. However, by the 1970s, the old dam began to show weak spots. A new American Falls Dam was completed in 1978. The American Falls Dam was and still is Idaho's largest irrigation project.

Review Questions

1. In 1905, 1919, and 1924, the Snake River was too low to ____________________. [*180*]

2. A time when there isn't enough water is called a __________. [*180*]

Ideas To Talk About

1. Why do rivers have less water in some years?

2. Why did the Snake River need a storage dam?

3. What were some of the problems of building a storage dam at American Falls?

Many fields are now irrigated with sprinklers instead of ditches. Why would some farmers choose to use sprinklers? IDAHO DEPARTMENT OF COMMERCE

Sprinklers Water Some Of The Land.

For many years, all irrigation was done by running water through canals and ditches to the fields. To water this way, the land must be nearly flat with a little slope. Also the land must be below the canal—water won't run uphill. In 1947, Julion Clawson drilled a deep well near the Minidoka Irrigation Project. He found a large amount of water deep in the ground. In only four years, he was sprinkling 24,000 acres of land

This huge sprinkling rig easily moves around the field in a great circle. How does this help the farmer? U. S. BUREAU OF RECLAMATION

with water pumped from under the ground.

By this time, electricity had arrived on most of Idaho's farms. With electricity and powerful electric pumps, more farmers began to sprinkle their land. Sprinklers can put water on land that isn't flat enough to irrigate from a ditch. Today thousands of acres of Idaho land are irrigated with sprinklers.

It has been found that sprinkling saves water. It spreads the water over the ground evenly. On the other hand, ditches often bring too much water to some places, and not enough to others. Sprinkling takes about one-fourth less water for an acre of land.

Northern Idaho. There is very little irrigation north of the Salmon River. The rich prairie land grows fine harvests of peas and wheat without irrigation. Most farms receive plenty of rainfall for crops. This is an important reason why northern Idaho was settled early.

Most northern Idaho farms do not need irrigation. Why not? VIRGIL YOUNG

Nearly all the good farmland was filled during the 1860s and 1880s.

When irrigation is needed, most is done by sprinkling. Much of northern Idaho is rolling prairie land. Ditches are impossible on such land. Lewiston, being lower, gets very little summer rain. Farms there are watered by sprinkling and with ditches. Rathdrum Prairie, north of Coeur d'Alene, is the largest piece of irrigated land in northern Idaho.

Ideas To Talk About

1. Why is some land irrigated with sprinklers instead of ditches?

2. How is farming different north of the Salmon River

Roger Wells. VIRGIL YOUNG

Life On a Farm.

By Roger Wells

In the morning I get up, get dressed, have breakfast, and feed the cats and my rabbits. I then walk up the road ¼ mile to catch the school bus with my brother. When I get home I watch some TV, then I practice the piano. After some work outdoors, I might watch TV, read, or play on the computer.

I have two does (female rabbits) and one buck (male rabbit). My brother has four rabbits. We take our rabbits to the fair as 4-H projects. We're both taking our bucks this year. My buck's name is Velvet, because he feels like it.

We grow alfalfa, wheat, barley, beans, and corn on our farm. My dad doesn't have any livestock. I pick rocks from the fields every spring, and pull weeds from the bean fields during the summer.

Last year I rode the bean combine to help my dad with threshing. My dad drove the tractor, and I would wave to signal him when the beans

Horses and wagons once hauled Idaho's famous potatoes to the train. The train took the potatoes to far-off markets. This Twin Falls picture was taken between 1910 and 1920. Notice how muddy the railroad yard is. BISBEE - TWIN FALLS PUBLIC LIBRARY

were up to the top of the bin. Then we would dump the beans into metal boxes that were on the truck. When the boxes were full, we took them to the place that bought the beans from us.

Sometimes I help my grandfather irrigate. I carry irrigation siphon tubes so he doesn't have to bend over. My grandfather's name is Frank Wells. He sold his farm to my dad and some of my dad's brothers. He still likes to help farm. My grandmother, Emma Wells, used to be a school teacher. Now she gardens and does things for her grandchildren. I'm glad that she lives on the farm near us.

My mother's parents are Arline and Ellis Fuller. He is a retired farmer who now enjoys carpentry. He built on to our house and built us a new garage. We got to help him because he had no helpers.

I enjoy living on a farm.

Roger Wells, Fourth Grade, Castleford Elementary School. Roger lives on a farm near Castleford, Idaho. His parents are Jon and Carol Wells.

Idaho Grows Many Kinds Of Crops.

It is easy to understand why early farmers came to Idaho and stayed. Just look at the choice of crops that can be grown in Idaho. The list of Idaho crops is long. There is room here to describe only the most important, however.

Horses worked well in the snow. These milk cans are full and on the way to the creamery. VIRGIL YOUNG

Beef cattle are Idaho's most valuable farm product and have been for many years. You have always heard of Idaho's famous potatoes. Idaho is indeed known around the world for its fine potatoes. Potatoes, hay, and wheat are Idaho's leading field crops. Potatoes rank first, but in recent years, hay has moved into second place ahead of wheat.

Beef cattle, hay, and wheat are raised in all parts of Idaho. Most of Idaho's potatoes are grown

Important Crops Grown in Idaho

Fruit Crops	Field Crops	Seed Crops	Livestock	Other Products
apples	barley	alfalfa	beef cattle	butter
apricots	beans (dry)	beans	chickens	cheese
cantaloupes	corn (canning)	corn	dairy cattle	eggs
cherries	corn (livestock)	grass	hogs	honey
grapes	hay	peas	horses	milk
peaches	hops	sheep	yogurt	
pears	lentils (dry)	trout		
prunes	mint			
	oats			
	onions			
	peas (dry)			
	potatoes			
	pumpkins			
	sugar beets			
	wheat			

This big team of horses is harvesting Palouse Country wheat. The machine is a combine, and the year is about 1900. #7-17-14 U OF I LIBRARY

Today large wheat ranches harvest their wheat this way. The combine mows the wheat, separates it from the straw, and dumps it into the truck. Is this a better way than using a combine that is pulled by horses? Why or why not? IDAHO WHEAT COMMISSION

Grain elevators are used to store wheat and other grain. This photo was taken at Genesee. VIRGIL YOUNG

in the Snake River Valley. The light desert soil and irrigation are ideal for potatoes. More than half are grown in eastern Idaho, and about one-fourth are grown in Magic Valley.

The farms of northern Idaho are well known for their wheat. The world record for the most pounds of wheat grown on an acre of land was earned by a Palouse farm. Latah and Nez Perce counties are famous for dry peas and **lentils**. Moscow calls itself "The Dry Pea Capital of the World."

Lewiston and the nearby canyon farms have many fruit orchards. Fruit and vine crops grow well in these deep canyons because of the warm temperatures. There is a long, frost-free growing season at less than 1,000 feet above sea level. Other northern Idaho crops are oats, barley, hay, beef and dairy cattle, hogs, and sheep.

The irrigated farms of southern Idaho grow more kinds of crops. Sugar beets are an important crop in the Snake River Valley. The Snake River Valley is well suited for seed crops. The soil is free from serious weeds and plant diseases. Some of the seeds grown are alfalfa, clover, beans, onions, corn, and garden vegetables. These seeds are sold in all parts of the United States.

Western Idaho grows most of Idaho's fruit and vine crops. The Payette and Boise valleys have a longer, frost-free growing season that is important for growing fruit. Fruits grown there are cherries, apples, prunes, peaches, pears, and apricots. Vine crops are watermelons, cantaloupes, cucumbers, and pumpkins. Many other crops grow on the farms of southern Idaho. A few of them are grain (several kinds), alfalfa, onions, green beans, cabbage, garlic, strawberries, tomatoes, popcorn, peppermint, and hops.

There are also dairy cattle, hogs, sheep, chickens and eggs, turkeys, and honey (from bees, naturally). There is almost nothing Idaho soil can't grow with water and the right temperature.

Ideas To Talk About

1. What are three of your favorite foods grown on Idaho farms?
2. Where in Idaho do you think your favorite foods are grown?

Much Idaho wheat is shipped to far-off markets through the Port of Lewiston—Idaho's "seaport." Here you see wheat pouring from an overhead pipe into a huge barge. The barge will carry the wheat down the Snake and Columbia rivers to Portland. From there, it will be shipped to Japan or Korea. VIRGIL YOUNG

Dams Are Found In Most Parts Of Idaho.

Today Idaho has dams almost everywhere: north, south, east, and west. Dams have four important uses. (1) They prevent floods. (2) They store water for irrigation. (3) They make electricity. (4) They make lakes for boating and fishing. The most important of these fight two of our oldest enemies: flood and drought.

Preventing Floods. Snow piles deep in the mountains during the winter. When the warm spring sunshine comes, the snow begins to melt. Often it melts so fast that the water flows over the river's banks and floods everything in its path. A flood can wash away farms and towns, drowning people and animals caught in its path. Before the 1930s, there were terrible floods in the Boise, Payette, and lower Snake river valleys.

Irrigation. Storage dams help slow down the rush of water before it gets to the farms and towns. Some of the heavy spring flow is caught and stored in the reservoirs behind the dams. They fill with water during the spring runoff. Later in the summer, the water is let out more slowly, and the farmers can use it for irrigation. Before there were dams, many rivers flooded every spring.

Electricity. Dams can also make electricity. The water falls through long tunnels inside the dam. The weight of the falling water turns a turbine. The turbine turns a generator, which makes the electricity. Most of the large dams in Idaho make electricity.

Recreation. A fourth use for dams is recreation—fun on the water. People love the lakes that form behind our dams. People by the thousands rush to the reservoirs (and natural lakes) to fish, swim, boat, and water ski. Nearly everyone in Idaho lives within an easy drive of a reservoir or lake.

Dworshak Dam is on the North Fork of the Clearwater River, just a short way from the main Clearwater. This photo shows several things: (1) Dworshak Dam is near the top center. (2) The North Fork flows into the main Clearwater at the lower left. (3) The main Clearwater flows from right to left across the picture. (4) The village of Ahsahka lies below the dam on the left side of the North Fork. (5) A government fish hatchery sits on the point of land between the two rivers. What town is just four miles upstream from this point?

IDAHO DEPARTMENT OF COMMERCE

Gasoline-powered street cars were being used in Caldwell in 1910. Later, other towns had electric street cars and trains. Why do you think street cars went out of use? IDAHO HISTORICAL SOCIETY

Review Questions

1. What are the four important uses of dams?
(a) ____________________
(b) ____________________
(c) ____________________
(d) ____________________ *[185–186]*

Idaho Must Plan For The Use Of Its Water.

When the first explorers saw the great Snake River, little did they dream that someday somebody might "drink it dry." However, as Idaho has grown, the need for water has grown. A study in 1975 reported that the Snake River could run dry if everybody with a water right were to take his full share.

Idaho irrigates more than 2.3 million acres of land. Only Texas, California, and Colorado irrigate more land than this—and they are larger states than Idaho. The lower Snake River Valley has at least 2 million more acres of good desert land. The Snake River may not have enough water to irrigate this land. Cities and factories also need water. As Idaho's cities grow, and more factories are built, more water will be needed. If the water behind the dams gets too low, we could run short of electric power.

Idaho's citizens are trying to plan for the best uses of Idaho's water. There are many different needs, and careful choices must be made. Farmers need water. Cities need water. Factories need water. People need water. Fish and wildlife need water. Everyone needs electricity. Deciding on the right plan will be a tough job.

Water Conservation. Each of us must help with **water conservation**. This means protecting our water and using it wisely. It is important not to waste water, because we could run out of water. Also we must protect our water against **pollution**. Trash, sewage, or poison chemicals sometimes pollute water. Then we can't use it for drinking and other things we need.

Our dams help conserve water by storing it for irrigation. Nature has its own ways to store water, too. Our mountains and forests catch the winter snow and let it melt slowly. Trees, forest soil, grass, and other plants catch rain and let it run slowly into the streams. In places where plants don't cover the soil, the rain runs off quickly and washes soil away with it. You can see that protecting our forests also protects our water.

Almost everyone agrees that our water must be protected. However, not everyone agrees on "wise use." Some people believe that our water should be used for farms, cities, factories, and

As the years went by, Idaho towns became more modern. This was a Rexburg drug store in 1920. What things do you see that make it modern? IDAHO HISTORICAL SOCIETY

electricity. They believe that other uses are not important.

Other people are interested in saving some of our streams the way nature made them. Some people believe that enough dams have been built, and that the rest of our streams should remain free flowing. A free flowing stream singing between tree-lined banks is one of the oldest human joys.

Dams have been built on most of Idaho's major rivers. Only the Salmon River still has a long stretch of "wild" water. The government has made part of the Salmon River a "Wild River." No dams can be built on that part of the Salmon River.

Deciding the best use for Idaho's water raises some very tough questions. People's jobs depend on how our water is used: farmers, factory workers, business people. Often it is hard to know the wisest thing to do. In only a few short years, you will be a grown-up citizen of Idaho. Then it will be up to you to help decide how Idaho should grow. Until then, you will want to go on thinking about Idaho so you can help make wise decisions.

Ideas To Talk About

1. How is it possible that the mighty Snake River could someday run dry?
2. Why is it important for Idaho to plan for the use of its water?
3. Why is water conservation important to you?
4. What can you do to help with water conservation?

Chapter 9 Skill Activities

Words and Ideas

In Chapter 9, you will find a number of key words printed in **bold** print. Each key word stands for an important idea. Answering these questions will help you understand some of the key words.

You can find the key words in the Glossary at the back of the book. The number after each question is the page where the idea is found in the book. Answer each question with a complete sentence.

1. What does a **canal** do? [*174*]
2. What is a **drought**? [*180*]
3. Why do some farms need **irrigation**? [*173*]
4. What are some examples of **pollution** that get into our water? [*172*]
5. What kinds of water do we measure when we measure **rainfall**? [*173*]
6. How is a **reservoir** different from a lake? [*181*]
7. What part of the **soil** is **topsoil**? [*172*]
8. What is meant by **soil conservation** [*172*]
9. How does a **storage dam** help farmers irrigate their land? [*181*]
10. What is meant by **water conservation**? [*187*]
11. How are **wind erosion** and **water erosion** similar? [*172*]
12. What was a **water right**? [*174–175*]

Research Projects

1. **Farm Products in Your County.** What are the chief farm products that are grown in your county?

(a) Call the **agricultural agent** at your County Extension Office. Ask for a list of the chief crops grown in your county, and where these products are sold. Are they used mostly in your own county, or are they shipped to market somewhere else?

(b) Write a report on the chief crop grown in your county. Use the encyclopedia or other source material.

2. **Making a Booklet.** Make a booklet of Idaho farm products. (a) Survey your grocery store to identify foods grown in Idaho. Collect food labels, make drawings, or cut pictures out of advertisements. Ask questions at the store if you aren't sure whether a product is from Idaho.

(b) Arrange your collection into your booklet, and add a sentence or two about each product.

3. **Checking Out the Restaurant.** What Idaho farm products are served in your favorite restaurant?

(a) Next time you go there, study the menu. Make a list of the Idaho products on the menu. Ask questions if you need to.

(b) Write a report about your visit.

4. **Taking a Field Trip.** Take a farm-related field trip. There are many interesting possibilities. Some of them are: egg farm, dairy, cheese

factory, canning factory, sugar factory, irrigation system, and many others.

(a) Prepare for the field trip by reading about the things you will see. Plan some good questions to ask while you are there.

(b) When you get back, make a mural that shows the entire process you saw.

(c) Follow up by making a booklet. Write a story about what you saw, then add pictures.

Using Your Imagination

1. **World Fair Exhibit.** The governor has placed you in charge of preparing an Idaho Agricultural Exhibit at the World's Fair. Use a classroom bulletin board and pictures for your display.

(a) Use the crops shown in the chart on page [184]. You may draw pictures, or use actual product labels from the store.

(b) Arrange the display attractively on the bulletin board. It is a good idea to lay the display out on the floor before fastening it up on the wall.

2. **Planning a Lunch.** Plan a lunch with Idaho farm products.

(a) Make a list of products, and write a lunch menu. Then look for recipes in a recipe book. Write out the recipes to go with the menu.

(b) Collect recipes from other class members, and make a class cookbook of Idaho recipes.

(c) If you want to be adventurous, prepare the meal at school for lunch one day.

Reviewing Chapter 9

Main Ideas In This Chapter

1. More than half of Idaho's people depend on farming, farm business, and food processing to make a living.

2. Idaho's farmland has rich soil that can grow many different kinds of crops.

3. With careful use, soil can be farmed almost forever.

4. Railroads make it possible to sell Idaho farm goods in far-off places.

5. Irrigation made it possible to farm the desert land in southern Idaho.

6. It takes a LOT of water to grow crops.

7. The Mormons were pioneers in irrigation.

8. Most of the irrigation water used in southern Idaho comes from our rivers.

9. Irrigation came to Magic Valley only when the Snake River was tamed by Milner Dam.

10. Irrigation brought farms and towns to Magic Valley.

11. The town of American Falls was moved when American Falls Dam was built. This was done so that Magic Valley could irrigate.

12. Some land is irrigated by sprinklers.

13. North of the Salmon River, most of the farmland gets enough rainfall to grow crops without irrigation.

14. Dams are built to prevent flooding, store water for irrigation, and make electricity. The lakes are used for recreation.

15. Dams are found on most Idaho rivers.

16. Idaho must plan for the future use of its water.

17. All of us must conserve water and soil.

Further Reading For Children

Halberstadt, Hans. *The American Family Farm*. St. Paul, Minnesota: Motorbooks International, 1996. [A seasonal theme compares the modern farm with farming in the early twentieth century. Spectacular photographs.]

Halley, Ned B., and Geoff Brightling. *Farm (Eyewitness Books).* New York: Alfred A. Knopf, 1996. [Animals, vegetables, grains, and machinery used in farming throughout history. Excellent photographs and brief text.]

Hansen, Ann Larkin. *All Kinds of Farms (The Farm).* Edina, Minnesota: Abdo & Daughters, 1998.

Peterson, Chris, and Alvis Upitis. *Century Farm: One Hundred Years on a Family Farm.* Honesdale, Pennsylvania: Boyds Mills Press, 1999. [A personal look at a real family's farm showing change over a 100-year period, including photographs from the family album.]

Plowhead, Ruth Gipson. *Lucretia Ann on the Sagebrush Plains.* Caldwell, Idaho: Caxton Publishers, n.d. [Lucretia Ann and Benjamin, the tortoise-shell cat, crossed the plains on the Oregon Trail and made their home by the bank of a rushing stream.]

Saunders-Smith, Gail. *The Farm (Field Trips).* Mankato, Minnesota: Capstone Press, 1998. [A Pebble Book]

Time Line

	1776 A.D.	Declaration of Independence; USA begins.
1800		
	1805	Lewis and Clark explore Idaho.
	1860	Franklin becomes Idaho's first permanent settlement. E.D. Pierce discovers gold and sets off Idaho's gold rush.
	1861	Lewiston becomes Idaho's first city.
	1863	New Fort Boise, Boise City, Olds Ferry, Weiser, Paris. Idaho becomes a territory, and Lewiston is made capital.
	1863–64	Fruit and vegetable growing begins around Lewiston and in Payette and Boise valleys. Cattle, horse, and sheep raising spreads throughout Idaho.
	1864	Emmett, Montpelier, Bloomington, St. Charles. Boise City becomes capital of Idaho Territory.
	1865	Glenns Ferry, Eagle Rock/Idaho Falls.
	1868	Fort Hall.
	1869	Albion, Bruneau.
	1871	Moscow.
	1873	Utah and Northern Railroad comes to Franklin from Utah.
	1875	Weippe Prairie. 1876—Grangeville.
	1877–79	Coeur d'Alene/Fort Sherman. Utah and Northern Railroad build through eastern Idaho.
	1880	Sandpoint.
	1882	Northern Pacific Railroad built across Idaho's panhandle.
	1883	Oregon Short Line Railroad; Glenns Ferry (new town), Mountain Home, Caldwell, Payette.
	1885	Nampa.
	1886–87	Hard winter kills many cattle; "Old West" ends in Idaho.
	1889	St. Anthony.
	1890	Idaho becomes a state.
1900		
	1976 A.D.	USA celebrates its Bicentennial
	1990	Idaho Centennial

Chapter 10
Idaho's Forests And Mines

Forests Serve Many Purposes.

Enjoying Our Forests. In Idaho, we are lucky to have so many great and beautiful forests. Our forests are favorite places for outdoor fun. People enjoy camping, hiking, and picnicking under the trees and beside the lakes and streams. Wild animals live in the forests, and they are exciting to watch. Forests protect these animals and provide food for them.

Storing Water. Forests are important because they collect and store water. Much of the water in our rivers came from our forests. Winter snow piles up in the forests, and the trees shade it from the sun. The shade lets the snow melt slowly. Without the shade, the snow would melt quickly. Also the soft spongy forest floor stores some of the water. Forests let the water trickle slowly, clean and clear, into the streams.

Roots from trees and other plants also help hold the soil in place. Without plant roots, the soil would wash down the streams and rivers in a big, muddy rush. There would be a huge, muddy spring flood, then no water later in the summer.

Forest Products. We use many things made from trees that grow in the forests. These things are called **forest products**. Trees are used to make houses, furniture, matches, and fence posts. Wood is used for making rayon. Rayon is used to make clothing and rubber tires. Paper is made from wood. This book, the newspaper, and the carton that holds your morning milk were all made from trees.

Forests are important because they collect and store water. A. B. CURTIS #13–653 U OF I LIBRARY

Jobs. Many people in Idaho depend on the forests for their jobs. Loggers cut the trees into logs. Mill workers cut the logs into lumber. Paper mill workers turn wood scraps and chips into paper. Truck drivers haul the logs, lumber, wood chips, and paper. Businesses sell lumber and paper. Carpenters use lumber to build houses and other buildings. We could find other jobs, too, if we looked.

Forests bring a great amount of wealth to Idaho. Idaho forest products are sold in all parts of the United States. Logs, lumber, paper, telephone poles, wooden matches, and railroad ties are just a few of them. Even food comes from our forests. Many sheep and beef cattle graze on Idaho's forest land.

Review Questions

1. What are three kinds of things people enjoy doing in the forests:
(a) ____________
(b) ____________
(c) ____________ [*191*]

2. Name five different forest products:
(a) ____________ (b) ____________
(c) ____________ (d) ____________
(e) ____________ [*191*]

3. Name three different kinds of jobs that depend on our forests: (a) ____________
(b) ____________ (c) ____________ [*191*]

Two lumberjacks are using a hand saw to cut logs into lumber in this 1890 photo. How long would it take you to make a board this way? #6-86-1B U OF I LIBRARY

Forests In Idaho's History.

Indians and Explorers. People have been using Idaho's trees for a long, long time. Indians used small trees to make poles for their tipis and lodges. They made **dugout canoes** by cutting and burning out the inside of larger trees. Lewis and Clark made canoes this way near Orofino in 1805. They rode those canoes down the Snake and Columbia rivers to the Pacific Ocean.

Miners and Pioneers. Trappers and gold miners built cabins from logs. The nicer buildings in the mining camps were made from boards cut with a two-handed saw. This saw was six or seven feet long. A log was laid out so one person could stand above the log and another could stand below it. The person under the log pulled the saw down and got sawdust in the eyes. The one above pulled the saw back up. The saw was pulled back and forth until the log was cut from end to end. It was slow work, and it took two cuts to make the first board! Heavy timbers sometimes were squared off on each side with a two-handed saw. More often, the sides were squared off with an ax.

Sawmills. Henry Spalding built Idaho's first sawmill in 1840 on Lapwai Creek. The mill sawed logs into boards and ground grain into flour. It was powered by a water wheel. Small water-powered sawmills appeared in all parts of Idaho during territorial times. These small mills served the mining and farming towns.

The demand for lumber was never ending. Government laws allowed people to cut trees for home and farm use. A person could buy as many

Today huge electric saws cut logs into lumber. BOISE CASCADE CORPORATION

as 160 acres of forest land. However, when those trees were gone, that person was out of the lumber business. Large lumber companies were not allowed to cut Idaho trees until 1892, when the laws were changed. Even the railroads could not cut Idaho's trees. When the railroads built their tracks across Idaho, they had to haul their wooden ties from as far away as the Black Hills of South Dakota.

Ideas To Talk About

1. How do forests store water?
2. How do forests help keep our water clean?
3. How did the miners and pioneers make lumber?
4. Why was there such a demand for lumber during pioneer times?

Theodore Roosevelt Saved Idaho's Forests.

Idaho might have no forests today if it had not been for President Theodore Roosevelt. This story begins in the eastern United States. During the 1800s, lumber companies thought only of cutting down all the big trees in the forest. Then they would move on to a new forest. They gave no thought to saving the younger trees for future forests.

After the lumber companies moved on, other people burned the stumps and trash. Much of the trash was crushed trees that were too small for lumber. The cleared land was then plowed for farming. Those forests were lost forever. The state of Maine lost much of its forest very early.

The tales of **Paul Bunyan** and Babe, the Blue Ox, came from this part of America's history. Starting at the Atlantic coast, the forests filled with lumberjacks and lumber camps. Strong loggers with sharp axes cut down the forests, leaving almost nothing behind them. Stories say that Paul Bunyan was there too, doing the impossible. As the trees were cut down, the camps moved west. Paul Bunyan came west, too.

By 1900, most of the good forests were gone in Wisconsin, Michigan, and Minnesota. Lumber companies were looking for new forests to cut. The forests of Washington, Oregon, Idaho, and Montana seemed ideal. After the railroad

Trees were cut the hard way in the early days. These men are cutting down trees in about ten feet of snow. A lot of lumber will be wasted in that tall stump. #5-58-1B U OF I LIBRARY

These loggers are using small tools to cut giant white pine trees. In what part of Idaho would they be cutting white pine? #5-14-1G U OF I LIBRARY

Horses were used to pull logs in the early days of lumbering. #5–75–1AC U OF I LIBRARY

As lumbering became more modern, trains were used to haul logs out of the forests. How are logs hauled out of the forests today? #5–75–1 U OF I LIBRARY

was built across northern Idaho, lumber was easy to ship. Idaho's white pine was a special prize that sold for high prices.

President Theodore Roosevelt loved the outdoors. He worried that all of America's forests might be destroyed. While he was president (1901–1909), he set aside 148 million acres of forest. He then set up the **Forest Service** to take care of that forest land. Today these forest lands are called **national forests**.

Idaho has 16 national forests, and they cover more than 20 million acres. This is more acres of forest than any other state except Alaska. Idaho's national forests are the Bitterroot, Boise, Cache, Caribou, Challis, Clearwater, Coeur d'Alene, Kaniksu, Kootenai, Lolo, Nez Perce, Payette, Salmon, Sawtooth, St. Joe, and Targhee.

Ideas To Talk About

1. Why did President Theodore Roosevelt fear that all of America's forests might be destroyed?
2. What did Theodore Roosevelt do about this problem?

The Forest Service Protects Our Forests.

Cutting and Replacing Trees. The Forest Service has the job of taking care of our national forests. The forests must be put to the best use for all Americans. The Forest Service sells trees to lumber companies, but the companies must not destroy the forests. Trees that are cut for lumber must be replaced with new trees. In this way, trees are harvested like a crop instead of being mined like gold and silver.

This is not Paul Bunyan. It is Billy Musch. He was known as one of the best lumber camp cooks in the Northwest. Billy cooked 600 to 700 pancakes for breakfast on an ordinary day. #12–196 U OF I LIBRARY

Many new trees grow from seeds dropped by older trees. A few grow from the stumps of trees that were cut down. In places where all the trees

Idaho's forests are protected from forest fires. This fire is seen from an airplane. #13-3544 U OF I LIBRARY

For many years, lookout towers have been used to watch for forest fires. People live in them during the summer and watch for fires. Would you like to spend a summer this way? IDAHO HISTORICAL SOCIETY

A smoke jumper is a fire fighter who gets to fires in a hurry by jumping out of an airplane. Would you like to do this? U. S. BUREAU OF LAND MANAGEMENT

have been cut down, people must go out and plant young trees. These young trees are grown from seeds in a forest nursery. America can have both trees and lumber as long as the forests keep growing new trees.

Forest Fires. The Forest Service also protects the forests by fighting fires. Each year, fires kill millions of trees. Before 1940, fire burned more trees than were cut by the lumber companies. The Forest Service now has roads and telephone lines in the forests to help fight fires, and airplanes fly over watching for fires.

It is known that some fire is helpful to the forest. Without some fire, the forest grows too thick and can become unhealthy. Fire is a natural part of the forest. It thins out the trees, and this lets in more sunshine. The burned areas then grow up with young trees and other new plants. The new plants provide food for deer, elk, and other wild animals. The Forest Service still fights wildfires, but it also burns certain parts of the forest to make it healthy.

The Great Fire of 1910. The Great Fire of 1910 was one of the worst fires in the history of North America. In only two days, the fire swept across northern Idaho and western Montana. In that short time, it destroyed 3 million acres of forest. It left a burn 160 miles long and 50 miles wide.

More than 100 people died in the fast-moving flames. Four towns were destroyed. The east end of Wallace burned to the ground. Elk City, however, was saved by its women and children, who carried buckets of water to put out the fire. One-sixth of all the forests in northern Idaho burned. Scars from the Great Fire could be seen along U.S. Highway 10 (the old Mullan Road) for more than 50 years.

One good thing came from this terrible fire. It made more Americans want something done to save our forests. Before the Great Fire, the Forest Service didn't have much money to fight fires. The Great Fire changed all that. The Forest Service got the money it needed. Since then, the Forest Service has grown large and strong. Today it does a fine job of protecting our forests.

Ideas To Talk About

1. What kinds of things does the Forest Service do?
2. Why is it important for the Forest Service to fight fires?
3. Why is the Great Fire of 1910 still remembered today?

These tools are ready for fire fighters to use. Name as many of the tools as you can. What do you think each one is used for? #13–567 U OF I LIBRARY

The Jordan Tree may be the largest western red cedar in North America. The trunk is more than 17 feet across. It is thought to be between 1,000 and 3,000 year old. A. B. CURTIS #13–12513 U OF I LIBRARY

Idaho's Forests Today

Idaho has more than 35,000 square miles of forest land. This is about two-fifths of all the land in Idaho. Idaho's forest lands cover a larger area than four northeastern states put together: Vermont, New Hampshire, Massachusetts, and Connecticut.

Several important kinds of trees make up Idaho's forests. The most valuable is the western white pine. This is a clear, straight-grained wood that makes fine lumber and wooden matches. Idaho has the largest forest of white pine left in the United States. Next in value are the yellow pine and the Douglas fir. These make excellent lumber and heavy timbers.

Another interesting and valuable Idaho tree is the red cedar. It is used for furniture, fence posts, and telephone poles. The largest living tree in Idaho is a red cedar growing in Clearwater County near Elk River. It is called the Jordan Tree. The tree is more than 17 feet through the trunk, and about 150 feet tall. It is thought to be between 1,000 and 3,000 years old.

Logging Has Changed. The ways that trees are cut down and logs are hauled has changed with the rest of Idaho. Machines have taken the place of the ax and the two-handed saw. One logger with a chain saw can do the work of several old-time lumberjacks. Helicopters carry logs from steep hillsides and other places where there are no roads. The exciting log drives

For many years, logs were floated down the Clearwater River to the mill at Lewiston. This rare photo shows a "river of logs" moving down the North Fork of the Clearwater. These log drives stopped when Dworshak Dam was built on the North Fork. A. B. CURTIS #13–1 U OF I LIBRARY

These loggers are on the river, walking on the logs. They push and turn the logs to keep them moving down the river. Why would a lumber company want to float logs to their mill? #6–121–3 U OF I LIBRARY

down the Clearwater River to Lewiston are only a memory. Dams have made that impossible. Logs still float down Lake Coeur d'Alene to the mills, however. Most logs are hauled on trucks and trains.

Forest conservation and today's machines have given Paul Bunyan a long rest. We can thank President Theodore Roosevelt for saving Idaho's forests.

Forest Conservation

Forests are important to everyone. They help keep the air clean and fit to breathe. They store water by catching the rain and snow. Our beautiful lakes and streams would be muddy and ugly without the forests to keep the water clean. Forests are home to many different kinds of **wildlife**. Besides giving us trees for wood, they are favorite places for outdoor fun. People like to camp, hike, and picnic in the forests.

Forest conservation is important. This means we must protect our forests and use them wisely, so they will always be there for people to use. Each of us in our own way can help protect the forests.

We must not waste trees. Sometimes people cut down trees for no good reason. A little tree may not seem important, but it is. A young tree is important, just like a young animal or young person. A young tree can grow into a forest giant. Trees grow very slowly, however. It takes a person's lifetime for a forest tree to grow tall.

Sometimes people kill trees without knowing it. They may carve their names on them, or they may mark trees by cutting off some bark. Such things allow insects and diseases to attack the trees, and these may kill the tree.

Fire is the worst enemy of the forests. In the summertime, forests became dry, and they catch fire easily. Each year, forest fires are started by people who are careless with fire. Forest fires can start from matches and cigarettes, camp fires, and chain saws. We must be very careful in the forest. One careless fire, started by one person, can burn thousands of acres of forest—and millions of trees.

Review Questions

1. About two-fifths of all the land in Idaho is ____________ land. [*196*]
2. Name three different kinds of trees found in Idaho forests: (a) ____________ (b) ____________ (c) ____________ [*196*]
3. Protecting our forests and using them wisely is called forest ____________. [*197–198*]
4. The worse enemy of the forests is ____________. [*198*]

Ideas To Talk About

1. How has logging changed in the past 100 years?
2. Why should we be happy that Paul Bunyan will never visit Idaho's forests?
3. Why is forest conservation important to you?
4. What are some ways that people waste trees?
5. What can you do to prevent forest fires?

This giant mining dredge was used to mine gold in the Idaho City area. The huge buckets scooped up great amounts of gravel to be washed for gold.
IDAHO HISTORICAL SOCIETY

Mining Changed After The Gold Rush.

When we think about mining, we often think of gold-rush miners. They carried picks, shovels, gold pans, and perhaps had a burro. The truth is that most of those old-time miners made very little money. It took five or ten minutes to wash the sand and gravel out of the pan. What if the pan had only five or ten cents worth of gold in the bottom? Often that is all there was. Few miners "struck it rich." Most miners made only a few dollars a day. When the "easy" gold ran out, the gold rush ended.

Hard-rock mining began after that. Mining takes **minerals** out of the ground. Minerals are the natural materials that make up the earth. Many are used to make things people need. Idaho has many different minerals, not just gold and silver. Most minerals are found in rocks, and machinery is needed to get them out.

Mining Companies Took Over.

Early miners had looked only for placer gold. Placer mining took gold only from the soil and gravel near the top of the ground. When these mines began to run out of gold, the miners left them to look for others. Most of Idaho's placer gold was gone by 1870. The gold rush to the Coeur d'Alene country in 1883 and 1884 did not last very long.

Dredge Mining. The early miners left a lot of gold in the ground. Groups of miners sometimes formed companies that could buy heavy mining machinery. A large machine called a **dredge** could dig up great amounts of soil and gravel and remove the gold. It did the work of dozens of miners. The dredge even washed gold from soil and gravel that the miners had already mined! Mining companies made a lot of money from gold the early miners had missed.

The Boise Basin had dredge mining for many years. Today around Idaho City, you can see piles of gravel in every direction. These piles were left by huge machines that washed the gravel for gold.

Hard-Rock Mining. Some miners knew that gold was also found in certain kinds of rock. In the West, gold was found in a kind of rock called **quartz**. When quartz gold was found, miners called it a mother lode. The gold in the soil and streams came from such rock. This made the rock the "mother" of the gold in the streams. A miner could make a **hard-rock claim**, but heavy machinery was needed to crush the rock and get the gold.

In 1982, this small mining dredge was working in the Salmon River near Riggins. VIRGIL YOUNG

Some miners were able to form companies to buy the heavy machinery needed for hard-rock gold mining. A number of rich hard-rock gold mines were started around Rocky Bar and Atlanta. These mines were worked for many years before they closed down.

Review Questions

1. A dredge was ______________________. *[198–199]*

These hard-rock miners were tunneling into a hillside along the old Idaho City road. IDAHO HISTORICAL SOCIETY

Silver City looked like this on September 24, 1895. Why was Silver City famous? IDAHO DEPARTMENT OF COMMERCE

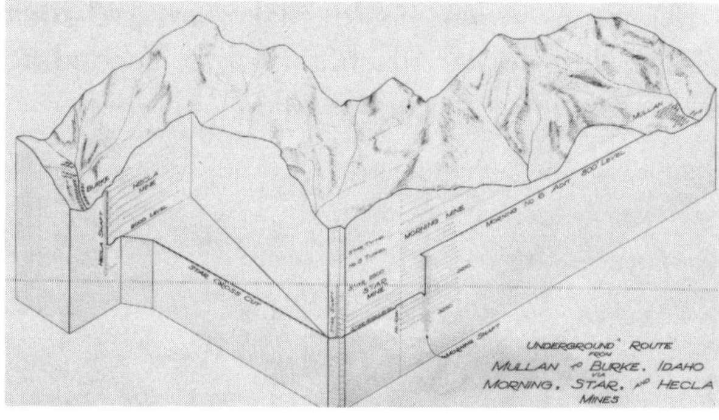

The towns of Burke and Mullan are several miles apart. However, they are connected by the tunnels of three underground mines. You could travel from Burke to Mullan by following the tunnels shown here. This map is old, and all the mines are much deeper now. BARNARD-STOCKBRIDGE COLLECTION #8-B86 U OF I

2. Quartz rock with gold in it was called a ____________. [*199*]

3. Mining in which gold or silver must be taken out of solid rocks is called ____________ mining. [*199*]

Ideas To Talk About

1. Why did some miners form mining companies?

2. What kinds of things did the mining companies do?

Silver And Other Metals Became Important.

A few gold miners looked for gold in the **Owyhee Mountains** south of the Snake River. They found gold on Jordan Creek, a small tributary of the Owyhee River. This strike wasn't nearly as rich as the gold in the Boise Basin, and didn't seem very important. However, somebody found a different kind of wealth—Silver. **Silver City** quickly arose high in the Owyhees!

Silver City was not named by accident. In October 1863, rich pockets of silver ore were found. Excited miners rushed into the Owyhees, and a silver rush was on. Silver City, **DeLamar**, and other Owyhee towns rapidly appeared. Mining companies shipped in heavy mining equipment, and hard-rock silver mining was quickly

These elevators are in the Morning mine at 800 feet down. They lift miners and ore to the surface of the ground. BARNARD-STOCKBRIDGE COLLECTION #8-B13–1 U OF I

Deep in the earth, these miners are drilling holes in the hard rock. Later the holes will be filled with explosives to blast the rock loose. Would you like to work here? IDAHO MINING ASSOCIATION

Many years ago, the Morning mine tunnel looked like this at 800 feet below the ground. This is part of the tunnel that runs between Mullan and Burke. Notice the many "train tracks." At the left, you can see a small train of cars filled with ore.
BARNARD-STOCKBRIDGE COLLECTION #8-B13–2 U OF I

The main street of Burke looked this way one snowy day in 1910. The canyon at this point is so narrow that there is room for only one street. Do you think Burke needed a railroad? Why do tracks run down the middle of the street? #5-65-2A U OF I LIBRARY

In the early 1980s, these buildings were all that remained of Burke. The mine at the left was still in business. However, the buildings across the street were empty. One or two families lived further up the canyon. VIRGIL YOUNG

under way. Before long, the rich Owyhee mines were world famous for their silver. Millions of dollars were taken out of these mines by 1870. Silver mining in the Owyhees went on for many years.

Today Silver City is a living ghost town. Though almost no mining is done there, some people do live at Silver City. The town looks very much like it did 100 years ago. Many buildings and fine old homes still stand. Some may need paint. Still Silver City gives us a first-hand look at a real old-time mining town.

The DeLamar Mine. Silver mining is not dead in the Owyhee country, however. Not far from Silver City is the **DeLamar mine**. Today the DeLamar mine is one of the largest **open-pit** silver mines in the United States.

The DeLamar mine was a rich silver mine about 100 years ago, and DeLamar was a busy mining town. Large amounts of silver were taken from the DeLamar mine between 1891 and 1912. However, by 1912 all the high grade silver ore was gone. The mine closed that year, and DeLamar became a ghost town.

The DeLamar mine was not forgotten. A new mining company opened the mine again in 1977. This time a huge pit was dug where the old mine had been. An open-pit mine is far different from the **underground** mines of 100 years ago. The old DeLamar mine, like most early silver mines, was an underground mine. Such mines were made up of tunnels under the ground. Some old tunnels are many miles long, crisscrossing under mountains and valleys.

On the other hand, an open pit is an open hole in the earth. You can stand at the edge and look down into it—and see the whole thing! Open-pit mining costs less than tunnel mining. The lower cost allows the mining of lower-grade ore. Million of ounces of silver and thousands of ounces of gold have been taken from the DeLamar mine since 1977.

The "Silver Shaft" of the Lucky Friday mine sinks more than a mile into the earth. This hole is 7,500 feet deep, making it the deepest shaft in North and South America. We can see only the steel tower that rises 135 feet into the air above the mine. The Lucky Friday is near Wallace. IDAHO MINING ASSOCIATION

Silver Valley and the Coeur d'Alene Mines. The richest mines in Idaho were—and still are—the **Coeur d'Alene mines** in northern Idaho. These are **underground** mines, world famous for their rich silver, lead, and zinc ore. They are found along the upper Coeur d'Alene River around Mullan, Wallace, and Kellogg. This mining area is often called **Silver Valley**.

The Coeur d'Alene silver mines grew out of the placer gold rush of 1883 and 1884. Gold miners quickly filled the stream beds of the Coeur d'Alene River and its tributaries. Other miners couldn't find land along the stream beds, so set out searching the nearby mountains. It was the search for gold on the hillsides above the streams that led to the finding of silver.

In 1885, a prospector named **Noah Kellogg** discovered silver and lead on the side of a mountain above the Coeur d'Alene River. This became the famous Bunker Hill mine. A legend grew up that Kellogg's burro had discovered the ore. It was said that the animal wandered away, and Kellogg found it standing beside some "interesting" rock.

However, Kellogg's "interesting" rock was

Not all Silver Valley mines are huge. When driving through Silver Valley, you can see a number of smaller mines such as this one. VIRGIL YOUNG

Tall and powerful, this steel figure stands just off the highway near Kellogg. It is a monument to 91 miners who died in a terrible fire at the Sunshine mine in 1972. VIRGIL YOUNG

The mining town of Wallace is surrounded by mountains. This picture was taken in 1929.
BARNARD-STOCKBRIDGE COLLECTION #8-B93 U OF I

more important than all the "easy gold" put together. It uncovered more wealth than the gold miners ever dreamed of. Soon silver, lead, and zinc were found up and down the Coeur d'Alene River. After the railroads came, hard-rock mining grew rapidly.

Idaho still has vast mineral deposits. However, miners no longer need a mule, a pick, and a shovel to find ore. Now they use state-of-the art survey maps, and they drill holes deep into the earth to take rock samples. Studies are made, including an Environmental Impact Statement. This is a plan to help prevent the mine from polluting Idaho's air and water. Modern technology now helps make mining easier, cleaner, and more friendly to the environment.

Review Questions

1. Mines in the Owyhee mountains became famous for their ____________. [200]
2. A famous Owyhee mining town was ____________. [200]
3. The ____________ silver mine, near Silver City, has produced millions of ounces of silver since 1977. [202–203]
4. The rich silver mines in Silver Valley are called the ____________ mines. [203]
5. Now state-of-the-art survey maps and holes drilled deep in the earth are used to ____________. [204]

This 1927 view of Wallace shows stores, cars and good streets. Burke was only about five miles from Wallace. Why do think Wallace grew into a nice town while Burke slowly disappeared?
BARNARD-STOCKBRIDGE COLLECTION #8-B63 U OF I

6. A plan to help prevent a mine from polluting air and water is called an ____________ __________ __________. [204]

Ideas To Talk About

1. Why do you think the DeLamar mine was made into an open-pit mine in 1977?
2. What is a ghost town?
3. Why does a town become a ghost town?

Hailey is an old mining town, and old miners' cabins can still be seen there. Why do you think these buildings have steep metal roofs? #5-71-2 U OF I

Other Kinds Of Mining In Idaho.

Other Metals. When we think of mining, we most often think of gold and silver. However, these are not Idaho's only valuable metals. During the 1980s, nine different metals were mined in Idaho. There were **antimony**, **cadmium**, copper, gold, lead, **molybdenum**, silver, **vanadium**, and zinc.

It is interesting to note that two or more metals may come mixed together in the same ore. In the Coeur d'Alene mines, silver often comes mixed with lead and zinc and other metals. The Lucky Friday mine is the richest **silver-lead** mine in the United States. In the Sunshine mine, silver comes mixed with lead and antimony. Because of this mixing of metals, the giant Coeur d'Alene silver mines also produce large amounts of other metals.

Other Mines. Not all of Idaho's mines are found in Silver Valley and at DeLamar. Mines are found in other places. Lead and zinc are mined in the Wood River mines in Blaine County. Vanadium is mined in Bear Lake and Caribou counties. Lead, zinc, copper, and cadmium are all mined with silver at the Clayton mine near Challis. Also near Challis is the Cyprus Thompson Creek molybdenum mine.

Phosphate Mining. Idaho has large **phosphate** mines in southeast Idaho. Phosphate is not a metal. It is a **mineral** used in a large number of things we use every day, from pudding to insect poisons. Phosphate is used in such things as bread, cheese, drinks, frozen foods, animal feed, and machine oil. It is best known for its use in fertilizer.

Idaho's phosphate mines are important. Phosphate rock is Idaho's second leading mineral. Silver is the only mineral that brings more wealth to our state. It is believed that more than half of America's phosphate rock lies buried in Bear Lake, Bingham, Bonneville, and Caribou counties. Florida is the only state that mines more phosphate rock than Idaho.

Idaho's largest phosphate mines are Conda mine near Soda Springs, Gay mine on the Fort

A huge truck is being loaded with phosphate ore at the Henry mine near Conda. Is this an open-pit mine or an underground mine? IDAHO MINING ASSOCIATION

Phosphate ore is passing by on a belt at this phosphate factory. Phosphate rock is Idaho's second leading mineral. IDAHO MINING ASSOCIATION

Hall Reservation, Henry mine near Soda Springs, Mabie Canyon mine near Conda, Smoky Canyon mine in Caribou County, and Wooley Valley mine near Soda Springs.

Review Questions

1. Name four metals (other than silver and gold) that are mined in Idaho:
(a) ____________ (b) ____________
(c) ____________ (d) ____________. [205]

2. Not all of Idaho's mines are found in Silver Valley and at Delamar. Name three other places where there are mines:
(a) ____________
(b) ____________
(c) ____________ [205]

3. In eastern Idaho, there are large ____________ mines. [205]

4. Name three products in which phosphate is used: (a) ____________
(b) ____________ (c) ____________ [205]

Chapter 10 Skill Activities

Words And Ideas

In Chapter 10, you will find a number of key words printed in **bold** print. Each key word stands for an important idea. Answering these questions will help you understand some of the key words.

You can find the key words in the Glossary at the back of the book. The number after each question is the page where the idea is found in the book. Answer each question with a complete sentence.

1. Why did mining companies use **dredges**? [*199*]
2. What is meant by **forest conservation**? [*197–198*]
3. How is **hard-rock** mining different from placer mining? [*198–199*]
4. Where do **minerals** come from? [*198*]
5. What person saved the forests that are now our **national forests**? [*193*]
6. How is an **open-pit** mine different from an **underground** mine? [*202–203*]
7. What valuable mineral is sometimes found in **quartz**? [*199*]
8. Name some of the **wildlife** found in Idaho forests. [*24, 37, 191*]

How Many Can You Find?

For this activity, you will need a **good** map of Idaho. The Idaho Official Highway Map is excellent because it shows all of Idaho's national forests.

A. On a plain outline map of Idaho, mark and label the following:

1. Coeur d'Alene mines
2. DeLamar mine
3. Silver City
4. Silver Valley

B. On the same map, mark Idaho's national forests. On the Official Highway Map, they are shown in red letters. See if you can find all 16:

1. Bitterroot
2. Boise
3. Cache
4. Caribou
5. Challis
6. Clearwater
7. Coeur d'Alene
8. Kaniksu
9. Kootenai
10. Lolo

11. Nez Perce
12. Payette
13. Salmon
14. Sawtooth
15. St. Joe
16. Targhee

Thinking About Idaho Minerals

A. **What Are They Used For?** Using this book, encyclopedias, or other sources, look up each of the following minerals and list its uses.

Mineral *Uses*

1. antimony _______________
2. cadmium _______________
3. copper _______________
4. gold _______________
5. lead _______________
6. molybdenum _______________
7. phosphate _______________
8. silver _______________
9. vanadium _______________
10. zinc _______________

B. **Checking Out Your Home.** Look around your home and find some of the minerals in the list above. They might be found in the kitchen, in the TV set, in toys, in the family car, and many other places. Then write a story about the ways that these minerals are used in your home.

Research Projects

1. **How are trees harvested and replaced?** Several different systems are used. Read about these in the encyclopedia under "Forestry."

(a) Write a report that explains how trees are harvested and replaced. Be sure to draw some pictures that show how the systems are different.

(b) Make a forestry poster for the bulletin board. Using pictures, show the several ways that trees are harvested and replaced.

2. **How are trees made into lumber?** Read in the encyclopedia under "Lumber." Your encyclopedia may have some pictures of the ways that boards are cut from a log.

(a) Write a report that follows one tree (your tree) from the forest to the sawmill. Add pictures to your report.

(b) Make a poster that shows how logs are cut into boards.

3. **What is an underground mine really like?** If we could go into one, we would find many shafts and tunnels. Look in the encyclopedia under "Mining." You should find a drawing of an underground mine.

(a) Make a poster that shows the parts of an underground mine. Be sure to label the parts.

(b) Write a report that explains what is shown on the poster.

Reviewing Chapter 10

Main Ideas In This Chapter

1. Forests are important for collecting and storing water.
2. We use many things made from trees that grow in the forests.
3. Forest products bring wealth to Idaho.
4. Many Idaho people depend on the forests for their jobs.
5. President Theodore Roosevelt saved the forests of the West by setting aside millions of acres of forest land. Today these lands are called national forests.
6. It is the job of the Forest Service to protect our forests.
7. Idaho has more than 35,000 square miles of forest. This is about two-fifths of all the land in Idaho.
8. Idaho's forests have several kinds of valuable trees.
9. Forest conservation is important to all of us.
10. Mining companies took over mining in Idaho after the gold rush was finished.
11. Hard-rock gold mining replaced placer gold mining.
12. Silver mining became important in Idaho after the gold rush. Today both silver and gold are still mined in Idaho.
13. The DeLamar mine in the Owyhee Mountains was opened again in 1977 as an open-pit silver mine.
14. The richest silver mines in Idaho are the Coeur d'Alene mines in Silver Valley.
15. Mining today must avoid polluting Idaho's air and water.
16. Nine different metals were mined in Idaho during the 1980s.
17. Large phosphate mines are found in eastern Idaho. Phosphate is an important mineral.

Time Line

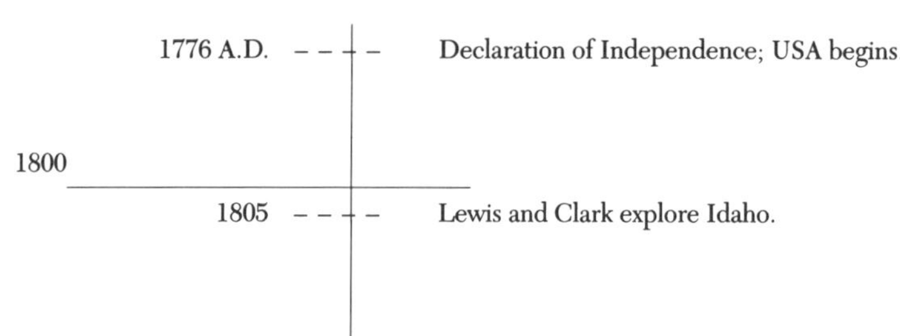

1776 A.D. — Declaration of Independence; USA begins.

1800

1805 — Lewis and Clark explore Idaho.

1860 — Franklin is settled. Franklin builds the first Idaho school for white children.

1861 — Lewiston becomes Idaho's first city. Steamboats begin bringing miners and supplies to Idaho.

1862 — Idaho's first newspaper is begun at Lewiston.

1863 — Idaho becomes a Territory and Lewiston is made the capital.

1864 — Lida Johnson is born at Eagle Island. First public school is opened at Florence. Stage lines begin to replace saddle trains. Idaho's first laws go into effect. Vigilantes in Virginia City hang Henry Plummer. Idaho's Second Territorial Legislature decides to move the capital to Boise City.

1866 — Vigilantes in Boise City hang David Updike.

1868 — Lars Frederickson moves to Weston. Franklin gets first telephone in Idaho.

1869 — Weston pioneers get log houses. School is built at Weston. Franklin gets first telegraph station in Idaho.

1871 — Gasoline lamps in Idaho.

1873 — Utah and Northern Railroad is built to Franklin from Utah.

1875 — Telegraph arrives in Boise City.

1877–79 — Utah and Northern Railroad is built through eastern Idaho.

1879 — Idaho's Indian wars are over.

1882 — First electricity in Idaho. New large school built in Boise City. Northern Pacific Railroad crosses panhandle.

1883 — Oregon Short Line Railroad crosses southern Idaho.

1887 — Electricity comes to Hailey and Boise City.

1889 — University of Idaho established at Moscow.

1890 — Idaho becomes a state.

1900

1947 — Most of Idaho's country schools are closed.

1976 A.D. — USA celebrates its Bicentennial

1990 — Idaho Centennial

Chapter 11
Idaho's Government—By The People

What if your house caught on fire or you were robbed? What if the bridge on your street washed away in a flood? What if nobody came when you called for help?

We expect the fire truck to show up at a fire or police officers to come. We expect somebody to fix our streets and bridges. Where do we get fire fighters, police officers, and road workers? They work for our government.

What Is Government?

Government is the set of laws we live by. When people live together, they need laws, or rules to live by. Laws help us live together in peace. Some laws tell us not to hurt each other or not to steal. Some laws tell us not to drive cars at dangerous speeds. Other laws give us police officers, fire fighters, and road workers. When

Idaho's handsome domed Capitol building is located in the capital city of Boise. What is the Capitol building used for? IDAHO DEPARTMENT OF COMMERCE

You are looking into the heart of Idaho's state government. The Capitol stands in the center of the picture, with the Idaho Supreme Court building on the far left. Across the street from the Capitol, you can see two other state office buildings: the "Hall of Mirrors" and the Len B. Jordan Building. VIRGIL YOUNG

each of us obeys the laws, all of us are safe from harm, and we get along better.

Our **government** is run by people who hold certain **offices**. The **mayor** holds the highest office in a city, and the **governor** holds the highest office in the state. There are other important offices besides these. You will learn more about these **officials** later in this chapter.

In America, we **elect** or choose the men and women who will run our government. When people **vote**, it is called an **election**. The people of a city vote for persons who run for mayor. The person who gets the most votes becomes the mayor. In the same way, the people of Idaho elect the governor and other state officials.

An election is held every two years in November. Election years are those that end with an even number (2008, 2010, 2012). Some officials must be elected every two years, and others are elected every four years. We elect Idaho's governor every four years.

We expect our government officials to follow our wishes. We expect them to be honest and to do their jobs well. We expect them to protect us through police officers and firefighters. We expect them to build us schools and streets. If we don't like what our officials do, we can vote for somebody else next time. In America, we expect good government.

Review Questions

1. Government is ______________. [209]
2. In America, we ______________ our government officials. [210]

Good Government Was Slow Coming To Idaho Territory.

When Idaho Territory was formed in 1863, the United States government didn't give it any laws. There were no laws of any kind in Idaho for almost a year! The Idaho legislature passed the first laws in 1864, a year later. These laws made little difference, however. Most people in the camps and towns of Idaho paid no attention to them.

Good government had little chance during the gold rush. Many people were fortune hunters. They intended to make money quickly and move on. They weren't interested in government or laws. Some people were from different countries and weren't used to American laws. There was a feeling of "live and let live" and "everyone for himself." It was hard to get laws to work during the gold rush.

Troubled Times.

Trouble began almost as soon as trappers and miners arrived. There was trouble over mines, horses, gold, and almost everything else. Matters were often settled with fists or guns. At first there was a **miner's code**. The miners looked out for each other, and anyone making trouble was sent away. After the camps became flooded with people, this no longer worked. Camps and towns began making their own laws.

Miner's court was one way of settling trouble. All the miners in the camp had a meeting and made a set of rules. Then they chose **officers** to see that the rules were followed. Mostly they would choose a judge, a recorder, and a **sheriff.** Someone charged with breaking a rule could ask for a **trial**. Anyone who didn't like the results of the trial could call a meeting of the miners. They would then decide the case. Often there were lawyers in camp to help people who got into trouble.

Gangs. Early camps and towns were troubled by gangs of robbers and murderers. Such gangs followed all the gold rushes. When a gang moved into a camp, there was little that anyone could do about it. They stole gold and found ways to cheat honest people out of their hard-earned money. They stole horses, cattle, and mining claims. They would pass fake gold, run crooked games, steal, rob stages and miners, and often kill people. Sometimes they would do terrible things to people "just for fun."

Sheriffs who tried to stop the gangs were often killed. Sometimes the sheriff was one of the gang. Other gang members might be store clerks, gamblers, workers at the **livery stable**, town officers, and keepers of stage stations. Gangs kept their members secret as much as possible. It was hard to have gold shipped without having it stolen. Miners, business people, farmers, and ranchers feared for their lives.

Vigilantes. Honest people saw no end to the trouble unless strong action was taken. Several camps and towns formed **vigilance committees** to fight the gangs. These people were called **vigilantes**. They would meet in secret and make plans for getting rid of the gangs. They wore masks so the gang members wouldn't know who they were. Otherwise, the gang might try to kill them.

One of the most famous vigilante deeds took place in Virginia City and East Bannack in 1864. These Montana towns were then part of Idaho Territory. The sheriff, Henry Plummer, was leading a "double life." He was also the leader of a large gang of murdering robbers. In January 1864, vigilantes in those towns hanged Plummer and several of his gang. The rest of the gang ran for their lives. They were never seen again in those parts.

Vigilantes worked in Payette Valley, Boise Valley, and eastern Idaho. They broke up and drove out many gangs. They hanged at least 27 murderers and other gang members. In 1866, vigilantes in Boise City hanged their sheriff, David Updike. Like Henry Plummer, he was the leader of a murdering gang.

After the hangings began, a warning was often enough to send a gang riding away to other parts. Gangs and their leaders were warned with a sign: "3–7–77" or "XXX." Nobody today knows just what those signs meant. It is thought, though, that "3–7–77" may have meant a grave three feet wide, seven feet long, and 77 inches deep!

Government Becomes Stronger. After the vigilantes broke up the gangs, life became better. Laws slowly took over. In the beginning, the government of Idaho Territory was quite weak. However, it became stronger as the years went by. The Legislature passed laws to start schools and to build roads, bridges, and ferries. Other laws gave towns and counties the power to collect taxes and hire police officers. Many, many laws were passed. These laws built a government that would help the people.

Ideas To Talk About

1. Why didn't government work well during the early years of Idaho Territory?
2. The miner's code worked when a mining camp was small. Why didn't it work when a camp had thousands of people?
3. Were vigilantes a good idea or a bad idea? Why?

Idaho Becomes A State.

Idaho's Constitution. In 1890, Idaho Territory became a state. With this change, Idaho got a state government and a **state constitution**. A state government takes care of things that are not done by the United States government.

A **state constitution** is a set of laws that explain the state's government. It can't be changed unless the people of the state vote to change it. It tells what **officials** there will be, and how they will be chosen. It tells how long they will stay in office, and what their jobs are. Our state officials must do exactly what the Idaho Constitution tells them.

In 1889, a group of Idaho citizens met at a **constitutional convention**. At this meeting, they wrote the Idaho Constitution. Later the

Dirk Kempthorne, governor. The governor is Idaho's highest state officer. OFFICE OF THE GOVERNOR

United States government accepted the constitution, and Idaho became a state on July 3, 1890. With few changes, the 1889 Idaho Constitution is the one we use today.

Idaho's Branches Of Government.

The Idaho Constitution gives our state three branches of government. These are the (1) **executive branch**, (2) the **legislative branch**, and (3) the **judicial branch**. Each of these three branches has a different job to do.

Executive Branch. This branch carries out the laws of the state. It runs most of the state government. The highest official is the **governor**. Next after the governor are six others. They are the **lieutenant governor**, the **secretary of state**, the **state auditor**, the **state treasurer**, the **attorney general**, and the **superintendent of public instruction**. Each of these seven state officers is elected every four years by the citizens of Idaho.

The state officials hire people to do many different jobs. Those people collect taxes, build highways, and look after our banks and schools. They protect the health of our citizens, arrest lawbreakers, and guard the state prison. Their job is to do the things that help Idaho's people.

Idaho's state officials have offices in Boise. The governor's office is in the capitol building, also called the statehouse. The other offices are found in nearby buildings. These buildings make up an area called the capitol mall. (A **capitol** is a building that houses a government. A **capital** is the city where the capitol is found.)

Review Questions

1. When Idaho became a state, it got a state ____________ and a state ____________. *[211]*
2. A state constitution is ________________________. *[211]*
3. Idaho's constitution was written by Idaho citizens who met at a ____________. *[211–212]*
4. Idaho's constitution gives our state three branches of government. These branches are the ____________ branch, the ____________ branch, and the ____________ branch. *[212]*
5. The highest official in the executive branch is the ____________. *[212]*

Linda Copple Trout, Chief Justice of the Idaho Supreme Court. PARKER PORTRAITS

Legislative Branch. The **legislature** is the legislative branch. The legislature makes the laws for our state. All of its laws must be allowed by the Idaho Constitution.

The Idaho Legislature has two parts that are called **houses**. These are the **senate** and the **house of representatives**. Members of the senate are called **senators**. Members of the house of representatives are called **representatives**. Members of both houses are called **legislators**.

Each legislator is elected to office for two years. The Idaho Legislature meets for several months each year, starting in January. During this time, the members study Idaho's needs and pass laws to meet those needs.

What is a Law? A law is a rule made by the government. These laws are written by the legislature. Then they must be signed by the governor. The Idaho Legislature has made many, many laws in the past 100 years. These laws fill large books. When the legislature meets each year, it passes new laws and changes some of the old ones.

The Idaho Senate is seen at work here. The Idaho legislature has two houses. What is the other house called? VIRGIL YOUNG

In 1898, the first women were elected to the Idaho legislature. They were Mary Wright (standing), Clara Campbell (left), and Hattie Noble. IDAHO HISTORICAL SOCIETY

The laws cover many things. Some provide services to the people of Idaho. Certain laws give money to the poor and to people who are out of work. Others create state highways, state parks, state colleges, and state universities. Public schools, state police, and state buildings were all created by laws.

Some laws deal with crimes. We all know that certain acts are against the law. Speeding, damaging property, harming other people, and murder are all crimes. There are laws that deal with each one of these crimes—and many more.

What is a Tax? A **tax** is money collected from citizens to pay for their government. A very large amount of money is needed to run the state government and its services. The legislature decides how much money the state will spend. Then it

Idaho has 26 state parks. These are provided by laws passed by the legislature and signed by the governor. VIRGIL YOUNG

must supply that amount of money. The legislature gets this money by setting certain taxes. The taxes are paid by working people and by businesses. The most important state taxes are the **sales tax** and the **income tax**. These taxes are used to pay for all state services—roads, parks, police, schools, and many other things. Every citizen of Idaho is helped by the taxes we pay.

Review Questions

1. The legislative branch is called the ______ ____________. [*213*]
2. It is the legislature's job to ____________ ________________________. [*213*]
3. The Idaho Legislature has two parts that are called ____________. [*213*]
4. The two houses are called the ____________ and the ____________ of ____________. [*213*]
5. A law is ________________________. [*213*]
6. A tax is ________________________. [*213*]

State highways crisscross our state. Every Idaho state highway has signs like the one shown here. Each highway has its own number. VIRGIL YOUNG

State taxes help to pay for Idaho's state universities and colleges. UNIVERSITY OF IDAHO

Ideas To Talk About

1. What kinds of things do our laws do for us?
2. Where does tax money come from?
3. What kinds of things are taxes spent for?

Judicial Branch. **Courts** make up the judicial branch of our government. The courts are run by **judges**, also called justices. They explain the laws and settle disputes. Disputes may arise between persons or businesses, or between persons and the government. Judges are elected by the citizens of Idaho.

Idaho has two different kinds of state courts: (1) **trial courts**, and (2) **appeals courts**.

Criminal Trials. We often hear about courts because of a **trial** reported in the news. Mostly we hear about **criminal trials** for crimes like robbery or murder. A criminal trial is held when a person is accused of a crime. When the person is arrested, the case goes to court for a trial.

The trial is held in front of a group of citizens called a **jury**. The jury decides whether the person is guilty of the crime. A person who is found "not guilty" goes free. Anyone found guilty may be sent to jail or prison.

Civil Trials. Not all trials are for crimes. Some are over disputes between citizens or businesses. These are called **civil trials**. Civil trials are of two kinds.

The first is a **suit for damages**. What if somebody hurts another person, or damages property? The person who is hurt may **sue** the other person for damages. If somebody kills a tree in your yard, you may sue that person for the damage to your tree. If you win, you may get money from the other person.

A second kind of civil suit is one that asks for a **court order**. A court order tells someone to **do** or to **stop doing** something. Pretend that somebody wanted to build a skunk oil factory next to your home. You might not like that. You could go to court and ask for a court order to stop the factory. If the court agreed with you, it would send an order that the factory could not be built.

Appeals Courts. A person who loses the case in trial court may **appeal** to an **appeals court**. Idaho has two appeals courts: the Idaho

The Idaho Supreme Court is the state's highest court. The justices are (left to right) Jesse R. Walters, Cathy R. Silak, Linda Copple Trout, Gerald R. Schroeder, and Wayne L. Kidwell. Linda Copple Trout is Chief Justice. Daniel T. Eismann replaced Cathy R. Silak in 2000. PARKER PORTRAITS, 2000

Supreme Court and the Court of Appeals. Both courts review the rulings made by trial courts. **The appeals court may let the trial court ruling stand, or may change it**.

Think about that skunk oil factory. What if the trial court had ruled against you? You could appeal the ruling to the Idaho Supreme Court. Perhaps the Supreme Court would agree with you. If so, that court would order that the factory couldn't be built.

A person found guilty of a crime may appeal also. In this case, the person must show that the trial was not fair. The appeals court will decide only whether the trial was fair. It won't decide whether the person was guilty. The appeals court may let the trial court ruling stand, or may change it. Perhaps the court will decide that the person didn't receive a fair trial. If so, the court may free the person, or order a new trial.

Review Questions

1. ____________ make up the judicial branch of our government. [*214*]
2. Courts are run by ____________. [*214*]
3. It is the job of the courts to ________________________. [*214*]
4. A person accused of a crime is given a criminal ____________. [*214*]
5. A trial is held in front of a group of citizens called a ____________. [*214*]
6. A person loses a case in trial court may ____________ to an appeals court. [*214*]
7. Civil trials settle disputes between ____________ or ____________. [*214*]

Ideas To Talk About.

Why do we need courts?

How Laws Are Made.

Idaho's laws are made by the legislature and signed by the governor. A law begins as a **bill** in either the senate or the house of representatives. The bill may propose a new law, or it may change or kill an old law. The bill is then voted on by each house. If the bill is passed by both houses, it is sent to the governor to sign.

The governor may choose to sign the bill or not. There are three choices:

1. The governor may sign the bill, and it becomes a law.
2. The governor may **veto** (reject) it. Then the bill is sent back to the legislature with a message explaining the veto. The bill can't became a law unless both houses vote to **override** the veto. If both houses vote to override, the bill becomes law.
3. The governor may choose not to sign the bill. In that case, the bill becomes a law in 10 days without the governor signing it.

Review Questions

1. Laws are made by the ________________________. [*215*]
2. Before a bill can be sent to the governor, it must be passed by ________________________. [*215*]
3. The bill becomes law if the governor ____________ the bill. [*215*]
4. Instead of signing the bill, the governor may ____________ it. [*215*]

Local Governments Have Important Jobs.

The state government has created **local** governments to do some of its work. These smaller governments are (1) counties, (2) cities, (3) school districts, and (4) special districts. Citizens pay a different kind of tax to pay for local governments. They pay taxes on property that they own. **Property taxes** are used for local government, but not for state government.

County Government. Idaho is too large for everybody to go to Boise for government business. This was even more true in 1890,

The Shoshone County Courthouse is located in Wallace. What is the purpose of the county courthouse? IDAHO HISTORICAL SOCIETY

when Idaho became a state. Travel was slow and often hard. The writers of the Idaho Constitution felt strongly that government should be close to every citizen. For this reason, they made county government the chief unit of local government.

Since 1890, county government has served as an arm of the state government. Counties provide roads and bridges, police officers, and a place to pay taxes. The county keeps records of property and water rights. These needs, and more, are served by county government.

County government is set up in a building called the **county courthouse**. Every county has one. The city having the courthouse is called the **county seat**. County officials have offices in the courthouse. A jail may be built in or near the courthouse.

In early times, people expected the county seat to be nearby. They needed to ride there by horseback or buggy and return home the same

The county sheriff protects people who live outside the city. VIRGIL YOUNG

day. For this reason, the courthouse seat was placed near the greatest number of people. Early cities were eager to have the county seat. They felt it would bring business and help the city grow. Indeed today's map of Idaho shows this to be true. Many county seats have grown to be the biggest city in the county.

Most county services are used by all the citizens living in the county. However, a few county services are used only by people who live outside of cities. The most important of these is police protection. The **sheriff** protects people living outside the cities. City police protect people living inside the cities.

Today Idaho has 44 counties. The Idaho Constitution describes the officials that each county will elect. Since 1970, there have been (1) three **county commissioners**, (2) a **county assessor**, (3) a **county clerk**, (4) a **county treasurer**, (5) a **coroner**, (6) a **sheriff**, and (7) a **prosecuting attorney**. All these officials share the legislative powers of the county government.

The **county commissioners** are the legislative branch of the county. They make county laws.

This was a lively meeting of the Ada County Commission. TV stations sent reporters and cameras. Many interested citizens attend the meeting, and several spoke their opinions. What are the duties of the county commission?

Review Questions

1. There are four kinds of local government. They are: (a) ____________
(b) ____________ (c) ____________
(d) ____________ *[216]*

2. People pay ____________ taxes for local government. *[216]*

3. The chief unit of local government is the ____________. *[216]*

4. The town that has the county courthouse is called the ____________. *[216]*

5. The county ____________ provides police protection for people living outside the cities. *[216]*

6. County laws are made by the ____________. *[216]*

Your county commission is responsible for the streets and roads in your county. VIRGIL YOUNG

7. How many counties does Idaho have? ____________ *[216]*

City Government. You may already know some of the services that your city provides. Most cities have libraries, parks, fire fighters, and police officers. Cities take care of streets, bridges, and sidewalks. They direct traffic. They look after water, sewer, and garbage service. Cities hire health officers to see that

Boise's 1903 horse-drawn fire pump used steam power to pump water onto fires. IDAHO HISTORICAL SOCIETY

The Boise mayor and city council are seen here at a weekly meeting. Any interested citizen may attend and speak. VIRGIL YOUNG

Police work for the people . . . CITY OF BOISE

. . . as do our firefighters. IDAHO HISTORICAL SOCIETY

businesses serve food and drinks that are clean and safe. City officers check plumbing, electrical work, and buildings to see that they are safe and built well.

Cities are not formed by the legislature or the Idaho Constitution. They are formed by the people who live in them. The legislature has made some general laws that govern cities. Otherwise, cities are free to choose their own ways to handle the needs of their citizens.

Most cities have a **mayor** and a **city council**. The mayor is the executive branch of city government and looks after the day-to-day business of the city. The city council is the **legislative** branch of city government. They make city laws. City council members and almost all mayors are elected by the citizens of their city.

City business is carried on in the **city hall**. The mayor's office is found there, together with other city offices. There may also be other city buildings: a police station, fire station, and jail.

School Districts. Have you ever wondered why you have to go to school? You must go because Idaho people believe strongly that everybody should be educated. The people who wrote the Idaho Constitution believed this also. The Idaho Constitution directed the legislature to provide schools for all the children of Idaho. The legislature, in turn, believed schools to be

The airport is another city service in many Idaho cities. (There are also some county airports.) This is the Boise Air Terminal. CITY OF BOISE

This was also the Boise Air Terminal—in 1928. America's first U. S. Airmail flight landed here on April 6, 1926. The air route ran from Pasco, Washington, through Boise to Elko, Nevada. Later the airport was moved, and today Boise State University stands on this spot. IDAHO HISTORICAL SOCIETY

important. It created special units of government that do nothing but take care of the schools. These are called **school districts**.

Idaho has 114 school districts. Each school district is run by a **school board**. School board members are elected by the people who live in the school district. The school board hires somebody to run the day-to-day business of the school district. This person is called the **superintendent**. The school board also hires your principal and your teachers!

Schools are paid for by taxes. Some of this money comes from local property taxes. However, most of it comes from the Idaho Legislature. The legislature gets the money from the sales tax, income tax, and other state taxes. A small amount of money comes from the United States government.

Some schools in Idaho are **not** run by school districts. These are called **private schools**. They are run and paid for by other groups, most often churches. If they wish, people may send their children to private schools instead of public schools.

Special Districts. Sometimes people want a service that the city or county can't provide. If they wish, the people can form a **special district**. The district will provide the service and set a special tax to pay for it. Many special districts are found in Idaho. They pay for cemeteries, fire protection, sewers, irrigation, libraries, highways, junior colleges, flood control, and other services. It is very likely that you live in more than one special district.

Review Questions

1. The ____________ is the executive branch of city government. [*218*]
2. The ____________ is the legislative branch of city government. [*218*]
3. City business is carried on in the ____________. [*218*]
4. Special units of government that do nothing but take care of the schools are called ____________. [*218–219*]
5. Each school district is run by a ____________. [*219*]
6. The ____________ runs the day-to-day business of the school district. [*219*]

Ideas To Talk About

1. What good are special districts?
2. Are taxes a good idea? Why or why not?

The city swimming pool is a favorite summer treat. CITY OF BOISE

Ann Morrison Park is a city park that lies between the Boise River and downtown Boise. CITY OF BOISE

Sewage disposal is an important city service. CITY OF BOISE

Summary of Idaho Government

STATE

Executive *(Carries out the Laws)*	**Legislative** *(Makes the Laws)*	**Judicial** *(Settles Disputes)*
Governor	Legislature	Supreme Court
Lieutenant Governor	Senate	Court of appeals
	House of Representatives	District Courts
		Magistrate Courts
Secretary of State		
State Auditor		
State Treasurer		
Attorney General		
Superintendent of Public Instruction		

COUNTY

Executive	**Legislative**
Commissioners (3 members)	Commissioners (same persons)
Sheriff	
Treasurer	
Coroner	
Prosecuting Attorney	
Clerk-Auditor-Recorder	

CITY

Executive	**Legislative**
Mayor	City Council

Chapter 11 Skill Activities

Words And Ideas

In Chapter 11, you will find a number of key words printed in **bold** print. Each key word stands for an important idea. Answering these questions will help you understand some of the key words.

You can find the key words in the Glossary at the back of the book. The number after each question is the page where the idea is found in the book. Answer each question with a complete sentence.

1. Where does a **bill** begin? [*215*]
2. What will you find in a **capital**? [*212*]
3. Who writes a **constitution**? [*211–212*]
4. What is a **county seat**? [*216*]
5. What is a **government**? [*209*]
6. Who elects the **school board**? [*219*]
7. The **sheriff** gives police protection to which people? [*216*]
8. What are **taxes** used for? [*213–214*]
9. What did the **vigilantes** do? [*211*]
10. Who do we vote for in an **election**? [*210*]

Where Do They Belong?

The following terms can be divided into four groups. On a piece of paper, write the four headings shown below. Then, below each heading, list the terms that belong in that group.

Headings: Executive Branch, Legislative Branch, Judicial Branch, Building

Terms:

1. capitol
2. county commissioners
3. city council
4. city hall
5. county courthouse
6. court
7. governor
8. house of representatives
9. judge
10. jury
11. legislature
12. mayor
13. senate
14. trial

Applying What You Have Learned

Who Passed That Law?

The following laws might be found in any part of Idaho. Discuss each situation with other students, then decide who passed the law: city, county, or state government.

1. A new snow plow was purchased to remove snow from county roads.
2. People are allowed only six trout each day when fishing in Idaho.
3. Sewer and water services are provided.
4. Farmers may not herd cattle on paved country roads during certain hours of the day.
5. The swimming pool is open only from noon to 5:00 P.M. each day.
6. State police officers patrol the freeways.
7. The sheriff was given a raise in salary.
8. Somebody is hired to take care of the flowers around the capitol.

9. People who have lost their jobs receive money to live on.

10. The old bridge is being replaced at Clover Creek on the south county road.

Using Your Imagination

Many new laws are passed every year. What new laws do you think we should have?

1. Pretend your class is a one-house legislature. Choose a governor by drawing one name from a hat.

2. Invent some new laws that you think are needed. (They are bills until they become laws.) Vote on each bill. A bill must get more than half the votes to pass. (The governor does not vote with the legislature.)

3. Send to the governor any bills that are passed by the legislature. Go back and read "How Laws Are Made" to find out what to do next.

Research Projects

1. **Watching the Newspaper** .

(a) Read your local newspaper for a week. Watch for news articles about state, county, and city government. The news might be about roads, traffic, health, schools, elections, zoning, police, and many other things. Cut out the articles and collect them.

(b) At the end of the week, sort them into three groups: state news, county news, and city news. Make a list of the topics in each group. These topics will give you a good sample of the kinds of things that governments do.

(c) Make three posters to hang in the classroom, using the three lists of topics (from "b" above). They should be labeled State News, County News, and City News.

2. **Invite a Government Official.**

(a) Invite a government official to visit your class to talk about government. This could be your mayor, a city council member, a county commissioner, a legislator, or a state official. Officials are happy to visit schools when they have the time.

(b) Plan some good questions to ask your guest. After the visit, write a report on what you learned.

Reviewing Chapter 11

Main Ideas In This Chapter

1. When people live together, they need laws or rules to live by.

2. In America, citizens elect our government officials.

3. Good government was slow coming to Idaho Territory.

4. When Idaho became a state, it got a new, stronger government.

5. Idaho's state government is built on the Idaho Constitution.

6. The Idaho Constitution gives our state three branches of government: executive, legislative, and judicial.

7. The executive branch carries out the laws of the state.

8. The legislative branch makes the laws for our state.

9. The judicial branch explains the laws and settles disputes.

10. Tax money is collected from citizens to pay for their government.

11. A law begins as a bill in the legislature. If it is passed by the legislature and signed by the governor, it becomes a law.

12. The state government has created smaller, local governments to do some of its work.

13. Counties were created by the state to bring services close to the people.

14. Cities are formed by the people who live in them. They provide many services that the state and county don't provide.

15. School districts are special districts that do nothing but look after the schools.

16. Special districts are sometimes formed to provide services that cities and counties can't provide.

Time Line

	1776 A.D.	Declaration of Independence; USA begins.
1800		
	1805	Lewis and Clark explore Idaho.
	1847	Mormons begin irrigation in Utah.
	1855	Mormons begin irrigation at Fort Lemhi. In 1858 they return to Utah.
	1860	Mormons settle in Franklin and irrigate the land.
	1862	The Homestead Act.
	1863	Bear Lake Valley is settled.
	1864	Malad Valley is settled.
	1871	Canal is built at Preston.
	1873	Utah and Northern Railroad is built to Franklin from Utah.
	1877	The Desert Land Act.
	1877–79	Utah and Northern Railroad is built through eastern Idaho.
	1883	Building of the Oregon Short Line Railroad causes a land rush in the Snake River Valley.
	1884	I.B. Perrine starts his Blue Lakes Ranch.
1900	1900	Perrine claims Snake River to irrigate Magic Valley.
	1902	The Reclamation Act.
	1903	Milner Dam is built. Settling of Magic Valley begins.
	1904	Town of Twin Falls is begun.
	1905	Bad drought in southern Idaho.
	1911	Bridge at bottom of Snake River Canyon replaces ferry between Twin Falls and Jerome.
	1919	Bad drought in southern Idaho.
	1924	Bad drought in southern Idaho.
	1927	Steel rim-to-rim bridge built between Twin Falls and Jerome. Town of American Falls completes its move to higher ground.
	1937	Toll is removed from rim-to-rim bridge, and it is named Perrine Memorial Bridge. The name Magic Valley is born.
	1947	Julion Clawson begins sprinkler irrigation. Most of Idaho's country schools are closed.
	1975	It is discovered that the Snake River could be run dry from too many people using its water.
	1976	Old Perrine Memorial Bridge is replaced by a new stronger bridge. Work is begun on a new American Falls Dam. USA celebrates its Bicentennial
	1990	Idaho Centennial

Chapter 12 Idaho's People— Our Greatest Pride

Idaho's People Have Come From Everywhere.

Do you know what part of the world your family lived in before they came to America? Each one of us has **ancestors** who came from other parts of the world. Those people brought their languages, **customs**, and names with them to America. The Indian people, who were here when the Europeans arrived, came to America from Asia many thousands of years ago. It is the same in Idaho as in the rest of America.

Some families have lived in Idaho longer than others. Your family may have lived here for one year, or a hundred years. Perhaps it was a grandparent who first came, or perhaps even a great-great-grandparent. It makes no difference. We are all Idahoans. Idahoans respect one another, both when we are alike and when we are different. America was built on this idea.

The telephone book gives us interesting clues about the people of Idaho. Some names clearly belong to one country or group of people. Smith is British and Schmidt is German. HighEagle and TopSky are Indian, while O'Leary is Irish. Johnson is Swedish. Martin may be either French or British, but Martinez is Spanish or Mexican. Wong is Chinese, and Tran is Vietnamese. Hayashi is Japanese; McDonald is Scottish; Epeldi is Basque.

The telephone book is not a perfect guide to names and countries. Some names are not easy to connect with a country, and sometimes family names have been changed. However, the telephone book does show that many Idaho family names trace back to Europe. Also it shows that the largest number of European names have come from Ireland and Great Britain. Great Britain is made up of England, Scotland, and Wales.

Even if we are Americans, it is fun to think about where our families have come from. The following pages introduce some groups of Idaho people. We begin with the Indians or Native Americans, of course, because they were here first. They were followed by explorers and settlers. Early newspapers reported a few blacks and Mexicans, too. Soon after, Chinese people arrived in Idaho's towns and mining camps. Japanese and Basque people arrived later. These are not all of Idaho's people, either. New people continue to arrive in Idaho every year.

Idaho's people have come from everywhere.
BALDEMAR ELIZONDO

Review Questions

1. Name five different countries that Idaho people have come from: (a) ___________ (b) ___________ (c) ___________ (d) ___________ (e) ___________ [223]

2. Name three things that our ancestors brought with them from other parts of the world: (a) ___________ (b) ___________ (c) ___________ [223]

Hattie Enos and her grandchildren are celebrating her 90th birthday. #6-24-1E D. E. WARREN U OF I LIBRARY

Indians Today Live Like Everyone Else.

By Laverne Sheppard

Many first-time visitors to Indian reservations are surprised. They find Indians living in houses, driving cars, going to school, and working just like everyone else. Indians no longer have to live on reservations. Some live and work in the cities. Others like the slower pace of reservation life with its farms and small towns. Here Indians still own much of the land, and families stay close together.

Indians give older people a great deal of respect. It is the older people who teach the younger people about their tribe. Young people are encouraged to learn the language, history, legends, art, and religious customs of their people. They may also take Indian language classes taught at the reservations.

Many schools on and near reservations in Idaho have an Indian Day each September. On this day, people honor the contributions that Indians have made to our state and country. Indian speakers visit the schools to talk about their tribes, and many Indian students take part in Indian dances.

Some of Idaho's Indians are quite well known in their fields. Jeanne Givens, a Coeur d'Alene Indian, serves in the Idaho Legislature. Hattie Kauffman, a Nez Perce Indian, is a reporter for the television show *Good Morning America*. Others are well-known lawyers, teachers, business people, and leaders of their tribes.

Each tribe chooses its own leaders. The leaders meet in a **council**, which is the tribe's government. They spend much of their time deciding how to make the best use of reservation land and resources. They want the greatest good for their people.

Jobs are scarce on reservations because tribes have been slow to change to the modern way of life. Many Indians must move away from the reservation just to find work. During the past several years, some Idaho tribes have started their own businesses to make jobs and income for Indian people. In 1978, the Shoshone-Bannock Tribes opened a grocery store, clothing store, gas station, and restaurant. Later, the Coeur d'Alene Tribe built a shopping mall, and the Kutenais built a hotel. The Nez Perce Tribe has bought land in northern Idaho to start a timber business.

The tribes want their young people to stay on the reservations to help improve the lives of their people. The young people are encouraged to go to college. However, it is hoped they will return to run the businesses and manage the reservations's resources. The State of Idaho also helps Indian businesses. Indian businesses can sell groceries and other goods without charging state taxes. State leaders passed this law to help Indian businesses earn money and make jobs for Indian people.

Hunting and fishing are still an important part of life on reservations. Some families even yet depend on wild animals and salmon for food. Many Indians think of hunting and fishing as a way to teach young Indian people about their tribe's older way of life. The tribes, however, protect the fish and wild animals so that not too many are killed.

The Nez Perce enjoy traditional dances. This dance is in a high school gym. #6-24-2F D. E. WARREN U OF I LIBRARY

Each year, the tribes in Idaho hold celebrations. Here Indians from all over the country come to dance, sing, feast, and play Indian games. These **powwows** give Indian young people the chance to dance for prizes and to meet Indians from other places. Indians enjoy giving each other gifts at "giveaways" held during these powwows. Giving and sharing are two important parts of Indian life that tribes want to bring into the modern world.

Laverne Sheppard is a member of the Shoshone-Bannock Tribes and is editor of their newspaper, the Sho-Ban News.

Ideas To Talk About

1. In what ways do today's Indians live like everyone else?
2. In what ways is Indian culture different from that of other Idaho people?
3. How could you learn more about the Indians who live in Idaho?

White Americans Came From Europe.

The largest number of Idaho people are white. Their families came from Europe. When Idaho's land filled with settlers, these were mostly white people who came from the United States. Their families had come as immigrants from Europe at an earlier time. Besides these, other people came to Idaho directly from Europe. They came from Great Britain, Ireland, Germany, Sweden, Norway, Poland, Czechoslovakia, Russia, Finland, and other countries.

The map of Idaho gives many clues about the Europeans who explored or settled Idaho. Lewiston was named for Meriwether Lewis, an American whose family came from England. Payette was the name of a French-Canadian trapper. Weiser was the name of a trapper and miner who had a German name. McCall is a Scottish name, and Murphy is Irish. Shelley is English and Hansen is Scandinavian. The names Boise, Coeur d'Alene, and Pend Oreille all come from French words used by early French-Canadian trappers.

Because so many Idaho people are white, much of Idaho's history is written about whites. However, we must not forget the other groups of people scattered through Idaho's history. We will see several of them on the following pages.

Review Questions

1. Name five countries that are in Europe:
(a) ____________ (b) ____________
(c) ____________ (d) ____________
(e) ____________ [225]

2. Name five places in Idaho that have been given European names: (a) ____________
(b) ____________ (c) ____________
(d) ____________ (e) ____________ [225]

Idaho Ebony: Black Americans In Idaho History.

By Mamie O. Oliver, Ph.D.

Black history in Idaho began with York, the black man who came west with Lewis and Clark in 1805. The Indians had never seen a black person before and were surprised when the color wouldn't wash off. They admired his shiny black skin and great strength. In the years to come, the Indians were to see more blacks in Idaho. After York, there came black trappers, fur traders, miners, soldiers, railroad workers, horse trainers, and rodeo riders.

Though blacks have lived in Idaho just as long as whites, this fact is not well known. Early newspapers did not report much news about them.

Elvina Moulton was a former slave who came to Idaho in 1878. She became a charter member of First Presbyterian Church in Boise. IDAHO HISTORICAL SOCIETY

Newspapers reported mostly funny things that blacks did, or reported those charged with a crime. This lack of news made Idaho's early blacks "invisible" when history was written. Most of Idaho's black citizens have passed without much notice from anyone.

Even so, we know about a few of the blacks who came to Idaho. Jane Allen may have been the first black baby born in Idaho. She was born in Ada County in 1861. Bella Carvan was born in Idaho City in 1865. Lewis Walker was a Silver City miner, who also worked as a barber. "Aunt Vinney" Moulton had been a slave. In 1867, she crossed the plains, walking barefoot part of the way. Tired of walking, she stopped in Boise and stayed. In 1878, she became the only black member of the Boise Presbyterian Church.

A number of blacks became cowboys. Some worked as camp cooks, while others roped cattle or broke horses. They rode hard, working the cattle alongside the other cowboys. A few joined outlaw gangs. All in all, they did the same things that all the cowboys did.

A small number of black families homesteaded in southern Idaho. One of these was Ned Leggroan of Mississippi. He became a Mormon and came west to Utah. In 1899, he settled on a farm near Idaho Falls. Other black families also settled on farms in that part of Idaho. Some of those families still live in Idaho. Clara Stevens Terrill, now of Boise, belongs to one of these. "I was born and raised in Rigby," she tells us. "My father was a farmer, and for years we were the only black family in that area."

Many early blacks in Idaho had to work at low paying jobs. Addie Carvan (baby Bella's mother) was a housekeeper in Idaho City. Her husband, Andrew, worked at such jobs as he could find. Whites liked to use blacks as workers, but often looked down upon them. As a rule, black people were not treated well.

The Army, Navy, and Air Force have brought a number of black people to Idaho. There were black soldiers in Idaho at least as early as 1900. During World War II, soldiers and sailors were sent to Idaho for training. Later, Air Force men and women came to Mountain Home Air Force Base. Many of these people, both black and white, decided to stay and make Idaho their home.

Idaho has never had a lot of black people. Records showed only 60 black people in Idaho in 1870, and only 53 in 1880. The number has grown in the past 100 years, but it is still small. The last count was made in 1980. There were about one million people in Idaho then, but only 2,711 of them were black.

Since early times, black families have known that going to school would make life better for

Ned and Suzanne Leggroan came west from Mississippi after they were married. They homesteaded near Milo, Idaho, in the 1880s. IDAHO HISTORICAL SOCIETY

their children. For more than 100 years, black students have been a part of Idaho schools and colleges. In 1899, Jennie Hughes, a black woman, graduated from the University of Idaho. Now it is common to see black students playing football, basketball, and other sports in Idaho high schools and colleges.

Today black Americans are part of everyday life in Idaho. In 1976, Les Purce became mayor of Pocatello, Idaho's first black mayor. Idaho blacks are teachers, professors, business people, and government workers, among other things. Though small in number, black Americans are an important part of Idaho.

Dr. Mamie O. Oliver was formerly Professor of Social Work at Boise State University.

Ideas To Talk About

1. What are some reasons that Idaho's black citizens were "invisible" when history was written?
2. Why was life hard for the early blacks who came to Idaho?
3. How does education make life better for black people?
4. Why do you think there are so few black people in Idaho?

Chien and Lily Wai are Chinese Americans who live in Moscow. Both are professors at the University of Idaho. Pictured here in 2001 are three generations of the Wai family. LILY WAI

The Chinese Of Idaho: A Small But Important Group

By Dixie L. Ehrenreich, Ph.D.

The number of Chinese in Idaho today is small but important. In 1986, there were only about 700 in all of Idaho. Of these, many were well educated and worked in professional jobs. Most spoke Chinese at home, as well as English.

Today's Chinese in Idaho are not like those we read about during the gold rush. Those Chinese were mostly miners, railroad workers, farmers, and others who did heavy work. They wanted to make lots of money in America and take it back home to China. They did not want to become Americans. They kept their Chinese dress, food, and language. Most of them were men, and they lived close together in boarding houses and other settlements. Very few Chinese women and children came, because the Chinese men expected to go back home to their families in China.

Because of the way they lived, it was easy for Americans to notice these different-looking people who didn't want to be Americans. Some of the Chinese took jobs that others thought they should have. Bad feelings against the Chinese became so strong that the government made a law against them in 1882. This law stopped most Chinese from coming to America. Only a few well-educated Chinese people were allowed to come after that. Very few of these came to Idaho.

This law was kept for 61 years—until 1943. In 1943, China was our friend in a terrible war, so the law was changed. By that time, very few Chinese were left in Idaho. A few Chinese families remained from the early days, but most of the old men had died or gone back to China. For 61 years, hardly any Chinese had moved to Idaho.

Since 1965, the number of Chinese in Idaho has grown slowly larger. The laws have been changed again to make it easier for them to come to America. More Chinese families are arriving, and more babies are being born. The new Chinese families are made up of two separate groups. The first group has come from parts of China, mostly mainland China, Taiwan, and Hong Kong. These are mostly professional people, because these are all the law will allow. Because these Chinese are well-educated professional people, they like to live in cities and college towns. They also like to go where there are other friendly Chinese. It is easy to see why few come to Idaho. Our cities are small, and we have very few Chinese already here.

A second group of Chinese has come to America since 1975. These people were living in other countries of Asia, mostly Vietnam, Laos, and Cambodia. Because of the war in Vietnam, Chinese people were forced out of those countries. They became homeless people. Our government passed special laws that allowed many of them to come to the United States. Some have moved to Idaho.

Most of this second group are less well educated. They are often farmers, laborers, and others who do heavy work. They may have run away from wars in several countries before coming to America. Many speak little English when they arrive. The Chinese in this group often move to smaller towns. Small towns offer them a better chance to find jobs and American friends to help them.

It is believed that the number of Chinese in the United States will grow faster in the years to come. More babies will be born, and more families will arrive from other countries. Some of these people will come to Idaho to live. The Chinese will be continue to be an important group of Idaho people.

Dr. Dixie L. Ehrenreich is a Research Scientist in the Laboratory of Anthropology at the University of Idaho.

Ideas To Talk About

1. How are today's Chinese in Idaho different from those who lived here during the 1870's?

2. Why do you think there are only a few Chinese people in Idaho?

3. Why do you think people have bad feelings about other people who look different or have different customs?

4. How have wars and laws affected the number of Chinese people coming to Idaho?

Idaho's Japanese Americans.

By Robert C. Sims, Ph.D.

Japanese immigrants came to the United States in a very short period, mostly between 1880 and 1910. Although they did not arrive in large numbers, they have been important to our country and our state. The Japanese people came to America to find jobs.

We already learned that a law in 1882 stopped Chinese people from coming to the United States. This was just at the time when the western states needed more workers for mining, farming, timber, and railroads. The law did not prevent Japanese workers from coming to America. Japanese immigrants were able to get jobs that would have gone to Chinese workers.

Many Japanese workers came to Idaho during the next several years. The first came to Idaho in the 1890s to work on the railroads. That was a time when several railroad lines were being built through the state, and most of the workers were Japanese. In 1892, there were more than 2,000 Japanese working on railroads in Idaho. Large numbers could be found around Pocatello and Nampa, both railroad centers.

Sugar beets also brought immigrants from Ja-

Some members of this baseball team are Japanese Americans. They played in southwest Idaho in the early 1930s. ROBERT C. SIMS

Beginning in the 1890s, many Japanese men worked on railroads in Idaho. ROBERT SIMS

pan. In 1903, more than 600 Japanese workers were brought in to help open the state's first sugar beet factory at Idaho Falls. Soon after they came to work on railroads or in sugar beets, some of the Japanese started businesses or farms of their own. Many were successful.

A number of Idaho people did not like to have Japanese in the state. Beginning in 1915, they tried to get laws passed that would prevent Japanese from owning land in the state. Such a law was passed in 1923. Just a year earlier, the United States Supreme Court had ruled that Japanese immigrants could not become citizens.

The children of Japanese immigrants were citizens, however. Any child born in the United States is an American citizen. The American children of Japanese immigrants are called **Nisei**. This means the second generation. The name Nisei is sometimes used to mean any Japanese-American citizen.

In spite of their problems, the Japanese and Nisei in Idaho made progress. In the 1930s, Japanese Americans were becoming successful in many kinds of businesses and professions.

World War II put a stop to this progress. In 1941, Japan went to war against the United States, and many Americans became angry at Japanese Americans. During the war, the United States removed more than 112,000 Japanese immigrants and their children from their homes along the west coast. These people were moved to relocation camps and kept under military guard. Over 70,000 of them were American citizens. One of the camps was in Idaho. It was called Camp Minidoka, and it held 9,500 people.

During the war, Japanese Americans proved that they were good American citizens. Many got permission to leave the camps to work in jobs that would help America win the war. Hundreds of young Nisei men joined the Army. They formed an all-Japanese American fighting unit called the 442nd Regimental Combat Team. This unit fought fiercely and bravely in Italy and France. Because of its fine record, the 442nd received more honors and awards than any other fighting unit in World War II.

Life improved for Japanese Americans after World War II. They had proved to be good citizens during the war, and the bad feelings toward them began to fade. When the war was over, 3,500 Japanese and Nisei chose to stay and live in Idaho. Many went into farming, and their farms are among the most productive in Idaho. Others have gone into business, teaching, science, medicine, and many other kinds of work. Japanese Americans have become an important group of Idaho citizens.

Dr. Robert C. Sims is Professor of History and Dean of the School of Social Sciences and Public Affairs at Boise State University.

Review Questions

1. When did most of the Japanese immigrants come to America? [228]

2. The first Japanese workers came to Idaho to work on the ____________. [228]

3. The American children of Japanese immigrants are called ____________. [229]

Ideas To Talk About

1. Why do you think our government placed Japanese immigrants and their children in camps and kept them under guard during World War II?

2. After the war, Americans realized that our government had been wrong to lock up the Japanese immigrants and Nisei. Why do you think it was wrong?

The Basques Came To Idaho From Spain.

Idaho is the home of many **Basque** people who came here from northern Spain. They came for two important reasons. Some came to make a better living for themselves and their families. Others came to escape from an unfriendly Spanish government.

Basques came to California during the 1849 gold rush. They didn't do much gold mining, however. Though they came from Spain, they had their own language. Most of them spoke only Basque and had very little schooling. For these reasons, they had a hard time finding good jobs. Many turned to farm work and herding sheep because English was not needed to do these jobs. The Basques proved to be hard working and honest.

The news spread back to Spain that there were jobs in America. This brought many Basques to Idaho. The first to come were men. Many of them saved money and sent to Spain for their wives and sweethearts. The women came, and soon Basque families were living in Idaho. Boise Valley gained a large number of Basque families between 1900 and 1920. Boise City became an important Basque center.

Many Basques first came to Idaho as sheepherders. What do you think the wagon with the stove pipe was used for? #6–78–1A U OF I LIBRARY

Nearly all of Idaho's early Basque men started out herding sheep. Few of them really wanted to herd sheep, so most of them took other jobs as soon as they could. Often they were able to find other jobs as soon as they learned to speak English.

Hardly any Basques herd sheep now. Today's Basques work as doctors, lawyers, bankers, college professors, and teachers. Others work in stores or offices, or have their own businesses. Pete T. Cenarrusa, son of Basque immigrant parents, has been Idaho's Secretary of State since 1967. Many Idaho families have Basque names

Idaho's Basque Dancers have pleased crowds all over America. Basques are very proud of their old-country customs. What part of Europe did the Basques come from? IDAHO DEPARTMENT OF COMMERCE

that show that part of their family once lived in northern Spain. Among these names are Archabal, Bengoechea, Echavarria, Gabica, Uranga, and many, many others.

Today Boise Valley is one of America's most important Basque centers. A large number of American Basques live in this part of the country. Because of that, Idaho is an important place for Basques in Spain as well as those in America. It also gives this interesting group of Americans a special place in Idaho history.

Today's Idaho Basques are Americans. The children of the first Basques now have children and grandchildren of their own. They grew up in Basque-speaking homes, but few of them learned to speak Basque. As a result, most of today's Idaho Basques know very few Basque words.

Idaho Basques are taking a new interest and pride in their old-country Basque customs. The Basque people brought with them from Spain a strong love for freedom and a deep feeling for their religion. They also brought their old-country language, songs, music, and dances. These customs began to drop away as the Basques became Americans.

Now, however, many Basques have been working to teach these customs to their children. Idaho Basques have singing and dancing groups, and there are classes for young people to study the Basque language. Basque dancing has become part of life in Idaho. The Idaho Oinkari Basque Dancers have pleased crowds all over America. They danced at the New York World's Fair in 1964 and the Spokane Expo World's Fair in 1974. Idaho Basques also hold festivals each summer in Boise and in Sun Valley. Here they have Basque feasts, games, dancing, and contests.

Review Questions

1. The Basque people came to Idaho from what part of Europe: ____________ [*230*]

2. A large number of Basque families came to Idaho between the years ____________ and ____________. [*230*]

Ideas To Talk About

1. Today Idaho has a large number of Basque families, but a small number of Chinese families. How can we explain this difference?

2. Hardly any Basques herd sheep now. What did the Basques have to do get jobs in business or government, or become doctors, lawyers, or teachers?

Mexican Americans: Our Hispanic Citizens.

By Santos Salinas

Mexicans and Mexican Americans were living in Idaho as early as 1865. Several places in Idaho were given Spanish names during and after the gold rush: Orofino, Lago, Oreano, Buena Vista, and others. In 1870, Mexican gold miners were working between Boise City and Idaho City. The *Idaho Tri-Weekly Statesman* reported in 1871 that Mexicans in Idaho had held a celebration in honor of the Mexican Republic.

Mexican Americans are citizens of the United States. Mexicans are citizens of Mexico. Early records in Idaho often don't tell us if a person with a Spanish name was a Mexican or American citizen. Today these people are called **Hispanics**, meaning that their language and culture came from Spain.

At least two early packers in Idaho were Hispanic. One of them, Jesus Urquides, was well known in Boise City. "Spanish Joe" Gestal ran a

Judge Sergio A. Gutierrez is Idaho's first Hispanic judge, appointed to the Idaho Court of Appeals by Governor Kempthorne in 2002. Judge Gutierrez is the son of farm workers. Although he once dropped out of high school, he went on to college and successfully graduated from law school. PARKER PORTRAITS

Boise City restaurant for many years before and after 1891.

In the 1920s, Hispanic people began coming to Idaho to work at summer farm jobs. These were hard jobs like weeding fields, thinning sugar beets, irrigating farm land, and picking fruit and corn by hand. After the harvest, most of them would move on to other places. Workers who follow farm work from place to place are called **migrant** workers.

For many years, most Hispanics in Idaho were migrant workers. Migrant workers often lived in labor camps. These camps were a lot like villages, handling their own problems. Families lived there free or at low cost. In return, each person was expected to spend two hours a week cleaning and taking care of the camp.

Since the 1960s, many Idaho Hispanics have chosen to stay and make Idaho their home. Though some are still farm workers, other Hispanics have chosen other ways of life. These no longer live in labor camps. Their young people are staying in school, and many are going to college. Educated Hispanics are becoming teachers, professors, lawyers, writers, nurses, and musicians. Others have gone into business.

Hispanics are still proud of their language and culture. They want their children to be proud, too. When they celebrate Cinco de Mayo and Mexican Independence Day, they share their culture with other Idaho people, too.

Hispanics are the fastest growing group of Idaho citizens. In 1988, there were between 50,000 and 60,000 Hispanics in Idaho. In years to come, there will be many more. Their interesting names are all around us: Alvarado, DeLeon, Fuentes, Galvan, Lopez, Salinas, and many more. The Hispanic future in Idaho looks bright.

Santos Salinas is an Instructor in Bilingual Education at Boise State University.

Review Questions

1. A person whose name, language, or culture comes from Spain is called a ____________. [231]

2. Most of Idaho's Hispanic families have come from what country? ____________ [231]

3. Workers who follow farm work from place to place are called ____________ workers. [231–232]

Ideas To Talk About

1. Mexico is nowhere near Spain. Why should Mexicans be called Hispanics?

2. Why do you think people live as migrants instead of getting better jobs and living in one place?

3. Why is life getting better for many Idaho Hispanics?

Women in Idaho.

By Susan H. Swetnam.

If you believe some movies and television shows, you might think that pioneer women spent most of their time being rescued. If you look at the lives of real pioneer women in Idaho, however, you can easily see that this isn't true. In fact, the women of Idaho history have done a great number of important things.

Two famous Idaho women, Sacajawea and Eliza Spalding, show how important women could be. Sacajawea, you may remember, traveled with Lewis and Clark. In 1805, Sacajawea gave Lewis and Clark valuable help in finding a route over the mountains to the Pacific. She recognized her brother, Chief Cameahwait, among a group of Shoshoni in the Lemhi Valley. Afterward, Chief Cameahwait became friendly and gave Lewis and Clark directions and a guide.

Eliza Spalding and her husband, Reverend Henry Spalding, came to Lapwai in 1836. Eliza started the first school in Idaho. She taught Nez Perce adults and children reading, writing, religion, and home crafts.

Pioneer women began coming to Idaho with their families during in the 1860s. Their lives were filled with hard, useful work. Even housework in pioneer days wasn't easy. On wash days, women had first to chop wood, build a fire, and carry water. To wash, they soaked the clothes in hot, soapy water and scrubbed them on a washboard. Then they boiled the clothes in new water and rinsed them in a third change of water before hanging them out to dry. A pioneer wash took at least 50 gallons of water, and a gallon of water weighs eight pounds. Imagine how steamy a small cabin got with all that water boiling for hours, especially in winter! No wonder that one pioneer woman said that washday always made her feel "worse than a stewed witch."

Pioneer women had other, more pleasant jobs, of course. Some women made their houses pretty by digging up wildflowers in the hills and planting them in their yards. They often papered their cabin walls (with newspaper if there was nothing else), and made clothes and wove rugs. They improved their children's lives by teaching them to sing and read, and they improved their towns by starting the first schools, libraries, theaters, and music groups.

Pioneer women helped with making a living, too. Some sold homemade products like honey, eggs, berries, and quilts. Others worked outside their homes, managing post offices, driving school buses and mail wagons, and running family stores. Many pioneer women worked in the fields beside their husbands and fathers, and some liked this work very much. Marcia Hennefer, who lived in Thomas, helped her father build an irrigation canal when she was only 11 years old. She drove a team of horses while her father held the plow.

Some pioneer women were very brave in the face of danger. In 1912, Mary Elizabeth Waters Barzee moved with her husband and five children to a homestead in the Birch Creek Valley. One summer, while her husband was away herding sheep, she had to protect her tent home all by herself. She writes in her life history:

"The cattlemen in the area did not want us there . . . and would gather several hundred of their cattle, head them towards our tent, then whip them into a stampede in an effort to run them over our tent and drive us out. Nine-year-old Effie and seven-year-old Marcia stood on bumps a few steps from and on either side of me, and I stood on another bump directly in line with the tent, each of us yelling at the tops of our voices and waving our arms, and with the aid of our part bloodhound, part bulldog helper, Jack, we split the herd and saved the tent with the smaller children in it. . . . Stampeding the cattle towards our tent was repeated many times."

Even though pioneer women helped their families and towns in many ways, they could not vote. Things sometimes got rough at voting places, and women were thought to be "too delicate, too refined" to be interested in such things. In 1898, however, Idaho's men voted to give women the right to vote. Idaho was only the fourth state to do so. (The others were Wyoming, Utah, and Colorado.) It was not until 1920 that the United States Constitution was changed to give women in all the states the right to vote.

In Idaho's 1898 election, the first three women were elected to the Idaho Legislature. Also Permeal French, from Idaho City, was elected State Superintendent of Public Instruction in that election. Until 1932, all Idaho State Superintendents were women. After 1898, though, only four women were elected to the Idaho Legislature during the next ten years. The number of women in the legislature has increased slowly over the years.

Since the late 1800s, Idaho's women have worked in many different kinds of roles. Some have been leaders in ranching and farming, like Emma Russell Yearian, called the "Sheep Queen of Idaho." Emma, a mother of six, got a loan and brought the first sheep to the Lemhi Valley. She ran her own operation for 40 years. Others have been businesswomen. Mabel Kasiska Hillman, of Lava Hot Springs, became Idaho's first woman bank president. Georgia Davidson started Boise's first television station. A few have been well-known writers and artists, like Mary Hallock Foote. Her sketches of life in the Boise River Canyon were published in national magazines.

Some women have been leaders in education. Ethel E. Redfield served as Head of the Department of Education at Idaho State University from 1928–1947. Others have held important jobs in state government. Since 1947, seven out of eight Idaho state publishers, businesspersons, and teachers have been women. Of course, many women still, as in pioneer days, work very hard to help their families earn a living, teach their children to sing, and make their homes beautiful.

Women in Idaho have certainly been much stronger and have done many more things than movies and television would lead you to believe!

Dr. Susan H. Swetman is Associate Professor of English at Idaho State University.

Ideas to Talk About

1. Do you think pioneer women worked harder than women today? Explain your answer.

2. Women today are able to do many more kinds of jobs today than during pioneer times. Why do you think this has happened?

Famous Idahoans.

Most Idaho people are not famous and never will be. Still, they help Idaho by doing their daily work and helping their neighbors. They care about their neighborhood, their state, and their country. Most Idaho people lead good, useful lives, no matter what country their families have come from. They care; they work; they build a better state and a better world. Idaho can be proud of its people.

Some Idaho people have done outstanding work in their fields. They have given their very best, and they have become people for others to admire. Such people are special.

The following pages show a few of the many Idaho people who have become well-known. Some are living, and some are dead. This book has room for only a few of the many people who could be listed here. It is hoped that their fine example will make others want to follow in their footsteps.

Cecil D. Andrus was Governor of Idaho when President Jimmy Carter asked him to go to Washington to serve as United States Secretary of the Interior (1977–1981). He was Governor from 1971–1977 and again from 1987–1995. This is more years than any other Idaho governor. Mr. Andrus lives in Boise. IDAHO HISTORICAL SOCIETY

J. A. "Joe" Albertson started the Albertson's food markets. He built his first store in Boise in 1939. Today there are hundreds of Albertson's stores from California to Florida. IDAHO HISTORICAL SOCIETY

Moses Alexander was the governor of Idaho from 1915 to 1919. He was the first Jewish governor elected in the United States. IDAHO HISTORICAL SOCIETY

Dr. Marty Becker is America's favorite pet doctor. He is a regular on ABC-TV's *Good Morning America*, where he talks about pet care. Dr. Becker also appears on other popular TV programs, and writes about pets and their owners in magazines, newspapers, and books. He grew up on a farm in Magic Valley and now lives in Bonners Ferry. DR. MARTY BECKER

Carol Ryrie Brink wrote 26 books for adults and young people. Her best-known book is *Caddie Woodlawn*, a book for young people. *Louly* is another book for young people. It is based on Mrs. Brink's own life while growing up in Moscow. *Buffalo Coat*, a book for adults, is based on the life of Mrs Brink's grandfather during Moscow's early days. #3-791, HISTORICAL PHOTO COLLECTION, UNIVERSITY OF IDAHO

Mary Brooks was Director of the U. S Bureau of the Mint from 1969 to 1977. During that time, she was responsible for all the coins (money) made in the United States. Mrs. Brooks's home is at Carey. IDAHO HISTORICAL SOCIETY

James Castle was a "primitive" artist. He developed his own art style, even though he could not speak, hear, or use regular sign language. He began drawing pictures to communicate with other people. Mr. Castle grew up in Garden Valley, and later moved to Boise. He died in 1977. BOISE GALLERY OF ART

Carole Farley is a famous opera star. She has starred in New York, Washington, Boston, and other American cities. Her work also takes her to England, Germany, France, and other European countries. She has even sung in South America and Australia. Miss Farley graduated from Moscow High School in 1964. MELVIN FARLEY

Michael Hoffman is a well-known movie director. He grew up in Payette and graduated from Boise State University. In 1979, he won a Rhodes scholarship to Oxford University in England, where he studied literature and wrote and directed his first film. Since then he has directed nine movies, including *A Midsummer Night's Dream* and *The Palace Thief*. Mr. Hoffman lives in Boise. BOISE STATE UNIVERSITY ARCHIVES

Philo Farnsworth became the "Father of Television." In 1922, while a student at Rigby High School, he drew the world's first workable television design. In later years, Mr. Farnsworth developed more than 150 other inventions in the field of television. FARNSWORTH TV PIONEER MUSEUM

Vardis Fisher was a well-known writer. Not only was he born in Idaho, he wrote most of his 36 books at his home in Hagerman Valley. His most famous book was *Mountain Man*, which was made into the movie *Jeremiah Johnson*. Mr. Fisher died in 1968. IDAHO HISTORICAL SOCIETY

Joe Parkinson was co-founder and CEO of Micron Technology. In 1978, he and two other men formed a tiny company that operated out of the basement of a dentist's office in Boise. From these beginnings, Joe Parkinson helped build an Idaho company that has become one of the world's largest makers of computer chips. He began his career at the age of seven picking potatoes in the Blackfoot area, and earned his own way through college and law school. THE IDAHO STATESMAN

May Hutton was important in winning women the right to vote. She was Idaho's most important "suffragette," and she became known across the United States. She came to Idaho "on the hurricane deck of a cayuse pony" and got a job cooking for miners around Kellogg. Later she and her husband "struck it rich" with a silver mine and became millionaires. She died in 1915, just five years before women won the right to vote. IDAHO HISTORICAL SOCIETY

William Jardine was U. S. Secretary of Agriculture under President Coolidge. Later he became ambassador to Egypt. Besides these jobs, Mr. Jardine was the president of two different universities in Kansas. He was born near Malad in 1879. IDAHO HISTORICAL SOCIETY

Hattie Kauffman is a television reporter for the "Good Morning America" television show. She has won four Emmy Awards for her work in TV writing and reporting. Ms. Kauffman was born in Grangeville, and is a member of the Nez Perce Tribe. ABC ENTERTAINMENT

Harmon Killebrew was a famous baseball player for the Washington Senators and Minnesota Twins. He hit 573 home runs, giving him fifth place in the all-time records for home runs. Mr. Killebrew also played in several world series. He graduated from Payette High School in 1954. OFFICE OF THE IDAHO SECRETARY OF STATE

David Maxey was editor of *Psychology Today* and *GED* magazines. He also worked for *Look* and *Life* magazines. In his first writing job, he talked to many important people, including President Kennedy. Mr. Maxey grew up in Boise and graduated from the University of Idaho. IDAHO STATESMAN

Harry W. Morrison and his partner, Morris H. Knudsen, started the Morrison-Knudsen Company in Boise in 1912. The company grew from a few horses and simple tools to become one of the world's largest builders. The Morrison family gave Ann Morrison Park to the City of Boise. Later the family gave money to help build the Morrison Center for the Performing Arts at Boise State University. IDAHO HISTORICAL SOCIETY

Morlan W. Nelson is known in many countries for his work with birds of prey (hawks, falcons, and eagles). For years, he trained birds for Walt Disney movies. He helped create the Snake River Birds of Prey Natural Area in Idaho. Mr. Nelson lives in Boise. IDAHO DEPARTMENT OF COMMERCE

Picabo Street is a world-famous skier from Idaho. She has won two Olympic medals in skiing, a silver in 1994 and a gold in 1998. She joined the U.S. Ski Team in 1989, and she has won several world and U.S. championships. Picabo was born in Triumph, Idaho, in 1971. She was the only girl among the nine kids in town—and seven of those boys were her brothers! Her parents named her after the nearby town of Picabo (pronounced *peek-a-boo*). AP/WIDE WORLD PHOTOS

Arthur Troutner invented new kinds of building trusses and revolutionized the building industry. He called his Boise company the Trus Joist Corporation. When old-growth timber became scarce, he found ways to glue smaller pieces of wood together to make new lumber. His inventions included the now common I-shaped floor joists and large laminated beams. Mr. Troutner died in 2001. THE IDAHO STATESMAN

J. R. "Jack" Simplot started the J. R. Simplot Company. At the age of 15, he went into business for himself by renting 40 acres near Declo to grow potatoes. His farming business grew, and later he added potato storing and potato processing. The J. R. Simplot Company has become one of the largest potato processing companies in the United States. Mr. Simplot lives in Boise. IDAHO HISTORICAL SOCIETY

Chapter 12 Skill Activities

Words And Ideas

In Chapter 12, you will find a number of key words printed in **bold** print. Each key word stands for an important idea. Answering these questions will help you understand some of the key words.

You can find the key words in the Glossary at the back of the book. The number after each question is the page where the idea is found in the book. Answer each question with a complete sentence.

1. What do we mean when we say "our **ancestors**"? [*223*]
2. Where did the **Basque** people come from? [*230*]
3. What is a **council**? [*224*]
4. What is an example of a **custom**? [*223*]
5. Why are Mexican Americans called **Hispanics**? [*231*]
6. What is a **migrant** worker? [*231–232*]
7. Who are the **Nisei**? [*229*]
8. What do Indians do at a **powwow**? [*225*]

Research Projects

1. Write a Report. Write a report on one of the following groups of Idaho people: American Indians, Black Americans, Basques, Chinese Americans, Japanese Americans (Nisei), or Mexican Americans.

You can use this book, an encyclopedia, or another source.

2. Invite a Guest. Invite someone from one of these groups to visit your class and talk about their customs.

(a) Prepare for the visit by reading about the culture. Then plan some good questions to ask your visitor.

(b) After the visit, write a report on what you learned.

3. Discover Your Family's Flag. Find out from your family what country your ancestors came from. There could be more than one country.

(a) Find that country on a world map. Be able to answer the following questions: What is the name of the country? On which continent is it located? What countries are its neighbors?

(b) Find a picture of the country's flag. There should be one in your encyclopedia.

(c) Draw and color a **small** picture of the flag. (Make it three inches long and two inches wide.)

(d) Display everyone's flag. Trace an outline of Idaho on a large piece of butcher paper. Then display all the flags inside of Idaho.

Using Your Imagination

1. Writing a Diary. It is many years ago, and you are just ten years old. You are part of an immigrant family who has just arrived in Idaho. Your family belongs to one of the following groups: Black Americans, Basques, Chinese Americans, Japanese Americans, or Mexican Americans.

(a) Choose the group that your family belongs to.

(b) Write a diary for one week. You should tell about the following things: What do you see? How is it different from the place you came from? What are you doing? What are you thinking about and how do you feel? What are your parents doing? What do you think they are thinking? What do you think will happen in the future?

Reviewing Chapter 12

Main Ideas In This Chapter

Idaho's people have come from many parts of the world.

2. Indians today live very much like other Americans.

3. White Americans came from Europe.

4. Idaho's white families came from many different European countries.

5. Blacks have lived in Idaho since it was first settled.

6. Life was hard for Idaho's early black people.

7. The number of black people in Idaho is small.

8. The Chinese in Idaho today are different from the first Chinese who lived here.

9. A law was passed in 1882 that stopped most Chinese from coming to America.

10. Today there are two different groups of Chinese immigrants in Idaho.

11. Only a few Chinese people live in Idaho.

12. For many years, Japanese immigrants could not own property or become American citizens.

13. During World War II, Japanese immigrants and their children were unjustly confined in relocation centers.

14. During World War II, the American Japanese and Nisei proved to be loyal Americans.

15. Since World War II, Idaho's Japanese Americans have done well and have become an important group of Idaho citizens.

16. Boise Valley is an important Basque center.

17. While early Idaho Basques were sheep herders, many of today's Basques work in government, business, and the professions.

18. Present-day Idaho Basques are deeply interested in their old-country Basque customs.

19. Mexicans and Mexican Americans have been living in Idaho for a long time.

20. Most Mexican Americans came to Idaho as migrant workers.

21. Today many Idaho Hispanics are staying in school, going to college, and getting good jobs.

22. A number of Idaho people have become famous.

Appendix A
Idaho's Counties

The following is an alphabetical list of Idaho's 44 counties. The license plate symbol is shown after each county name.

County	Symbol	County	Symbol	County	Symbol	County	Symbol
Ada	1A	Camas	1C	Idaho	I	Owyhee	2O
Adams	2A	Canyon	2C	Jefferson	1J	Payette	1P
Bannock	1B	Caribou	3C	Jerome	2J	Power	2P
Bear Lake	2B	Cassia	4C	Kootenai	K	Shoshone	S
Benewah	3B	Clark	5C	Latah	1L	Teton	1T
Bingham	4B	Clearwater	6C	Lemhi	2L	Twin Falls	2T
Blaine	5B	Custer	7C	Lewis	3L	Valley	V
Boise	6B	Elmore	E	Lincoln	4L	Washington	W
Bonner	7B	Franklin	1F	Madison	1M		
Bonneville	8B	Fremont	2F	Minidoka	2M		
Boundary	9B	Gem	1G	Nez Perce	N		
Butte	10B	Gooding	2G	Oneida	1O		

Appendix B
Idaho's Elected Officials

OFFICE	NAME	BEGAN OFFICE	END OF TERM
U.S. Senator	Larry Craig	1991	2002
U.S. Senator	Mike Crapo	1999	2004
U.S. Congressman District 1	C. L. "Butch" Otter	2001	2002
U.S. Congressman District 2	Mike Simpson	1999	2002
Governor	Dirk Kempthorne	1999	2002
Lieutenant Governor	Jack Riggs	2001	2002
Secretary of State	Pete T. Cenarrusa	1967	2002
State Controller	J. D. Williams	1989	2002
State Treasurer	Ron Crane	1999	2002
Attorney General	Alan G. Lance	1995	2002
State Superintendent	Marilyn Howard	1999	2002

NOTE: These people were holding office in 2002.

Glossary and Pronunciation Guide

A simple pronunciation guide is included here to help the reader "sound out" unfamiliar words. Guide words are given below to illustrate the system used in this glossary. Accented syllables appear in capital letters. (Payette = pay – ET)

Oral Sound	*Guide Word*
a	bat, pan
ah	pot, arm
air	hair, bear
aw	saw, fought
ay	say, grey, pale
e	pet, said
ee	me, tree, eat
er	fur, father, girl
eye	fly, pie, sigh
i	sit, him, mill
ir	ear, deer
oh	go, low, dough
oo	hoot, flute, blue
or	for, door, north
ow	cow, trout, south
oy	boy, coin
uh	about, silent, pencil, love, cup
yoo	you, cue, fuel
g	game, pig
j	jack, giant
k	cat, kick
s	sun, circus
sh	she, shower, cash
th	three, both
th	the, mother
zh	treasure, measure

ANCESTOR. (AN-ses-ter) An ancestor is someone you have descended from, usually further back than a grandparent.

ANTELOPE. (ANT-uhl-ohp) The antelope is a fast-running animal that lives on the western deserts and plateau lands. It looks a little bit like a deer.

ANTIMONY. (ANT-uh-moh-nee) Antimony is a metal used in medicines and to make certain metal alloys.

APPALOOSA. (ap-uh-LOO-SUH) Appaloosa horses came from spotted horses that were bred by the Nez Perce tribe. The Nez Perce used the Palouse Country to pasture their horses. Because of this, spotted horses came to be called Palouse horses, then Appaloosa horses. Today most Appaloosa horses are spotted on the rear half of the body.

APPEALS COURT. (uh-PEELZ) A person who loses the case in a trial court may ask an appeals court to change the ruling. The appeals court may or may not change it.

AQUIFER. (AHK-wuh-fer) or (AK-wuh-fer) An aquifer is a layer of rocks, sand, or gravel that holds or carries water. The Snake River Plain aquifer carries water from the mountains south to the Snake River.

ARTIFACT. (AHRT-uh-fakt) An artifact is an item, usually very old, that shows something about the people who made it. Old weapons and tools are two kinds of Indian artifacts.

ASCEND. (uh-SEND) To ascend is to move upward. A mountain climber ascends a mountain.

ASTORIA. (as-TOR-ee-uh) Astoria was a fur-trading post near the mouth of the Columbia River. It was named for John Jacob Astor.

ASTORIANS. (as-TOR-ee-uhnz) The Astorians were the party of fur traders led by William Price Hunt from St. Louis to Astoria.

AWL. (AWL) An awl is a pointed tool for making small holes. The Indians used awls to make holes in leather.

BAND. A band of Indians was a group of closely related families. A tribe might have several bands or many bands.

BANNOCK. (BAN-uhk) The Bannock Indians lived in southern Idaho with the Shoshoni, mostly along the Snake River Valley. Today Bannock County is in eastern Idaho around Pocatello.

BASQUE. (BASK) The Basque people came from northern Spain. The Boise Valley is one of the largest Basque centers in the United States.

BILL. (BIL) A bill is a proposed law being considered by the legislature.

BLACKFOOT. The Blackfoot tribe, a powerful one, lived in Montana and Canada. Blackfoot is also a town in Bingham County.

BOISE. (BOY-see) The Boise Basin is the mountain area of the Boise River and its tributaries. Much of it is now in Boise County. The city of Boise is on the lower Boise River in the Snake River Valley. It is in Ada County.

BONNEVILLE. (BAHN-uh-vil) Captain Benjamin L. E. Bonneville was an Army officer who traveled around Idaho during the time of the fur trappers. His name is now remembered in the names of Bonneville County (eastern Idaho), Bonneville Dam (Columbia River), and ancient Lake Bonneville. During the time of the glaciers, ancient Lake Bonneville covered much of the Great Basin in parts of Idaho, Utah, and Nevada.

BORAH. (BOR-uh) Mount Borah is the highest point in Idaho. The peak was named for Idaho's famous U. S. Senator William E. Borah. He was born in 1865 and served in the U. S. Senate from 1907 until his death in 1940.

BOWIE. (BOH-ee) or (BOO-ee) A bowie knife was carried by mountain men, soldiers, and, sometimes, Indians. The knife was named after Jim Bowie, a famous American soldier.

BRAND. A brand is a special mark burned on the skins of cattle to show which ranch owns them. The brand of each ranch is different from every other brand.

BRONCO. (BRAHNG-koh) Bronco is a cowboy word for horse. "Bronco" comes from the Spanish word meaning "wild."

BRUNEAU. (BROO-noh) Bruneau is the name of a river and a town in southwest Idaho. Bruneau is in Owyhee County.

CACHE. (KASH) A cache is a hiding place or something hidden in a hiding place. Cache Valley was named because Jim Bridger often cached his furs there.

CADMIUM. (KAD-mee-uhm) Cadmium is a soft metal used in certain alloys. Some batteries contain cadmium.

CAMAS. (KAM-uhs) Camas is a lily that once grew in many parts of the West. Camas bulbs were used as food by most western Indian tribes. Camas Prairie, Big Camas Prairie, and Camas Meadow were all named because great amounts of camas grew there. Camas Prairie is in Idaho County around Grangeville. Big Camas Prairie is in Camas County around Fairfield. (Big Camas Prairie is smaller than the Camas Prairie in Idaho County.) Camas Meadow is on Camas Creek in Clark County.

CAMEAHWAIT. (ka-MEE-uh-wayt) Chief Cameahwait was a Shoshoni chief and Sacajawea's brother.

CANAL. (kuh-NAL) A canal is a large man-made waterway or stream used to carry irrigation water to farm land.

CAPITAL. (KAP-uh-tuhl) A capital is the city where the capitol building is located.

CAPITOL. (KAP-uh-tuhl) A capitol is the building where the legislature meets. In Idaho, the governor and other state officials also have offices there.

CARIBOU. (KAIR-uh-boo) A caribou is a type of large, antlered deer found in parts of Idaho. It is related to the reindeer. Caribou County is in eastern Idaho. Soda Springs is the county seat.

CASTOREUM. (kas-TOR-ee-uhm) Castoreum is a musky-smelling material taken from a beaver. Fur trappers used castoreum to bait their beaver traps.

CATALDO. (kuh-TAL-doh) or (kuh-TAWL-doh) Cataldo is the village where Father Ravalli built the Sacred Heart Mission, now known as the Old Mission Church. It is located in Kootenai County east of Coeur d'Alene on the Coeur d'Alene River.

CAYUSE. (KEYE-yoos) or (keye-YOOS) A cowboy often called his horse a cayuse.

CAYUSE INDIANS. (KEYE-yoos) or (keye-YOOS) The Cayuse Indians were a tribe that lived in Oregon and Washington.

CHARBONEAU. (SHAR-buh-noh) Charboneau was the French-Canadian husband of Sacajawea. He was a guide for the Lewis and Clark party.

CITY COUNCIL. (KOWN-suhl) The city council is a group of elected officials that make laws for the city.

CITY HALL. The city hall is the building that contains the offices of the city government.

CLAIM. (KLAYM) A claim is a piece of land staked out by a miner or homesteader.

CLIMATE. (CLEYE-muht) The climate is the average weather over a period of time. Climate includes the temperature, wind, and rainfall.

COEUR D'ALENE. (kor-duh-LAYNE) Lake Coeur d'Alene and the Coeur d'Alene River are in northern Idaho. The Coeur d'Alene Indians lived along the shores of the lake. The city of Coeur d'Alene now sits on the north end of Lake Coeur d'Alene. The Coeur d'Alene Indian Reservation is now located at the south end of the lake.

CONSERVATION. (kahn-ser-VAY-shuhn) Conservation means protecting our natural resources and using them wisely. These resources include our forests, our soil, and our water.

CONSTITUTION. (kahn-stih-TOO-shuhn) A state constitution is a set of laws that explains the state's government. Idaho's constitution was written by a group of citizens meeting at a constitutional convention. The U. S. Constitution explains the government of the United States.

CONSTITUTIONAL CONVENTION. A constitutional convention is a meeting of citizens for the purpose of writing a constitution.

CONTINENTAL DIVIDE. (kahnt-uhn-ENT-uhl) The continental divide is a ridge of rocky peaks (running somewhat north and south) that divide North America. The land to the east slopes away toward the Atlantic Ocean, and all the water on that side runs into the Atlantic Ocean. All the land to the west slopes away to the Pacific Ocean, and all the water on that side runs into the Pacific Ocean.

COUNCIL. (KOWN-suhl) A meeting of Indian chiefs to talk about the business of the tribe or tribes was called a council. Council Valley and the town of Council were named because the Shoshoni often held councils there.

COUNTY COMMISSIONER. (kuh-MISH-uh-ner) County commissioners make laws for the county. They are the legislative branch of county government.

COUNTY COURTHOUSE. (KORT-hows) This is the building that contains the offices of the county government.

COUNTY SEAT. The county seat is the city that contains the county courthouse.

COURT. The people who conduct trials are referred to as the court. These include the judge, jury, lawyers, and others.

COYOTE. (keye-OHT-ee) or (KEYE-oht) Coyote is a character from American Indian legends. The coyote is a smaller relative of the wolf and is found in many parts of the United States.

CRATERS OF THE MOON. Craters of the Moon National Monument is an area of unusual lava formations. It lies between Arco and Carey on U. S. Highway 93.

CUSTOM. (KUHS-tuhm) A custom is a habit or a way of doing things. Groups of people have long-time customs that they follow and often take them for granted.

DELAMAR. (DEL-uh-mahr) DeLamar was once a lively silver-mining town nine mines down Jordan Creek from Silver City. It became a ghost town after the DeLamar mine closed in 1912. In 1977 the DeLamar mine was opened again—this time as an open-pit mine. The new DeLamar mine is an important Idaho silver mine.

DESERT. (DEZ-uhrt) A desert is very dry land that needs irrigation before it can grow crops. Most of the Snake River Plain is desert land.

DE SMET. (Father Pierre Jean De Smet) (pee-AIR) (zhahn) (dee-SMET) The name is French, though Father De Smet was born in Belgium. Father De Smet was a Catholic missionary among the Indians of the Northwest. He started the Sacred Heart Mission at Cataldo, and he built other missions in Washington and Montana. The present Coeur d'Alene Mission is located at the town of DeSmet [sic] in Benewah County.

DREDGE. A dredge is a large machine that can dig up soil and gravel so that gold or other minerals can be removed.

DROUGHT. (DROWT) A drought is a time when there isn't enough water.

DUGOUT. (DUHG-owt) Dugout canoes were made from logs. The logs were made partly hollow by burning or carving. The dugout houses used by the first Idaho pioneers in the town of Weston were shelters dug into the ground. These were covered with roofs made from poles, grass, and soil.

DWORSHAK DAM. (DWOR-shak) Dworshak Dam is in northern Idaho near Orofino. It is on the North Fork of the Clearwater River.

ELECT. (ee-LEKT) Elect means to choose. We elect our government officials by voting for them.

ELECTION. (ee-LEK-shuhn) An election is the act of choosing public officials by voting. Election day is the day we vote.

ELEVATION. (el-uh-VAY-shuhn) The height above sea level is called elevation.

EROSION. (ee-ROH-zhuhn) Erosion is the wearing away of soil or rock by the action of wind or water.

EXECUTIVE BRANCH. (eg-ZEK-yuh-tiv) This branch of government carries out the laws.

EXPEDITION. (ek-spuh-DISH-uhn) An expedition is a journey made for a purpose. The purpose of the Lewis and Clark expedition was to explore the land west of St. Louis to the Pacific Ocean.

FERRY. (FAIR-ee) A ferry is a boat that carries people or things across a body of water such as a river.

FLATHEAD. (FLAT-hed) The Flathead Indian tribe lived mostly in Montana. The Kalispel Indians of northern Idaho were related to the Flathead tribe.

FOOFARAW. (FOO-fuh-rah) Foofaraw was the name given to the things that white trappers traded to Indians. Foofaraw might include brightly colored glass beads, colored cloth, earrings, mirrors, and anything else that might please Indians.

FORT BOISE. The first Fort Boise was a fur trading post on the Snake River at the mouth of the Boise River. Later it was moved to a spot near the present town of Parma. It was closed in 1855. This fort is sometimes called "Old Fort Boise." In 1863, the U. S. Army built a military post at Boise City and named it Fort Boise. Fort Boise today has a Veterans' Administration hospital.

FOSSIL. (FAHS-uhl) A fossil is a trace, found in the earth's crust, of a plant or animal that lived long ago. A fossil might be a footprint or the print of a leaf, a seashell, or a bone.

FOX. Fox is a character from American Indian legends. The fox is a wild member of the dog family. It is related to the wolf and the coyote, but it is smaller and has shorter legs, larger ears, and a long bushy tail.

FREMONT. (FREE-mahnt) Captain John C. Fremont explored and mapped much of the American West. He mapped the Oregon Trail in 1842 and 1843. Fremont County is located in eastern Idaho. St. Anthony is the county seat.

GEM. (JEM) A gem is a stone valued for its beauty.

GEOGRAPHER. (jee-AHG-ruh-fer) A geographer is a scientist who studies geography.

GEOGRAPHY. (jee-AHG-ruh-fee) Geography is the study of the earth's surface—its elevation, climate, and shape—and the plants, animals, and people who live there.

GEYSER. (GEYE-zer) A geyser is a spring that shoots hot water and steam into the air at certain times of the day. A geyser does not flow all the time. It flows part of the time and rests part of the time.

GLACIAL VALLEY. (GLAY-shuhl) A glacial valley is formed by a glacier. It is shaped like a giant letter U.

GLACIER. (GLAY-sher) A glacier is a large body of ice that moves slowly down a slope or valley. It may also spread out over a large area of the earth's surface.

GOVERNMENT. Government carries out the laws we live by. Our governments are run by people elected to certain offices. Within our state we have a state government, county governments, city governments, school districts, and special districts.

GOVERNOR. (GUHV-er-ner) The governor is the highest elected official in the state. He or she is part of the executive branch.

GYPSUM. (JIP-suhm) Gypsum is a mineral used for making fertilizer, plaster of paris, and plasterboard.

HARD-ROCK MINING. Hard-rock mining is the mining of ore. The ore (rock) has to be crushed so the metal or other minerals can be removed.

HELLS CANYON. Hells Canyon is the deepest canyon in North America and perhaps in the entire world. Reaching almost from Weiser to Lewiston, it forms the border between Idaho and Oregon. The Snake River flows north through Hells Canyon.

HISPANIC. (his-PAN-ik) The word Hispanic refers to things that are Spanish. Mexicans are called Hispanics because they speak the Spanish language and have other Spanish customs.

HISTORY. (HIS-tuh-ree) History is the record of things that people have done.

HOMESTEAD. (HOHM-sted) When the early settlers got empty land from the government and began farming it, those farms were called homesteads. The laws that let people settle on the land and farm it were called homestead laws.

HOUSE. The Idaho Legislature is made up of two parts, called houses. They are the senate and the house of representatives.

HOUSE OF REPRESENTATIVES. (REP-ri-ZEN-tuh-tivz) This is one of the two houses of the Idaho Legislature.

HYDRAULIC MINING. (heye-DRAW-lik) Hydraulic mining uses powerful streams of water to wash out large amounts of sand and gravel.

ILTSWETSIX. (ILT-swuh-chicks) Iltswetsix was a terrible monster that appeared in several Indian legends.

IMMIGRANT. (IM-i-gruhnt) An immigrant is a person who comes to a new country to make a home. The settlers who came west and made homes in the Oregon Country were immigrants to the Oregon Country.

INDIAN AGENT. (AY-juhnt) An Indian agent was a government official whose job was to work with the Indians.

INDIAN RESERVATION. (rez-er-VAY-shuhn) An Indian reservation is a piece of land set aside (or reserved) for a certain group or tribe of Indians.

IRRIGATION. (ir-uh-GAY-shuhn) Irrigation is watering the soil in some man-made way. Irrigation in Idaho is done with canals and ditches and with pumps and sprinklers.

JEDEDIAH. (jed-uh-DEYE-uh) First name.

JOAQUIN. (wah-KEEN) First name of the writer Joaquin Miller.

JUDGE. A judge is the court officer who hears cases or conducts trials.

JUDICIAL BRANCH. (joo-DISH-uhl) The courts make up the judicial branch of our government.

JURY. A jury is a group of citizens who sit in court and hear a trial. The jury decides if the accused person is guilty or not guilty.

KALISPEL. (KAL-i-spel) The Kalispel Indians were also called Pend Oreille Indians. They lived along the shores of Lake Pend Oreille.

KAMIAH. (KAM-ee-eye) Today Kamiah is a small town in Lewis County. Kamiah was a Nez Perce village long before explorers and settlers came to Idaho.

KOOSKIA. (KOOS-kee) Kooskia is a small town where the Middle Fork and the South Fork of the Clearwater River come together. Kooskia comes from an Indian word meaning "where the waters join."

KOOTENAI. (KOOT-nee) The Kootenai River and Kootenai County are both in northern Idaho.

KUTENAI. (KOOT-nee) The Kutenai Indian tribe lived along the Kootenai River of northern Idaho, western Montana, and southern British Columbia. The name of the tribe is sometimes spelled Kootenai or Kutenay.

LAPWAI. (LAP-way) Today Lapwai is a small town on the Nez Perce Reservation in Nez Perce County. Lapwai was a Nez Perce village in the Clearwater Valley long before explorers and settlers came to Idaho.

LATAH. (LAY-tah) Latah County is in northern Idaho. Moscow is the county seat.

LAVA. (LA-vuh) Lava is melted rock that flows out of the ground.

LEAD. (LED) Lead is a soft heavy metal used for making chemicals and many other products.

LEGEND. (LEJ-uhnd) A legend is a story from the past that is passed on from person to person.

LEGISLATIVE BRANCH. (LEJ-is-LAY-tiv) The legislative branch of government is the legislature.

LEGISLATOR. (LEJ-is-LAY-ter) State senators and state representatives are legislators. They are members of the state legislature.

LEGISLATURE. (LEJ-is-LAY-cher) The legislature is the branch of government that makes laws. The Idaho legislature makes laws for the State of Idaho.

LEMHI. (LEM-heye) Lemhi County is in eastern Idaho. Salmon is the county seat. Fort Lemhi was built on a tributary of the Lemhi River in 1855. The Lemhi Indians were a band of Shoshoni.

LENTIL. (LEN-tuhl) The lentil plant is a member of the bean family. The lentil seed is small, round, and flat. It is used especially in soups.

LIVESTOCK. Livestock are farm animals such as horses, cattle, sheep, and pigs.

LIVERY. (LIV-uh-ree) Livery is feeding and caring for horses for pay. A livery stable is a business place where this work is done. A livery stable also has horses for rent or hire.

LOCAL GOVERNMENT. (LOH-kuhl) City and county government are two kinds of local government. Other kinds include school districts and special districts.

LODGE. The Indian home was often called a lodge. The tipi was one kind of lodge. Other lodges were built of poles with reed mats or bundles of grass. Sometimes they were covered with earth. They might be round and about the size of a tipi, or long and narrow, housing as many as ten families. A few lodges were built in caves and holes dug in the ground.

LOUISIANA TERRITORY. (loo-ee-zee-AN-uh) (TAIR-uh-tor-ee)

MARSHAL. A marshal is a town law officer hired to enforce the laws. Some early mining towns had marshals.

MAVERICK. (MAV-rik) A maverick is an unbranded range animal (cow or bull) or a motherless calf.

MAYOR. (MAY-er) The mayor is the highest official in city government. His or her office is the executive branch of city government.

MESA. (MAY-suh) A mesa is a hill with steep sides and a level top. In Idaho, Mesa is a village in Adams County northeast of Weiser.

MIGRANT. (MEYE-gruhnt) Migrants are people who move from job to job, following crop harvests and other farm work.

MINERAL. (MIN-uh-ruhl) A mineral is a material taken from the ground that can be used to make things people need. Important Idaho minerals include silver, phosphate, zinc, sand and gravel, stone, and many others.

MINER'S CODE. The miner's code was an agreement among miners that they would look out for one another. Anyone making trouble for the miners was sent on his way.

MINER'S COURT. Miner's court was a special meeting of the miners in the camp. At this meeting, the miners would decide if an accused person was guilty of breaking the camp rules.

MINNETONKA. (min-uh-TAHNG-kuh) Minnetonka Cave is southwest of Paris in Bear Lake County. Minnetonka Cave is not an ice cave.

MISSION. (MISH-uhn) A mission is one or more buildings and some land used for religious work in a foreign country or territory.

MISSIONARY. (MISH-uh-nair-ee) A missionary is a person who works to teach his religious beliefs to other people in a foreign land. Missionaries usually work at a mission.

MOLYBDENUM. (muh-LIB-duh-nuhm) Molybdenum is a metal with a very high melting point. It is used to make steel harder and stronger for missiles, jet engines, and high-speed drills.

MORMON. (MOR-muhn) The Church of Jesus Christ of Latter-day Saints is often called the Mormon Church or the LDS Church. Members are known as Mormons or Latter-day Saints.

MORTAR AND PESTLE. (MOR-tuhr) and (PES-tuhl) A mortar used by the Indians was a stone with a dish-shaped hollow. Food and other materials were placed in the hollow and pounded, crushed, or ground with a pestle. A pestle was a club-shaped grinding tool made of stone.

MOSCOW. (MAHS-koh) Moscow is the county seat of Latah County. It is also home of the University of Idaho.

MOUNTAIN MAN. A mountain man was a fur trapper who lived very much like an Indian.

NATURAL RESOURCE. (NACH-uh-ruhl) (REE-sors) A natural resource is something from nature that people can use, such as trees, soil, water, and minerals.

NEZ PERCE. (NEZ-pers) The Nez Perce tribe lived in central Idaho along the Clearwater River and lower Salmon River, and also in parts of Washington and Oregon. The town of Nezperce is the county seat of Lewis County. Nez Perce County is in the Idaho panhandle, with Lewiston as the county seat.

NISEI. (NEE-say) or (nee-SAY) A Nisei is the American son or daughter of Japanese immigrant parents. Nisei means second generation, but sometimes Nisei is used to mean any Japanese-American.

NORTHERN IDAHO. Northern Idaho is usually thought of as the ten most northern counties of Idaho. It is also called the Idaho panhandle. The Salmon River and its rugged mountains form the southern edge of northern Idaho.

NORTHERN PAIUTE. (PEYE-yoot) The Northern Paiute tribe lived in Oregon, Nevada, and California. Two small bands lived in southwest Idaho along the Snake and Owyhee rivers. It is believed that the Bannock tribe came from Northern Paiute people who moved into southern Idaho and mixed with the Shoshoni people.

OFFICIAL. (uh-FISH-uhl) An official is a person who holds a public office. Officials are sometimes called officers.

OINKARI. (oyn-KAH-ree) Oinkari is the name of Idaho's Basque dancers.

ONEIDA. (oh-NEY-duh) Oneida County is in southeast Idaho. Malad is the county seat.

OPEN-PIT MINE. An open-pit mine is a mine that is just an open hole in the ground. You can see the whole mine when you stand at the edge and look down into it.

ORE. (OR) Ore is rock that contains metal or some other valuable mineral. Ore often contains more than one mineral.

OREGON COUNTRY. The Oregon Country was a huge piece of land that included the present states of Oregon, Washington, Idaho, and part of Canada.

OROFINO. (or-oh-FEE-noh) or (or-uh-FEE-noh) The word "Orofino" comes from the Spanish words meaning "fine gold." Orofino is now a small town on the Clearwater River in Clearwater County. Orofino City was a gold mining camp near the present town of Pierce.

OWYHEE. (oh-WEYE-hee) Owyhee County, the Owyhee River, and the Owyhee mountains are all in southwest Idaho. The name is said to have come from bad pronunciation of the name Hawaii. There is a story that a group of men from Hawaii disappeared in those mountains and were never found. Early miners and settlers called them the Hawaii Mountains, but the name came out "Owyhee."

PALOUSE. (puh-LOOS) Parts of northern Idaho and eastern Washington surrounding the Palouse River are called the Palouse country. Moscow and Genesee (in Idaho) and Pullman and Colfax (in Washington) are important Palouse towns. The name Palouse comes from the Palus (puh-LOOS) Indians who liked to dig camas in the area around Moscow and Pullman.

PANAKWATE. (puh-NAK-wayt) The Bannock Indians called themselves Panakwate, which was their word for being partners with the Shoshoni. Settlers couldn't pronouce the word and said "Bannock."

PANHANDLE. Northern Idaho is sometimes called the panhandle. If you look at a map of Idaho, you can see why. The panhandle is made up of the ten most northern counties of Idaho.

PAYETTE. (pay-ET) Payette County is in southwest Idaho and borders Oregon. The town of Payette is the county seat. The Payette River flows south from the Payette Lakes in Valley County (at McCall) and empties into the Snake River at the town of Payette. Francois Payette was a fur trapper for many years along the river that was named for him. He quit trapping in 1834 and became manager of "old" Fort Boise from the time it was built until he retired in 1844. Immigrants on the Oregon Trail remember him as a "merry, fat old gentleman" who was very kind and polite to them.

PEMMICAN. (PEM-i-kuhn) Pemmican is an Indian food made from dried meat pounded into fine pieces and mixed with melted fat.

PEND OREILLE. (pahn-duh-RAY) Lake Pend Oreille is in northern Idaho. The Kalispel Indians lived along its shores and were sometimes called the Pend d'Oreille Indians. The original French spelling (with the d') is often used with the name of the Indian tribe, but has been dropped from the spelling of Lake Pend Oreille.

PERRINE. (puh-REYEN) Ira B. Perrine started the work that brought irrigation water to Magic Valley—and the growth of farms and towns in that part of Idaho. The Perrine Memorial Bridge, named in his honor, crosses the Snake River Canyon between Twin Falls and Jerome.

PHOSPHATE. (FAHS-fayt) Phosphate is a mineral used for making fertilizer and other important chemicals.

PIERRE. (pee-AIR) First name.

PIONEER. (peye-uh-NIR) The first early settlers in Idaho are called pioneers. People who are the first to work and make new discoveries in a field are called pioneers in their fields. Philo Farnsworth was a pioneer in the field of television.

PLACER MINING. (PLAS-er) Placer mining is mining gold from gravel, sand, or soil by washing it out with water.

PLATEAU. (pla-TOH) A plateau is a large piece of land, mostly level, that is raised sharply above the land next to it on at least one side.

PLATINUM. (PLAT-uh-nuhm) Platinum is a metal used in making certain metal alloys. It is one of the most valuable metals and is sometimes used in jewelry and dental work.

POCATELLO. (poh-kuh-TEL-oh) Pocatello is a city in eastern Idaho named after Bannock Chief Pocatello. Pocatello is the county seat of Bannock County, and it is the home of Idaho State University.

POLLUTION. (puh-LOO-shuhn) Pollution is the poisoning of air, water, or soil by chemicals or other kinds of wastes.

PORTNEUF. (PORT-nuhf) The Portneuf River is a tributary of the Snake River in eastern Idaho.

PRAIRIE. (PRE-ree) A prairie is a large piece of rich farmland that grew mostly grass before it was plowed up for farming.

PROSPECTOR. (PRAHS-pek-tuhr) The men who filled the early West searching for gold were called prospectors. There are still a few prospectors today searching for gold and other valuable minerals.

QUARTZ. (KWORTZ) Quartz is one of the most common minerals. It is hard and forms glasslike crystals. Some quartz stone contains streaks of gold. Weather and water break quartz into small pieces. These small pieces make up most of the sand and sandstone that we see in nature.

RAINFALL. Rainfall is measured as the number of liquid inches of water that land receives each year. All forms of water are included—rain, hail, and snow.

RANGE LAND. Range land is a large area of land where livestock can graze. Open range means land that has no fences.

RAVALLI. (ruh-VAL-ee) Father Anthony Ravalli was a Catholic missionary in northern Idaho. He was sent by Father De Smet to build the Sacred Heart Mission at Cataldo.

RENDEZVOUS. (RAHN-day-voo) The rendezvous was a summertime meeting of mountain men and the fur companies. The mountain men would sell their furs and buy new supplies. It was also a good chance for them to meet friends and have a good time.

REPRESENTATIVE. (rep-ri-ZEN-tuh-tiv) A state representative is a legislator who serves in the Idaho house of representatives. A U. S. Representative serves in the U. S House of Representatives.

RESERVOIR. (REZ-er-vwor) A reservoir is a manmade lake created by building a dam on a river.

RHEUMATISM. (ROO-muh-tiz-uhm) Rheumatism is pain or stiffness in the muscles or joints.

SACAJAWEA. (SA-kuh-juh-WEE—uh) Sacajawea was the young Shoshoni woman who served as a guide and interpreter for Lewis and Clark. She was married to the French-Canadian Charboneau. Her name is sometimes spelled Sacagawea.

SALMON. (SAM-uhn) The salmon is a large fish that swims from the ocean up the rivers and into the smaller streams and creeks. The Indians living along these streams would catch the salmon and use them for food. The Salmon River of Idaho was named because of the great number of salmon that appeared in its waters. The town of Salmon sits where the Lemhi River flows into the Salmon River. It is the county seat of Lemhi County.

SCHOOL BOARD. A school board is a group of citizens who are elected to run a school district.

SCHOOL DISTRICT. A school district is a special unit of government that takes care of the public schools within its borders.

SCYTHE. (SEYTHE) A scythe is a long-handled tool with a long curved blade for cutting grass or grain.

SEA LEVEL. Sea level is the level of the ocean. The elevation of land is measured as the number of feet above sea level, or above the ocean.

SENATE. (SEN-it) The Idaho senate is one of the two houses of the Idaho legislature. The U. S. Senate is one of the two houses of the U. S. Congress.

SENATOR. (SEN-uh-ter) A state senator is a legislator who serves in the Idaho senate. A U. S. Senator serves in the U. S. Senate.

SETTLER. (SET-ler) A settler is a person who comes to live on "empty" land. The pioneers who began farming in Idaho were settlers on Idaho's land.

SHERIFF. (SHAIR-if) The sheriff is the county law official who protects people living outside the cities.

SHOSHONE. (shoh-SHOHN) or (shuh-SHOHN) Shoshone Falls, Shoshone County, and the town of Shoshone are spelled and pronounced this way. Shoshone Falls is on the Snake River near Twin Falls. The town of Shoshone, north of Twin Falls, is the county seat of Lincoln County. Shoshone County is in north Idaho, and is famous for its Coeur d'Alene mines.

SHOSHONI. (shuh-SHOH-nee) The Shoshoni Indian tribe's name is spelled and pronounced this way. Some people may spell the tribe's name Shoshone, but it will still be pronounced like Shoshoni. Idaho's Shoshoni Indians lived in southern Idaho, mostly in the Snake River Valley. Sometimes they were called Snake Indians.

SLUICE BOX. (SLOOS) A sluice box was a boxlike wooden tool used by the placer gold miner to make his work faster and easier.

SOUTHERN IDAHO. Southern Idaho usually means everything south of the Salmon River. Different parts of southern Idaho are called by different names. The mountain region south of the Salmon River is often called central Idaho. The main southern Idaho farming regions are called western or southwest Idaho, Magic Valley, and eastern or southeast Idaho.

SPOKANE. (spoh-KAN) The Spokane River flows from Lake Coeur d'Alene (and the city of Coeur d'Alene) west into Washington. The Spokane Indians lived in eastern Washington. Today the city of Spokane is the largest city in eastern Washington and is larger than any city in Idaho.

ST. MARIES. (saynt) (MAIR-eez) The name is pronounced like Saint Mary's. St. Maries is the county seat of Benewah County in northern Idaho. It sits where the St. Maries River flows into the St. Joe river.

SUMMIT. (SUHM-it) The summit of a mountain is its highest point. The summit of a trail or road going over a mountain is the highest point on that trail or road.

SYMBOL. (SIM-buhl) A symbol is a picture, a word, or a mark that stands for an idea. Idaho's symbols include a flower, a bird, an animal, a tree, a gem, and a fossil. Each of these symbols stands for an idea about Idaho.

TAX. A tax is money collected from citizens to pay for their government.

TERRITORY. (TEHR-uh-TOR-ee) Before an area became a state, it was given borders and called a territory. Oregon Territory and Idaho Territory are examples. Later, when more people settled there, the territory might become a state.

TETON. (TEE-tahn) The Teton River flows through the Teton Valley, which lies on the Wyoming border. Both are in Teton County, which has Driggs as the county seat. The famous Teton Mountain peaks, just across the border in Wyoming, tower high above the Teton Valley.

TIPI. (TEE-pee) (sometimes spelled tepee) A tipi is an Indian tent made from poles and animal skins. The Indian home was often called a lodge. The tipi was one kind of lodge.

TOLL. (TOHL) The toll is the money or tax paid for using a road, a ferry, or a bridge. Idaho Territory had many toll roads and toll ferries. Later, toll bridges were built.

TREATY. (TREE-tee) A treaty is an agreement between two nations. The U. S. government made treaties with many Indian tribes. Some of those tribes are still considered to be separate nations.

TRIAL. When a person is accused of a crime, he goes to court for a trial. At the trial, the jury decides if he is guilty or not. Some trials are held without a jury. In these cases, the judge does the deciding.

TRIBE. (TREYEB) An Indian tribe is a group of people who share the same ancestors, language, and customs.

TRIBUTARY. (TRIB-yuh-tair-ee) A tributary is any stream that flows into a larger stream. A tributary may have smaller tributaries of its own.

TURBINE. (TER-bin) The turbine in a dam is a machine that is turned by water passing through the dam. The turbine turns a generator, and the generator makes electricity.

UNDERGROUND MINE. An underground mine is a mine with shafts and tunnels under the ground. The mines in Silver Valley have hundreds of miles of tunnels that crisscross beneath the valley and the nearby mountains.

VALLEY. (VAL-ee) A valley is the land starting at a river and running to the higher land above it.

VANADIUM. (vuh-NAYD-ee-uhm) Vanadium is a metal used in certain metal alloys.

VERMILLION. (ver-MIL-yuhn) Vermillion is a bright red powder. Some Indians liked to use vermillion to paint their faces and bodies.

VETO. (VEE-toh) Veto means to reject. The governor may veto a bill instead of signing it. Instead of signing it, he stamps VETO on it in big red letters, then sends it back to the legislature.

VIGILANTE. (vij-uh-LAN-tee) A vigilante was a member of a vigilance committee. A vigilance committee was a group of citizens who joined together to fight gangs of robbers and murderers.

WALLOWA. (wuh-LOW-uh) The Wallowa Valley is in eastern Oregon near the area where the Salmon River flows into the Snake River. Chief Joseph's band of Nez Perce once made their home there.

WATER RIGHT. A water right is a water claim that gives a person the right to use a certain amount of water from a certain stream.

WEIPPE. (WEE-eyep) Weippe is a small town in Clearwater County. Near this spot, Lewis and Clark met Chief Twisted hair in 1805.

WEISER. (WEE-zer) Weiser is the county seat of Washington County, which lies on the Oregon border. The town sits where the Weiser River flows into the Snake River.

WICKIUP. (WIK-ee-uhp) A wickiup was a hut made of poles covered with grass, brush, or strips of bark.

WILDERNESS. (WIL-der-nes) Wilderness is land that is still the same as it was before people discovered it. Idaho has more wilderness than any other state except Alaska.

WILDLIFE. Wildlife means wild animals of any kind. Sometimes wildlife refers to wild plants.

WILLAMETTE VALLEY. (wuh-LAM-uht) The Willamette Valley is in western Oregon. The Oregon Trail ended in the Willamette Valley at Oregon City, south of Portland.

WYETH, NATHANIEL. (nuh-THAN-yuhl) (WEYE-uhth) Nathaniel Wyeth built Fort Hall in 1834.

ZINC. (ZINK) Zinc is a metal that is often used in making soft metal alloys.

Index